AT THE EDGE OF THE WORLD

Caves and Late Classic Maya World View

By Karen Bassie-Sweet

UNIVERSITY OF OKLAHOMA PRESS : NORMAN AND LONDON

Also by Karen Bassie-Sweet

From the Mouth of the Dark Cave: Commemorative Sculpture of the Late Classic Maya (Norman)

Bassie-Sweet, Karen, 1952–
   At the edge of the world : caves and late classic Maya world view
/ by Karen Bassie-Sweet.
      p.   cm.
   Includes bibliographical references and index.
   ISBN 0-8061-2829-1 (alk. paper)
   1. Mayas—Philosophy.   2. Mayas—Religion.   3. Caves—Religious
aspects. I. Title.
   F1435.3.P5B37   1996
   299'.784—dc20   95-45428
                                                         CIP

1 2 3 4 5 6 7 8 9 10

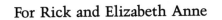

For Rick and Elizabeth Anne

at the edge of the world
at the edge of the sea
there live the angels.

Chorti text (Fought 1972:26)

Contents

Illustrations

FIGURES

MAP

TABLE

Unless indicated otherwise, all drawings are by Karen Bassie-Sweet.

Preface

Several areas of inquiry could not be pursued in depth in a previous publication (Bassie-Sweet 1991) because of time and space limitations. This book represents my research into one of these subjects, the role of caves in the Maya world view.

Most researchers use a variation of the model of the Maya world view presented by Sir J. Eric Thompson (1950:10) over forty years ago:

> The Maya appear to have believed that the sky was divided into 13 compartments, in each of which certain gods resided. These may have been arranged as 13 horizontal layers or as six steps ascending on the east to the seventh and then six more descending on the west, so that compartments 1 and 13, 2 and 13, etc. were on the same level. In the latter case there were 13 heavens but seven layers. The sky was sustained by four gods, the Bacabs, who were placed one at each side of the world. . . . Almost every element in Maya religion and not a few parts of the Maya calendar are connected with one world direction and its corresponding color. . . . At each of the four sides of the world (or perhaps at each side of one of the heavens) stood a sacred ceiba. . . . They appear to have been the trees of abundance, from which food for mankind first came.

In a later publication, Thompson (1970:175) expanded on his model of the Maya world view:

As to our world, it was regarded as a flat square block with skies above and underworlds beneath.

At the four points of the compass or at the angles between stood the four Bacabs who, with raised up hands, supported the skies. . . . There were thirteen "layers" of heaven and nine of the underworld. . . . the thirteen celestial layers were arranged as six steps ascending from the eastern horizon to the seventh, the zenith, whence six more steps led down to the western horizon. Thus there were really only seven celestial and five infernal layers. The sun followed this sort of stepped rhomboid on his daily journey across the sky and his nightly traverse of the underworld to return to the point of departure each dawn. . . . Countering this severely geometric structure, a giant ceiba tree, the sacred tree of the Maya, the *yaxche*, "first" or "green" tree, stands in the exact center of the earth. Its roots penetrate the underworld; its trunk and branches pierce the various layers of the skies.

Such a model fits with Mircea Eliade's archetype for traditional societies with its center-oriented axis mundi that provides access to heaven above and hell below (Eliade 1958). Variations on Thompson's and Eliade's models have been generated by numerous authors. As the study of Maya culture has progressed through the years, we have been presented with a vast amount of evidence that is at odds with these models. The primary task of this book is to refine Thompson's model using evidence from the forty years of intervening research and to demonstrate the fundamental role that caves played in this world view. My basic premise is that the Maya ordered and structured their world based on natural observations.

I would like to take this opportunity to acknowledge a number of people who have greatly contributed to the ideas in this book. I warmly thank Claude Baudez, Mary Ciaramella, John Fought, Nicholas Hopkins, Kathryn Josserand, and David Kelley for providing me not only with constructive criticism and debate but with support. They pushed me in many directions that I was reluctant to explore. It has been an honor to have worked with such fine scholars.

John Fought, Calixta Guiterras, Esther Hermitte, Oliver La Farge, Robert Laughlin, Maude Oakes, Robert Redford, John Sosa, Dennis and Barbara Tedlock, Alfonso Villa Rojas, and Evon Vogt have documented the rapidly disappearing culture of the twentieth-century Maya. The information published by these researchers has been invaluable to me.

The research of Vogt and Sosa concerning the cosmological foundation of ritual was particularly inspiring.

A number of archaeological investigations of caves have contributed to my understanding of the important role that these natural features played in Maya life. The works of Frans Blom, James Brady, Oliver La Farge, Barbara MacLeod, Carlos Navarrete, David Pendergast, Mary and John Pohl, Dennis Puleston, and Andrea Stone are exceptional in this regard. I would also like to acknowledge the importance of Sir J. Eric Thompson's paper concerning the use of caves. Like so much of Thompson's material, it is foundation work.

Phonetic decipherments and interpretations by John Carlson, Nikolai Grube, Stephen Houston, Barbara MacLeod, Martha Macri, Linda Schele, David Stuart, and Karl Taube have provided further evidence for many of my interpretations and generated a host of ideas. In particular, John Carlson's paper on geomantic models (1981) and Houston and Stuart's papers on the *way* sign and place names (1989, in press) opened numerous roads of investigation. Karl Taube's interpretation of the Post Classic Yucatec New Year ceremony added immeasurably to my understanding of that event.

Many cultures outside the Maya zone have similar world views. Although I have limited my discussion to evidence from Maya sources, I have been greatly enlightened by the research of several scholars who have examined world view in other Mesoamerican and South American cultures. In particular, the works of David Grove, Doris Heyden, John Pohl, Richard Townsend, and Gary Urton have stimulated new ideas and validated others.

Several people have directly assisted me in my writing. I thank Gillian Steward for her editorial work, criticisms, and support. I am also indebted to Wendy Ashmore and two anonymous readers for their thoughtful reviews of the manuscript. Their comments greatly improved the quality of the work. Ian Graham, Merle Greene Robertson, Catherine Kincaid, and the Peabody Museum have provided illustrations without which this book would be incomprehensible. Their generosity in sharing this material is appreciated. I would also like to acknowledge Elin Danien for inviting me to the University Museum Maya Weekend, where I was able to present a summary of my interpretations in a public forum. I thank her for her endorsement and friendship. I would especially like to express my sincere thanks to John Drayton of the University of Oklahoma Press for his encouragement and faith. I have been extremely fortunate to have such a supportive editor.

Finally, I acknowledge my husband, Rick, once again, for his endless editing, support, humor, and patience. So who's your best friend?

KAREN BASSIE-SWEET

Calgary, Alberta, Canada

AT THE EDGE OF THE WORLD

N

▲ Chichen Itza

Tortuguero ▲

Usumacinta River

Palenque ▲
Tila ▲

Tonina ▲

▲ Piedras Negras

Tikal ▲   ▲ Naranjo
          Yaxha

▲ La Pasadita

Yaxchilan ▲▲

Kuna Lacanja ▲▲ Bonampak

Pasion River

▲ Caracol

Dos Pilas ▲▲

▲ Seibal

Aguateca ▲▲   ▲ Machaquila
             ▲ Naj Tunich

Chixoy River

Motagua River

Quirigua ▲▲

▲ Copan

Graphic by C. Kincaid

Maya Region Showing Sites Discussed in Text

Introduction

All people structure their lives according to their culturally created concept of the universe. Cosmology or world view explains not only the creation of the universe but the birth of humankind, the ordering of the world, the place of humans in that order, and their obligation to maintain it. The Maya region is predominantly a low limestone shelf broken in numerous places by ridges, hills, and mountain ranges. Because limestone is particularly susceptible to water erosion, the entire area is honeycombed with caves and cave systems.[1] Caves played an important part in the Maya view of the creation and maintenance of world order.[2]

Ritual activity provides a method of validating and reinforcing a community's model of the universe. It ultimately gives a sense of control over the forces of life and death. By its very nature, ritual activity is directed toward and expresses this cosmological model (Sosa 1985:315). We can reconstruct the Classic Maya view of the universe and their place in it from the rituals recorded in their art and hieroglyphic writing. Basic concepts and themes in their art indicate that the Late Classic Maya had a standardized world view.

The Maya universe included a domed layered sky, the disk-shaped surface of the earth, a sea on which the earth floated, and a layered underworld. The deities created and destroyed humankind a number of times before they succeeded in making a suitable being. On the surface of the earth they established a quadrilateral space within which people could safely live if they acted appropriately. The corners of the square were formed by the rise and set points of the solstice sun.

On each side of the quadrilateral world was a mythological mountain aligned with the cardinal point. At these horizon mountains sky met earth and the sun, moon, and stars rose and set. Within these mountains lived the ancestors and guardian deities associated with lightning, rain, and wind. Access to the mountain and its supernaturals was through a cave opening marked by a ceiba tree. The ruling lineages believed that they originated from one of these great world trees. This sacred descent gave them exclusive ownership rights not only to the land but to its people.

The Maya replicated the quadrilateral world model whenever they constructed any area such as a community, house, cornfield, or ritual space. In doing so, they created a safe and ordered human space, separating it from the chaotic and wild as well as the supernatural. The Maya performed rituals in both natural and constructed locations that represented the horizon caves of the guardian deities and ancestors. This book concentrates on these direction-oriented rituals and their relationship to caves.

Many of the places illustrated in Classic art or named in hieroglyphic texts can be identified as replications of one of the world mountains or its cave and as sites for Period Ending rituals (see chapters 2 and 6). Because the Maya replicated the world model on many levels and at many locations, it is not always readily apparent whether these places represent a natural mountain and cave in the vicinity of a community, a structure at the border of the town, or an architectural feature within the town such as a temple/pyramid. For reasons cited in later chapters, I lean toward the belief that these Period Ending places refer to natural caves and elevations, but the evidence is not conclusive. What is certain is that they replicate one of the mythological mountains.

The most common event illustrated in Late Classic Maya monumental art is the direction-oriented Period Ending ceremony of the contemporary ruler. Some of these narratives also tell of the last destruction and re-creation of the world by the deities, which also occurred on a Period Ending date. This mythological event is given as background information leading to the ruler's Period Ending ceremony: just as the deities destroyed and re-created the world, the ruler symbolically destroyed and re-created the world during the renewal ceremony on the Period Ending. While these ceremonies share this common theme, there is significant variation in the details over time and from region to region, due to changing political, social, economic, and environmental factors. These variations made each site unique, but the standard elements illustrate the common beliefs of the Late Classic Maya, which are the focus of this book.

The ideas for most of my interpretations originated from Postclassic, postconquest, and contemporary Maya sources. Some researchers have questioned the validity of using such material to explain Classic culture because Maya society has undergone innovations and changes over the centuries. I believe this is a legitimate concern, but there has also been a great deal of continuity. The pervasiveness of the quadrilateral model through time has been demonstrated (Thompson 1934; Berlin and Kelley 1961; Vogt 1969; Gossen 1974; Coggins 1980; Carlson 1981; Tedlock 1982; Hanks 1984; Sosa 1985; Ashmore 1989, 1991; to name only a few). The belief in the quadrilateral world endured not only in the face of the Classic collapse but even following the cataclysmic events of the Spanish conquest. Throughout the colonial period and into this century, it continued to be a basic paradigm for many communities. Associated concepts such as animal counterparts and guardian supernaturals also persevered. While we need to be judicious in using this later material, I believe that it is one of our richest resources.

This book is organized into seven chapters and a conclusion. Chapter 1 reviews the structure of the Maya universe, focusing on the creation of the world and the establishment of its quadrilateral nature. Chapter 2 deals with the many ways in which caves are illustrated in Maya art and how they are related to the mythological mountains of the world model. Chapter 3 reviews architectural complexes and sculptures that replicate the mythological mountains. Chapter 4 discusses the cave ceremonies that sought to maintain the balance and order of the world. The idols used during these rituals are reviewed in chapter 5. Chapter 6 discusses the cave beliefs associated with the soul and the role of the elite in the world order. Chapter 7 deals with the spiritual power of the ruling elite, which they used to maintain world order, and how they obtained that power through cave rituals.

Certain concepts and conventions are fundamental to our understanding of Maya cave beliefs. Many of the following topics are discussed at length in later chapters.

HIEROGLYPHIC WRITING

Hieroglyphic signs represent words. On most stone sculpture hieroglyphs appear in square blocks. A block can consist of either one sign or a series of signs (compound sign). In a compound sign one sign is usually larger than the other and is referred to as the *main sign*. Smaller signs attached to the top, bottom and sides are called *affixes* (*prefix, subfix, superfix,* and *postfix*).

In the last two decades many epigraphers have focused on the phonetic decipherment of individual signs, producing important new readings and insights into the nature of hieroglyphic writing. In these studies the pictographic nature of a sign is often ignored in the quest for its phonetic value, but I stress that the pictographic value should not be lightly dismissed. For example, the Maya represented the word *witz* "mountain" with a pictograph that incorporates all the fundamental elements of the mountain: caves, lightning, water, and corn (see chapter 2). They wrote the verb that refers to the ritual preparation of space not with a combination of purely phonetic signs, but with the head of a deity (God N) whose duty was to maintain the structure and order of space. Pictographic hieroglyphs do more than represent words: they evoke images and concepts in the mind of the reader. Furthermore, Maya signs often represent multilayered concepts that are intrinsically interwoven.

J. Eric S. Thompson (1962) produced a catalogue of known signs. Thompson designations are preceded by the letter *T* (e.g., T528). Researchers often use nicknames to identify certain glyphs or iconographic elements, but these nicknames are by no means standardized. The best are descriptive but devoid of subjective meaning. For example, Heinrich Berlin (1959) identified Palenque rulers with neutral terms such as Topic 1 and Topic 2 or Subject A and Subject B. George Kubler (1972) gave nicknames to these subjects based on the pictographic elements in their name glyphs. Subject A was nicknamed Sunshield for his *kin* "sun" and shield components, while his successor became Jaguar-Snake because his name glyph is a conflation of these two animals. At the first Mesa Redonda de Palenque Moisés Morales suggested that instead of English nicknames Chol names should be adopted. In response to this, Peter Mathews and Linda Schele (1974) renamed Berlin and Kubler's subjects with Chol names. For example, Jaguar-Snake became Chan Bahlum "serpent jaguar."[3] Because phoneticism in the inscriptions was gaining acceptance, several rulers were named using what were thought to be phonetic renderings of their names. Sunshield thus became Pacal "shield." Over the years scholars have continued to work on the phonetic decipherment of these name glyphs.[4] Several recent publications have used the latest readings to describe these lords. I personally find this practice confusing. Given the dramatically changing and erratic state of phonetic decipherments, I have chosen to retain the nicknames with the understanding that they are precisely that.

The words found on Classic monuments do not merely list a series of events. These texts are narratives that often tell stories of a complex nature (Josserand 1991). They move both forward and backward in time, providing background information about the subjects and events. In longer texts the storyline is divided into episodes that build to a climax.

A basic assumption of modern research has been that the action in the image is the verb stated in the text or that it forms a couplet with the verb and provides additional information. This direct relationship is easily demonstrated on monuments where the verb is actually a pictograph of the action (Yaxchilan Stela 1) or where the verb has been phonetically deciphered and matches the action in the image (dance verbs accompanying actors dancing).[5] The text and image can also relate sequential actions of an event. For example, the text may state that the ruler set up a stone idol while the image illustrates another step in the ceremony.

When a text contains more than one event or when an image pictures more than one action, it is not always apparent what event matches what action. To clarify this situation the Late Classic Maya used a framing device in which glyph blocks were placed in proximity to the actions they were describing (Bassie-Sweet 1991:38–77). In some examples a sentence is so placed that in order to read it the viewer's eye is literally drawn across the action being described.

In applying the framing convention to Late Classic monuments it is apparent that many of the scenes that were initially interpreted to be accession ceremonies or underworld scenes are not. For example, at Piedras Negras the niche scenes are framed not by the accession text of the ruler but by his Period Ending narrative (Bassie-Sweet 1991:50–53). Many of the Palenque monuments are unquestionably illustrations of pre-accession rituals (Bassie-Sweet 1991:200–237).[6]

THE CALENDAR

A Maya date has two aspects called a Long Count date and a Calendar Round date. The Long Count gives the exact number of days that have elapsed since the beginning of the current era. The equivalent date in the Gregorian calendar system for this zero base date is 13 August 3114 B.C.[7] A Long Count date of 9.12.11.5.18 means that 9 periods of 400 years (*baktuns*), 12 periods of 20 years (*katuns*), 11 years (*tuns*), 5 months (*uinals*), and 18 days (*kins*) had passed since the beginning of the base date.[8] The zero base date was not the beginning of time but the end of a previous era and the beginning of a new one.

The Calendar Round consists of two parts called by modern scholars the *tzolkin* and the *haab*. The haab is a solar count of 365 days that is divided into 18 months composed of 20 days each (Pop, Uo, Zip, Zotz, Zec, Xul, Yaxkin, Mol, Ch'en, Yax, Zac, Ceh, Mac, Kankin, Muan, Pax, Kayab, and Cumku). An additional 5 days (called Uayeb) are added at the end of the haab, resulting in a close approximation to a solar year. A sequential series of days would have the haab positions of 1 Pop, 2 Pop, 3 Pop, and so forth. An unusual feature of the haab is that the twentieth day of any given month was also called the seating of the next month. For example, 20 Pop could be referred to as the seating of Uo.

The tzolkin is a count of 260 days. It is composed of the numbers 1 to 13 combined with 20 different day names (Imix, Ik, Akbal, Kan, Chicchan, Cimi, Manik, Lamat, Muluc, Oc, Chuen, Eb, Ben, Ix, Men, Cib, Caban, Etznab, Cauac, and Ahau). Each day both the day number and day name change. Hence, a sequential series of days would have the designation 1 Imix, 2 Ik, 3 Akbal, 4 Kan, 5 Chicchan, 6 Cimi, 7 Manik, 8 Lamat, 9 Muluc, 10 Oc, 11 Chuen, 12 Eb, 13 Ben, followed by 1 Ix, 2 Men, 3 Cib, 4 Caban, and so forth. Because 13 (the day number) and 20 (the number of day names) do not have a common denominator, the same day number and day name will not occur again for 260 days. Each day in the 260-day cycle had characteristics and aspects that influenced the events that occurred on that day.

The mathematics of the calendar dictate that a particular tzolkin date can only occur with the same haab date once every 52 years. For reasons we do not yet understand, the zero base date of the current era began on 4 Ahau 8 Cumku.

The first of Pop (New Year) can only occur with four day names, again because of the mathematics of the calendar. For the Classic period and Dresden codex these "Year-bearer" days were Akbal, Lamat, Ben, and Etznab; the Madrid codex and Bishop Landa's sources give the days Kan, Muluc, Ix, and Cauac.[9] During the days of Uayeb and the first of Pop, ceremonies were performed to usher in the New Year (see chapter 4). These ceremonies were reenactments of the destruction and re-creation of the world. The Classic Maya performed ceremonies at the end of each tun (360 days), but special attention was paid to the fifth, tenth, thirteenth, and fifteenth tun. The end of twenty tuns (the end of the katun) involved the most elaborate rituals, which also represented the symbolic destruction and re-creation of the world (see chapter 4). A katun ending would have a Long Count position such as 9.12.0.0.0. All katun endings occur on the day name Ahau. In addition to these celebrations, each month and each day had specific rituals that were carried out only at these times.

The calendar was directly related to the quadrilateral world model. This is evident in the 819 Day Count found in both Classic and Postclassic inscriptions (Thompson 1934; Berlin and Kelley 1961). These passages indicate that each day was assigned to a particular direction.[10]

Understanding and manipulating the calendar was a primary skill of the ritual specialists, which allowed them to structure time into recurring, predictable cycles. The calendar provided a means for calculating and anticipating the movements of the celestial bodies within the framework of the yearly cycle of the sun. They also used it to structure and maintain social institutions. For example, it was the mechanism for assigning the animal counterparts that were so important in establishing the hierarchy of the community (see below). The timing of all rituals was dictated by the calendar. The most venerated ritual location was the cave.

THE SACRED NATURE OF THE CAVE

The Maya were, and are, an agricultural society based on the production of corn. The importance of this staple in their life cannot be overstated. The Maya believe that without the sustenance provided by corn their souls would perish.

The central elements necessary for a productive crop are quality seed, fertile soil, sunshine, wind, rain, and fire. Sun, wind, and rain are the wild cards. The rain must come and go at precisely the right times or the crop suffers. Too much is as bad as too little. The wind must fan the fires of the milpa but not spread the fires out of control. It must bring the rainclouds and blow them away to let the sun shine. If the wind blows hard during the growing season it will break the stalks and ruin the crop. Because of the importance of agriculture, the Maya were most concerned with sun, rain, wind, fire, and corn. All of these elements were intimately associated with the cave.

The cave was naturally thought to be the source of surface water, for most of the caves in the Maya region are wet and many contain springs, streams, rivers, waterfalls, pools of water, or small lakes. The Maya also believed that rain, mist, clouds, thunder, lightning, and wind were produced in caves. There is often a cool or even cold wind blowing from the opening as the warm air of the outside world draws the cool air from the cave. This natural observation surely led to the conclusion that wind was created in caves. Moist environment and temperature changes often create mist. It is not unusual to find clouds of mist at the mouth of the cave and at vertical openings. In addition, clouds form on the slopes and tops of mountains. These phenomena have been used to explain why clouds and rain were thought to be formed in caves (Vogt 1969:82; MacLeod and Puleston 1978:73). During storms, lightning bolts flash around the mountain tops, giving the impression that lightning, a natural source of fire, originates there. The Maya also believed that corn was first procured from a mountain. This too may be based on natural observation. The slopes of elevations were usually the last to be cultivated due to the difficult nature of the terrain. These locations were sources of wild corn, which grew particularly well near cave openings with their sheltered environment, soil accumulation, and higher moisture levels.[11]

In addition, many Mesoamerican groups believed that their creators fashioned humans from the corn and water found in a cave and that humans first emerged from a cave. The theme of procreation was consistently associated with the cave throughout Mesoamerica, depicting it as a womb and as a source of life.

The deities associated with corn, rain, lightning, thunder, and wind were thought to reside in caves, particularly caves associated with the high elevations that surrounded the community. The cave deities guarded the community from the destructive forces of the outside world.

High elevations were not thought to be upthrust hunks of rock, but sacred beings. There was, and still is, an almost universal Maya belief that all elevations contain caves whether or not there is a physical opening. The world inside the mountain was thought to be much like the outside world. The supernaturals lived in houses and conducted their daily lives much as humans did. As the apparent source of corn, rain, lightning, and wind and as the home of the deities who owned or protected these elements, the cave was a powerful location for fertility rights and by extension cycles of creation, destruction, and re-creation (birth, death, and rebirth).

SUPERNATURALS

For the purpose of this study, a supernatural is a being not explainable by natural laws or phenomena. The term pertains to deities, spirits, and the souls of the ancestors as well as entities such as goblins, gnomes, and fairies. This book contains a general introduction to some of the major deities (these supernaturals and the lesser supernaturals associated with caves are the subject of a future volume).

Souls and Spirits

In the world of the Maya humans, plants, animals, objects, landscape features, and even phenomena such as darkness and thunder were thought to have a soul or spirit. For ease of discussion, I use the term *soul* to refer to humans and *spirit* to refer to all other categories of beings, objects, and phenomena.[12] These souls and spirits appear to have been separate entities that represented the essence of the individual or thing. It was the responsibility of the deities, the ancestors, and the ruling elite to protect these entities.

Many modern beliefs concerning souls are applicable to precolumbian beliefs. The modern soul has several different forms but is most often thought of as wind or at least as traveling like wind. The human soul exists in two locations at once: in the heart or blood of the body and in a supernatural animal (animal counterpart) who lives in a sacred ancestral mountain in the vicinity of the community. An animal counterpart, as the name implies, takes the form of a specific animal except in the case of the animal counterpart of a ritual specialist, which can take the form of lightning or whirlwinds.[13] Some modern Maya groups believe that a person may have as many as thirteen different animal counterparts, while others believe there is only one. The spiritual strength of the individual is determined by the species of the animal counterpart. Jaguars and lightning/serpents are at the top of the hierarchy. When an ordinary person is in a state of unconsciousness, the soul can leave the body and the animal counterparts can leave the ancestral cave. Ritual specialists, however, are in command of their animal counterparts at all times and use them to perform beneficial and harmful deeds.

All things have a spirit. The spirits of certain elements such as corn, water, wind, and lightning can also be contained in idols and objects to which offerings can be made (see below). For example, the spirit of lightning is contained in flint and obsidian. The concept that some forces can also have an animal form is fundamental to the understanding of Maya culture. The spirit of lightning is contained in certain snakes, while the spirit of corn is said to reside in a toad. The spirits of sacred elements can also take human form. In Tzotzil Chenalho the spirit of corn is manifested as the maiden daughter of the rain god (Guiteras 1961:40). There is a predominant belief that corn was first procured from a sacred cave with the help of the rain gods. One of the variations on this theme tells of a man's journey to the rain god's cave. The rain god gives his daughter, the spirit of corn, to the man to be his wife. She has the ability to produce abundant amounts of corn, but the man eventually loses her due to inappropriate behavior. The moral of the story is that the deity entrusts humans with the spirit of corn, but only if they act properly will the spirit provide for them.

In a Tzeltal tale a man finds an injured snake (the spirit of lightning) who asks to be carried to his cave in a nearby rock. A huge toad appears at the entrance and summons Thunderbolt, the owner of the cave. The snake turns into the handsome son of Thunderbolt and three toads in the cave turn into his beautiful daughters (Hermitte 1964:41). This sibling relationship between corn and lightning is reflected in the Tzeltal term for *Rhadinaea* snakes: "the big brother of the mother of corn" (Hunn 1977:243). These stories illustrate that the spirits of lightning and corn (two of the primary elements owned by the deity) can be personified as the deity's children and can have animal forms.

Deities

For the purpose of this book, a deity is neither a spirit nor the personification of a spirit but a separate entity who owns, protects, or controls some force, element, or object that humans think they must have to survive and thus must be respected, worshiped, or appeased.

Oral traditions, colonial period documents, and the depictions of deities in Maya art illustrate several themes such as the formation of the earth and its preparation for humans by the creator deities, the creation of humankind by these same deities, and the acquisition of patron deities. These sources reveal that the deities, like humans, were in competition and conflict with one another. They underwent trials, adventures, rites of passage, stages of growth, and transformations. A Maya deity could have both benevolent and malevolent intentions toward humans. Like other aspects of Maya life, the deities were structured into a hierarchy.[14] It is not always apparent how this hierarchy operated and whether it remained stable over time, space, and circumstance. Many of the major deities had a quadripartite nature directly related to the quadrilateral world model. For example, there was an East Bacab, North Bacab, West Bacab, and South Bacab.

In order to categorize the deities found in Postclassic codices, Paul Schellhas (1904) grouped deities with similar traits together and assigned an alphabetic designation. In Classic period contexts the same alphabetic designation used for a Postclassic deity is used when a Classic deity with similar diagnostic traits is identified. The four surviving Postclassic codices are divinatory in nature and were probably the property of priests.[15] They have survived through historical accident and are not a representative sampling of Maya codices; thus they do not portray all the deities. In similar fashion the deities depicted in Classic Maya art do not represent all Maya deities, merely those that were pertinent to the stories being told.

Several methods are used to identify deities. Isolating the diagnostic features of a deity and comparing them with the features of a deity known from colonial period documents has been the most successful to date. Matching the nominal glyphs that accompany these deities with known deity names has also been productive. Documents like the Quiche *Popol Vuh* indicate that deities can be grouped into categories by location and function, such as the creator grandparents of the sea, the patron deities specific to a lineage, and the patron deities of the leading lineages who protect the community and the world.

Some authors have suggested that the ruler experienced an apotheosis at death, but the illustrations of deceased rulers and ancestors at Palenque and Copan show no such transformation. The souls of the ancestors were worshiped and appeased, but they were supernaturals below and separate from the deities.[16]

A review of the hieroglyphic texts and art of the Classic period demonstrates that throughout the Maya region the major deities appear in the same contexts. I conclude from this that the Classic Maya elite held common beliefs concerning these deities, although regional variations were also present.

Idols

The Maya often directed their ritual offerings to idols. At least two kinds of idols have been identified: objects that represented a deity or ancestor and objects that were the receptacle for a spirit owned or protected by a deity.

Modern idols come in many forms, ranging from plain and carved stones to Catholic saint images. These idols may or may not have anthropomorphic features. Some are hollow and are also used as incense burners. Many of the modern idols, whether they are of precolumbian or modern origin, are thought to have been discovered in a cave (Laughlin 1977:2).[17]

Atitecos believe that most things have a spirit or "intangible co-essence" and that there is a hierarchy of spirits associated with each thing (Douglas 1969:78). Thus there is a specific spirit who resides in each ear or kernel of corn, a generic spirit of all corn who resides in two female stone fetishes called the heart of the corn, and the spirit in charge of corn called a spirit lord, who resides in a Catholic saint statue. In the last two examples, the spirit resides in the body of an object to which ritual activity can be directed.

Assuming that all things have a spirit that represents their essential character, it may be concluded that an idol also has its own spirit. Each of the Atitecos' stones should have a spirit. In addition, there is evidence that an idol can contain spirits relating to more than just one element.

Although they are often of secondary importance, the idol's physical properties can be related to the sacred spirit it hosts. For example, flint can be struck to produce sparks that are visually related to lightning and both elements are natural sources of fire. The Maya apparently believe that flint can produce sparks because it contains the spirit of lightning. It is frequently said that lightning is created when the rain god throws his axe (the literal translation of some of the terms for lightning is "the axe of the rain god"). The ancient axe heads found today in fields or near lightning strikes are considered to be just such axes. The modern Maya greatly prize these as sacred objects and often place them at ritual locations such as mountain shrines and church altars. These flint and obsidian stones are repositories for the spirit of lightning just as the Atitecos' stone fetishes are the repositories for the spirit of corn.

The Spanish reports of the contact period make references to the numerous idols worshiped by the precolumbian Maya. These idols took the form of clay and stone incensarios; wood, clay, and stone statues; and speleothems. There is nothing in the literature or archaeological record to suggest that these idols did not function in the same manner as modern idols: they represented the deity and/or contained a spirit owned or protected by the deity.[18]

Offerings to a modern idol are consumed by the spirit in the idol or by the deity who comes to the idol to partake of the offering. The Lacandon believe that the deity does not reside in the idol representing it. Their idols are said to be "treated as the person of the god in question, without being considered as such" (Bruce 1975:80). Landa noted that "they knew well that the idols were the works of their hands, dead and without a divine nature; but they held them in reverence on account of what they represented" (Tozzer 1941:111).

Offerings of food, drink, or incense can be left out for a deity on an altar or presented directly to the idol. The deity arrives at the site, eats the spirit of the offering, and leaves. In the case of burning incense, the deity consumes the spirit of the smoke. The incense is often mixed with the blood of a chicken or turkey and then burnt. The spirit of these birds, which is contained in their blood, is thus eaten by the deity. Spanish accounts of Postclassic human sacrifice describe the importance of extracting the still beating heart of the victim to offer to the deity. The intent of this practice seems to be capturing the victim's soul and offering it to the deity to be eaten. The practice of smearing the idol's mouth with blood ("feeding the idol") also appears to represent this concept. Many accounts describe how the deity arrives at the ritual location and partakes of the spirits in the burning incense. A number of Classic stelae illustrate deities in scrolls representing clouds (Houston and Stuart, cited in Schele 1992). These deities hover above the ruler, who is conducting a ritual that includes the burning of the incense. They are probably consuming the spirits in the incense.

The Ancestors

When the modern Maya refer to the ancestors, they may mean either the souls of departed kin group members or the souls of the founding members of the community and all subsequent leaders and ritual specialists. These latter souls, along with their animal counterparts, form a supernatural government whose duty it is to protect and punish the community. In conjunction with the guardian deities, they regulate and control the daily lives of the community members. The living leaders and ritual specialists are also members of this ancestral council. The hierarchy established in the natural world continues after death. The ancestors represent the great moral force of the universe (Bunzel 1952:269). Similar concepts are found in the Late Classic (see chapters 3 and 6).

Although the ancestors of the modern Maya are thought to live in the many caves surrounding the borders of the community, there is invariably one senior cave associated with a directional mountain. The concept of a senior ancestral cave oriented to one of the mythological mountains of the horizon was present in the Classic period. A compound glyph associated with specific sites was nicknamed the emblem glyph (Berlin 1958). As a title, this compound is composed of the hand-scattering drops, an *ahau* "lord" sign, and a main sign specific to the inscriptions of a particular area. It is paraphrased as "the holy lord of X." In several inscriptions the emblem glyph is used as a specific place name (Stuart and Houston in press). Many of these emblem place names are also the location of Period Ending events associated with one of the directional mountains.[19] The mythological locations called *Matawil* and *Na Ho Chan* are used as emblem glyphs in the name phrases of deities. In the case of *Matawil*, it is clear that this location is a place of origin (see chapter 3, note 2). Emblem glyphs designate a specific location associated with the sides of the world and a place of origin, surely the senior ancestral cave (see chapter 6).

The major sites were governed by a ruler who claimed patrilineal descent from the founding ancestors.[20] Some inscriptions contain episodes that relate the descent line of the ruling lineage, while others mention that the ruler was a particular number in the descent line. The founding ancestor of the lineage was invariably from the Early Classic period or earlier. The *ahau* title, which was carried by both males and females, indicated an individual's membership in a ruling lineage (see chapter 6).[21]

THE RULING ELITE

Classic leaders had administrative, judicial, military, and religious roles.[22] Two symbols represented the office and authority of the ruler: the mat and the jaguar (see chapter 7). The God C *ch'ul* title represented an office held by a subordinate lord (Stuart, cited in Houston 1993). This official seems to have had administrative and mediating functions in the house of the lord (Houston 1993:130). Other subordinate lords carried a title pronounced *sahal*, but the meaning of this title is unclear.[23] Some of these *sahal* lords lived within the main site, while others ruled communities in the vicinity. There is some indication that the brothers of the ruler could hold this title (Houston 1993:130).

It is known from several Classic hieroglyphic texts that the members of the ruling lineage were trained in the arts of divination, writing, and calendrics (Reents 1985; Stuart 1987). The ruler, certain women, and secondary lords acted as ritual specialists when they performed the state-sponsored ceremonies for the community such as the Period Ending events.[24] They petitioned the deities for a safe and ordered world. The political responsibilities of preserving life and perpetuating the group through its institutions were firmly rooted in religious responsibilities:

> By the preservation of life is understood the well-being of body and soul; this implies control over the powers of nature that will insure the regular succession of the days and the seasons, and the fertility of the soil; that will protect man against the evil powers in the world and his fellowman, and ward off violence and envy, illness and death. . . . To govern is to care for and protect; therefore he who governs wrestles with evil and through his sacrifice and efforts draws upon the people the blessings of the ever-reluctant gods. (Guiteras 1961:78)

With this background on the deities, the ancestors, and the ruling elite, the following chapter examines the physical environment of the Maya.

1
THE PARTS
OF THE UNIVERSE

All individuals and communities strive to order and structure their environment to bring under control forces that are ultimately uncontrollable. Creating a world view is about making and maintaining a safe place to live. This chapter describes the culturally ordered world of the Maya and how they believed that order was established, with an overview of the precolumbian concepts of sea, earth, sky, horizon, and underworld.

THE SEA

The concept that the flat disk of the world floats on a sea is frequently found in Maya sources. Water as the boundary between the flat earth and the underworld is also a common theme. In many modern sources the concepts of the precolumbian underworld and Christian hell have merged, but the notion of a sea separating the earth from the underworld remains. The ancestors of the Chorti said that "under the world which we live on, farther down, they say that there is just water. And they say that under the water, what there is is another place. Like here. And they say that that place there is filled with all the people called evil" (Fought 1972:371).

In a modern Yucatan prayer the edge of the world is described as a beach: "Bless me at the right hand of the beach, at the right hand where it thunders, at the right hand, at the eastern source of the sky [horizon]" (Sosa 1985:323). The *Ritual of the Bacabs* incantations make reference to the directions: the north shore, the north estuary, west shore, the west estuary, the south shore, the south estuary (Roys 1965:26–28). The Chorti ancestors are quoted as saying "at the edge of the world at the edge of the sea, there live the angels" (Fought 1972:374).

The sea is characterized as a layered body of water that contains both saltwater and freshwater animals as well as a host of supernaturals. It is the home of the creator deities of the sea and is represented by lakes, pools of water, and water shrines. The surface is often covered in waterlily plants. The T501 sign is a pictograph of a waterlily that can represent both the sea and water shrines (see chapter 2). In certain contexts it carries the value of *naab*, which means both waterlily and sea.

In Chorti belief, the sea is divided into four quadrants, each associated with a color: milk white, blood red, blue-green, and pitch black (Fought 1972:433). During the Quiche hero twins' journey to the underworld, they arrived at a crossroads of black, white, red, and blue-green roads, suggesting that these represent roads to the great sea, which was divided into quadrants. In Quiche and Yucatec Maya sources the creator couple of the sea is associated with the east sea (see below).

The Maya refer to the color that is midway between blue and green as *yax*, which also means "first." In the *Popol Vuh* the creator grandparents are said to be the makers of a *yax* plate and *yax* bowl, which were the first ritual dishes. They are described as glittering light in water, wrapped in blue-green quetzal feathers. The divination stones of Ix Chel (the Yucatec Maya ancestral grandmother) and the idols representing Itzamna (the ancestral grandfather) were also colored blue-green (Tozzer 1941:130, 154). This association is based on their roles as the first couple and their location in the blue-green water of the eastern sea.

All Maya homes contain three stones that form the fireplace. The Classic place name for the ancestral couple's home includes the phrase "the First Three Stones" (see chapter 6). Thus their home was in effect called the first home. The First Three Stones place was situated in the east quadrant.

THE EARTH

The Maya considered the earth to be a living, sacred entity. It was both the source of the sacred sustenance of corn and the place from which humans came and to which they would return in death. Metaphors alluding to the disk shape of the world are found in many contexts. For example, in Chenalho corn should not be planted during the three days centered around the new moon, for it is believed that seeds planted at this time will not sprout (Guiteras 1961:41). If corn must be planted during this time the farmer carries a miniature tortilla with three holes in it: because this imitation disk-shaped earth has holes, the young plants will be able to come through to the surface. The surface of the earth is frequently depicted or referred to as a turtle or caiman (Redfield and Villa Rojas 1934:207; Taube 1988b). Both these animals are appropriate symbols because they have the ability to float on the water of the mythological sea.

Most Maya sources describe the surface of the earth as a square with a defined center (Redfield and Villa Rojas 1934:114; Vogt 1969:297; Sosa 1989:132). The sides of the quadrilateral world were oriented to the four directions, just as most square spaces such as milpas, houses, and altars were. The midpoints on the sides of the quadrilateral world were aligned with the cardinal directions. Each directional side was assigned a specific color. The earliest combinations were red/east, white/north, black/west, and yellow/south (Thompson 1934:212; Berlin and Kelley 1961; Kelley 1976).

When the quadrilateral world model is superimposed on the flat disk of the earth, the horizon (where sky meets earth) is outside the boundaries of the quadrilateral model. In each of the four horizon areas was a mythological mountain centered on the midpoint (fig. 1). The deities and ancestors resided in these mountains. A cave opening marked by a tree/cross was found at each midpoint. The cave provided access to the mountain and its supernaturals, to the sea beyond the mountain, and to the underworld beyond that. Illustrations and descriptions of the mythological mountains appear in many sources. For example, in the Dresden New Year pages deities are illustrated presenting offerings to an idol and world tree. The Chilam Balam books describe the Pauahtun wind deities, seats, and trees at these locations.[1] The *Ritual of the Bacabs* incantations paint a rich

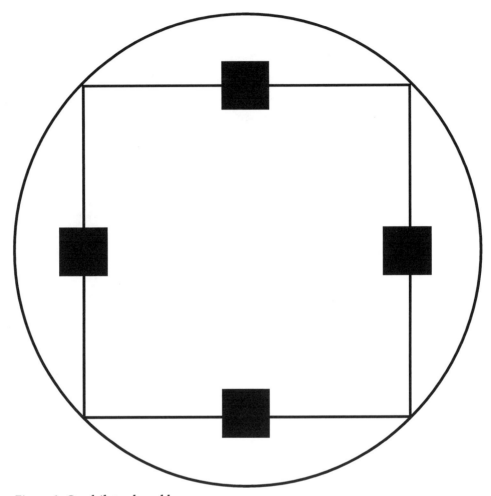

Figure 1. Quadrilateral world

and detailed picture of these sacred places.[2] Several chants refer to the horizon cave as the location of a world tree, the door to the house of a Pauahtun, a crossroads, and a resting place. These mountains are discussed more fully in chapter 3.

The perimeter of the quadrilateral world was conceived to be a road. Four roads also radiated from the center to each midpoint on the side (fig. 2). These ran on an east/west and north/south axis. The roads did not end at the midpoint but continued into the cave. The midpoint, where the road crossed the perimeter, was called a crossroads, as was the center where all four roads joined. Several *Ritual of the Bacabs* incantations

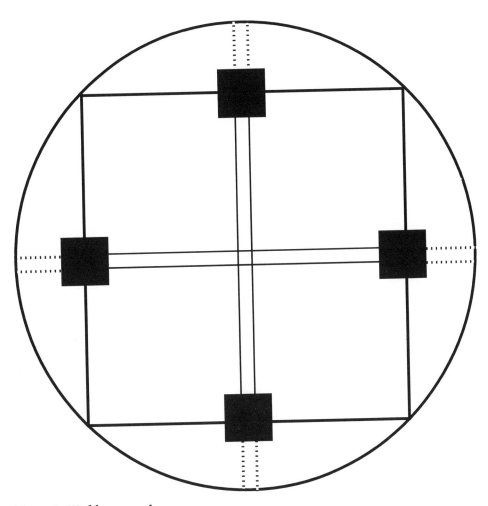

Figure 2. World crossroads

appropriately refer to the midpoints as the four crossroads. One of the deities named is Ix Hol-can-be "lady opening-at-the-four-crossroads" (Roys 1965:7, 149, 161). This name also refers to the caves at the midpoints: the term *hol* is applied to the holes or caves on the sides of a ritual space.

A number of Late Classic texts record a cycle of time referred to as the 819 Day Count, indicating that a God K or an idol representing him was set up at one of the midpoint seats at the end of every 819 days (Thompson 1934; Berlin and Kelley 1961). This demonstrates that the world of the Classic was conceived to be quadrilateral. The zero base date of the Long Count was the end of the previous era and the beginning of the new and current era. The Palenque Cross Tablet contains a passage that refers to the time before the beginning of the current era. It speaks of the birth of a female deity in 3121 B.C. and includes an 819 Day Count. This indicates that the world of the previous era was also thought to be quadrilateral.

In addition to the sources that refer directly to the world, a considerable amount of data about the center, sides, corners, and midpoints of the quadrilateral world model can be accumulated by reviewing the forms that use this structure. The Maya replicated the quadrilateral model when they built or established any human space such as communities, towns, temple/pyramids, houses, altars, beds, milpas, or ritual spaces.[3] These quadrilateral forms were often used as metaphors to describe the earth. For example, the corners of the earth were called corner posts of the house; the Yucatec phrase "the sun enters his house" refers to the sun entering the earth at sunset. The Chol say it is night when the sun is in his house.[4]

John Sosa (1985:315) noted that "ritual activity is directed towards and expresses a cosmological order." The placing of offerings at the midpoints of a quadrilateral ritual space was common. Ritual activity was directed toward locations that symbolized the midpoints of the world because they represented the sacred caves of the ancestors and deities. Offerings left at these locations were intended for these supernaturals.

Natural caves in the vicinity of the community were also thought to represent the horizon caves. Many modern communities still use four sacred mountain or caves to define their borders ritually. For example, each year the new Quiche Year-bearer is "greeted" with incense and fireworks on one of four Year-bearer mountains that surround Momostenango (Tedlock 1982:101). In Todos Santos there are four sacred mountains, each associated with one of the Year-bearers; ritual circuits to these locations are still performed in conjunction with important days in the native calendar (Oakes 1951). Four sacred mountains define the ceremonial center of Tzotzil Zinacantan (Vogt 1969:49), and four sacred mountain caves demarcate the sacred space of Tzeltal Pinola (Hermitte 1964:49).[5] A number of sources that refer to the creation of the world by the deities provide additional information about the Maya world view.

The Creation

In the *Popol Vuh* there are two kinds of gods who bring about the creation of the earth and humankind: sky and sea deities. The deities of the primordial sea were known by the names Maker, Modeler, Bearer, Begetter, Hunahpu Possum, Hunahpu Coyote, Great White Peccary, Tapir, Sovereign Plumed Serpent, Heart of the Lake, Heart of the Sea, Maker of the Blue-Green Bowl, Maker of the Blue-Green Plate, Xpiyacoc, and Xmucane.[6] The names of the sky deities were Heart of Sky, Hurricane, Thunderbolt Hurricane, New Born Thunderbolt, and Raw Thunderbolt. Through consultation with each other, these deities conceived of humans and a world in which they might live. The sky deities created the earth by making it rise out of the sea:

> And then the earth rose because of them, it was simply their word that brought it forth. For the forming of the earth they said "Earth." It arose suddenly, just like a cloud, like a mist, now forming, unfolding. Then the mountains were separated from the water, all at once the great mountains came forth. By their genius alone, by their cutting edge alone they carried out the conception of the mountain-plain, whose face grew instant groves of cypress and pine. . . .Such was the formation of the earth when it was brought forth by the Heart of the Sky, Heart of the Earth, as they are called, since they were the first to think of it. The sky was set apart, and the earth was set apart in the midst of the waters. (Tedlock 1985:73)

After creating the earth, the deities prepared it for human habitation. This preparation is specifically described as being quadrilateral in the *Popul Vuh:*

> The fourfold siding, fourfold cornering,
> measuring, fourfold staking,
> halving the cord, stretching the cord
> in the sky, on the earth,
> the four sides, the four corners. (Tedlock 1985:72)

This provides clear evidence that the Quiche believed the quadrilateral model was a product of divine creation. The Maya measure out their milpas using a cord, and Dennis Tedlock's informant observed that this passage "describes the measuring out of the sky and earth as if a corn-field were being laid out for cultivation" (Tedlock 1985:244). The cord is stretched out to its full length and folded in half. This suggests that both the corners (stretching the cord along the side of the square) and the midpoints (halfway along the side) were being measured. The making of a milpa is viewed by the Maya as the creation of a human space safe from the dangerous wild. It is, in effect, duplicating the crea-tion of the human world by the deities. This means that in addition to being viewed as a road the perimeter of the world was also demarcated by a cord or rope. During the modern Yucatec *loh* ceremony, Sosa (1985) noted that the space is symbolically tied and untied by ritual circuits around the quadrilateral. This allows the evil winds inhabiting it to escape through holes around the perimeter and prevents them from returning.

The Postclassic ceremonies were often initiated with the ritual crea-tion of a quadrilateral space (Tozzer 1941). Four assistants stood where the corners of the square were desired. A long cord was stretched between them to mark the perimeter of the square. Each of the four inner columns of Copan Structure 18 picture Yax Pac performing a dance that was related to the act of tying (Grube 1992:213). These tying dances formed a quadri-lateral space just as the deities tied off the quadrilateral world (the location of this Copan space is discussed in chapter 2).

In the *Popol Vuh* the deities prepared the earth for humans by creating the cycles of sun, moon, and stars (Tedlock 1985). These cycles are repre-sented by the epic adventures of the ancestral couple's children (Hun Hunahpu/sun and Vucub Hunahpu/Venus) and grandchildren (Hunahpu/sun and Xbalenque/full moon). This suggests that the fourfold siding/fourfold cornering that also prepared the surface of the earth for humans was related to these astronomical events. It was, in fact, the annual cycle of the sun that demarcated the quadrilateral space on the surface of the earth, as the following section shows.[7]

The Solar Basis of the Quadrilateral Model

From a visual perspective, the observer is at the center of the world. Most groups have an ethnocentric view in which the village is thought to be the center. For example, the Tzeltal villagers of Pinola and Amatenango consider their towns to be *yolil b'alumilal* "the navel of the world" (Hermitte 1964:45; Nash 1970:2). A ritual specialist in the Mam village of Todos Santos reported:

> My grandparents told me that the pueblo is as old as the world. . . . Tata Dios [father god] placed Todos Santos in the middle of the sky. . . . This pueblo is in the centre of the world; it is the heart of the world. . . . Domingo Calmos spread his arms out like a cross and turned halfway around so that he covered the four directions. (Oakes 1951:54)

The exact center is often marked: the Tzotzil communities of Zinacantan and Chamula have a small hill called "the navel of the world" or "the navel of the earth" (Vogt 1969:297; Gossen 1974:18). The Kanjobalan community of Santa Eulalia has a cross in front of its Rosario chapel that is called the "middle of the village" (La Farge 1947:112, 127). It must be noted that these occur in locations that are not the physical center of the communities. Yucatan village centers are marked by a cenote and its tree/cross (Redfield and Villa Rojas 1934:114). In Yucatec Valladolid the center of the world was thought to be marked by a giant yaxche tree with its branches ascending through the layers of the sky (Tozzer 1907).[8] In regard to the training of a Quiche daykeeper in Momostenango, Barbara Tedlock (1982:71) noted:

> During the following 260-day period, the daykeeper may be further trained concerning the "six-place" (*wakibal*) shrine. This is located on Paclom, a hill in the town center; it is the "heart" (*C'ux*) or center of the Momostecan world, spiritually connected to four inner hills of the four directions or corners, each located within a radius of about three kilometers.

When the sun attained its noon position on the day of zenith passage it was directly above the center of the quadrilateral model. Alfonso Villa Rojas (1988:130) noted:

> The sun's passage through the zenith is a subject of great interest to the Tzeltal Indians of Chiapas since it lends support to their contention that their land occupies "the center of the world." . . . I was asked, "Have you not noticed that on certain days the sun rests for awhile exactly above the church of our chief town?" A similar idea exists among the Mams of Guatemala.

The crossroads at the center of the world was also visually aligned with the rise and set points of the equinox sun.

At present there are no apparent means of establishing where the symbolic center of a Classic town and village was thought to be. For example, without the testimony of modern informants such as those in Zinacantan, it would be easy to conclude that the center of the world was the main plaza bordered by the church. Yet in Zinacantan the center is a physically insignificant hill near the outskirts of the town.

There has been considerable debate over what established the corners of the square; modern sources indicate it was either the intercardinal points or the rise and set points of the sun on the solstices (Thompson 1934; Redfield and Villa Rojas 1934; Villa Rojas 1945; Girard 1962; Vogt 1969:601; Villa Rojas 1988; Sosa 1989:132). Both models ultimately derive from the rise and set points of the sun. In a model based on the intercardinal directions, the corners of the square are calculated by observing the east and west rise and set points of the equinox sun and using these to extrapolate north, south, and the intercardinal points. In a solstice-based model, the corners of the quadrilateral space are established by direct observation of the solstice sun (observing when the sun "turns" and begins to rise and set at points closer to the equinox points). This is still an important event for the Maya, who beseech the sun to come back at this time.

In order to decide which of these two was the precolumbian model, we must review what directions mean to the Maya and the pivotal role of the sun. By definition the terms for east—"the exit of the sun (from the earth)"—and west—"the entrance of the sun (into the earth)"—can be applied to any point between the solstice rise and set points (see the appendix for discussion of Maya directions). These terms cannot be used to refer to the horizon area between the intercardinal points and the rise and set points of the solstice sun because the sun never reaches these areas. Accepting these directional definitions in a literal fashion means that the limits of east and west must be formed by the solstice points, not the intercardinal points. One of the drawbacks in a solstice model is that it is a rectangle not a square. How can we reconcile this discrepancy? I suggest that this model was idealized into a square, just as the modern Chorti and Yucatec who use the solstice model today have idealized it.[9]

The quadrilateral world model is used to define the borders of Yucatec towns. The corners have stone slab altars that are called resting places. During the period of the solstice, the sun appears to rise and set at the same location on the horizon for several days. The Maya interpret this to mean that the sun is resting there. The corners of the world were also thought to be the location of caves, for the sun rose out of a cave and set back into one (see chapter 2).

The solstice points formed the corners of the square, but the midpoints are aligned with the cardinal directions. The Early Classic buildings of Uaxactun Group E are noted for their astronomical alignment (Ricketson 1928; Aveni 1980:279) (fig. 3). When the observer is stationed on Pyramid E-VII, the sun rises over the northeast corner of Temple E-I on the summer solstice, over the center of Temple E-II on the equinox, and over the southeast corner of Temple E-II on the winter solstice. These buildings, an architectural model for the east side of the world, demonstrate that the eastern midpoint was aligned with the rising of the equinox sun.[10]

Ritual Circuits as Replications of the Sun's Path: Paths or roads are often associated with the perimeter of the spaces that replicate the world model. Examples of this are found in Yucatan, where the sides of the town are marked by a ritual path that connects the four corners (Sosa 1989:134). Ritual circuits are conducted around most spaces that are based on the quadrilateral world model. Part of the Yucatec Chan Kom ceremony to rid the village of evil winds, the *loh* "redeem" ceremony, involved such a circuit:

> Then all the participants went together to each of the four "entrances" of the village in turn, and at each, the *h-men* buried in the road, the usual preventives against the evil winds: a piece of obsidian (*tok*), a cross made of *tancaz-che* [prickly-ash], another of *halalche*, and a little salt. All of them returned to the altar and the h-men prayed again. (Redfield and Villa Rojas 1934:176)

Ritual circuits tend to follow the pattern east, north, west, and south. The solstice rise and set points established the corners of the square. The east and west sides of the quadrilateral space represented, in effect, the annual path of the sun. The north and south sides of the square represented the path of the solstice sun both above and below the earth

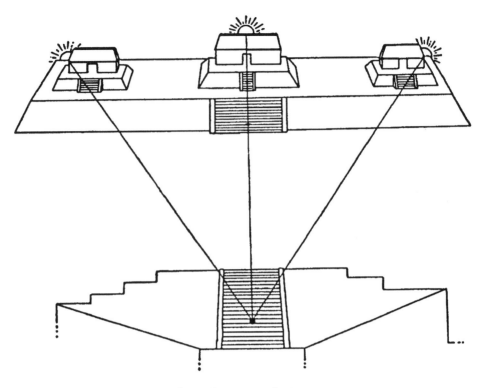

Figure 3. Uaxactun Group E (after Sylvanus Morley)

superimposed on the surface of the world. Thus these ritual circuits symbolically duplicated the annual path of the sun, creating safe human space.

The Tikal twin pyramid complexes are replications of the quadrilateral world (fig. 4; see chapter 3). The east and west mythological mountains are represented by radial pyramids. The top of the pyramid represents the midpoint and the four staircases represent the four roads radiating from this point. In terms of a vertical axis, the tops of the mythological mountains (the crossroads) were the locations where sky met earth, but they also had a direct relationship with the sun. From the perspective of a center-oriented viewer, the east and west tops were aligned with the rise and set points of the equinox sun and the north and south tops were aligned with the sun's noon position on the solstices. The sun, therefore, was directly related not only to the corners and center of the quadrilateral but also to the midpoints. While the deities were preparing the surface

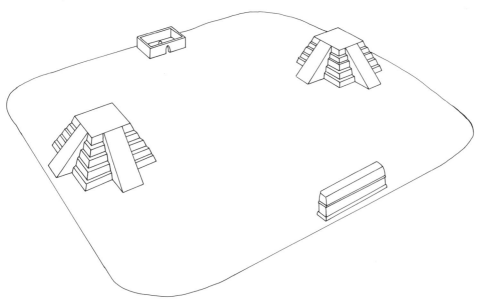

Figure 4. Tikal twin pyramid complex (after Norman Johnson)

of the earth by creating the sun and its cycle, they were also working on the creation of humans.

The Making of Humans and the Acquisition of Idols

The *Popol Vuh* creator deities stated that their purpose was to make beings that would admire and worship them. They did not succeed in their first attempts; these prototypes were either destroyed or transformed into animals. In the final creation the deities succeeded by using corn and water found in a mountain cave. The ancestral grandmother ground this corn into a fine paste that was modeled into four humans, who became the founding heads of the four major Quiche lineages, the first members of the ancestral council. Other men who became the lineage heads of their respective groups were also formed at this time, but the *Popol Vuh* only details those of the Quiche.

Before the sun appeared in the sky for the first time, the four lineage heads made a pilgrimage to a citadel called Seven Caves to acquire a patron deity (Tohil, Auilix, Hacauitz, and Middle of the Plain). At the instruction of Tohil, all the tribes journeyed to a mountain called Place of Advice.

To make the trip each of the Quiche deities was placed in a backpack or rack and carried by his respective lineage head. At Place of Advice, Tohil, Auilix, and Hacauitz requested that they be hidden in the surrounding countryside, where they would not be subject to attack or plunder by opposing groups and where the Quiche could come and worship them.[11] Jaguar Night took his deity Auilix to a deep canyon; Mahucutah and Jaguar Quitze placed their deities (Hacauitz and Tohil) high on mountains. Each patron deity was placed in an arbor. These three sacred places became known as Pauilix "at Auilix," Patohil "at Tohil," and Hacauitz.

On Hacauitz mountain the Quiche waited and prayed for the sun, moon, and stars to appear. When they finally did, there was great rejoicing and offerings were made to them. The appearance of the sun represented the establishment of the square on the surface of the earth and, thus, the beginning of safe human space. It also marked Hacauitz as the center of the world; the Quiche established their first community there.

This first appearance of the sun also turned the three patron deities to stone. It is not clear why this occurred, but the Quiche continued to hold these patron deities in the highest esteem and to leave offerings to these stone idols. When the community was threatened by invaders, the lineage heads called upon Tohil, a lightning deity, as guardian of the community. These episodes tell us that the creation of safe human space involved the establishment of a quadrilateral world based on the annual cycle of the sun and the setting up of patron deities at what eventually became the borders of the community.

The four lineage heads instructed their descendants to honor and call upon them after their deaths. Leaving behind a sacred bundle to which offerings could be made, the four departed (died) and became the founding members of the ancestral council, the ancestral fathers of their community. The last section of the *Popol Vuh* tells of the pilgrimage of the second generation of Quiche lords to another citadel, where they received important emblems of power. On their return the Quiche migrated to a number of sites in succession, gathering power and prestige along the way. Many generations later, they finally settled at Utatlan, where the shrines of the patron deities were replicated around the main plaza.[12] These final episodes deal with the establishment of the ancestral council, the acquisition of power symbols, and the replication of the world model when a new community was formed.

The Postclassic Re-creation of the World

One of the common themes in Mesoamerican creation myths is the idea that humans and their world were created and destroyed a number of times (Tozzer 1941:136; Thompson 1970:330-47). A small number of Classic texts refer to the beginning of the current era. Several authors have suggested that the era events refer to the creation of the world, the setting into motion of the night sky, or the appearance of certain constellations. It is highly likely that the era event represented not the first creation of the world but the last cycle of destruction and re-creation (Thompson 1950:149). The Classic re-creation texts refer to the setting up of stone idols representing the guardian deities (discussed in chapter 4).

In the *Popol Vuh* the deities destroyed the world with a black rainstorm and great flood. Most Maya references to the last destruction suggest that the devastation resulted in the surface of the world being flooded.

The destruction of the world is illustrated on Dresden page 74, preceding the New Year pages (fig. 5). In this scene water cascades from the mouth of a monster with a skyband body. Chac Chel (the ancestral grandmother), dressed in the costume elements of God A (a death deity), pours water from a jar. God L crouches below, brandishing spears and spearthrower.[13] The four New Year pages following this scene are each formatted into three scenes (figs. 6, 7, 8, and 9).[14] These illustrate what occurred following the destruction of the world.

The first scene on every page illustrates an opossum, each carrying a different supernatural in a backpack. The texts identify these supernaturals as Mams and indicate the directional association for the current year (Love 1991:295).[15] Diego Lopez Cogolludo, writing in A.D. 1688, refers to the Mam:

> They had a piece of wood which they dressed like those figures of boys made of straw that are used in bull fights and placed on a stool on a mat. They gave him food and gifts during the feast known as Uayeyab . . . and they called it Mam, grandfather, whilst the offering and feast lasted. (cited in Tozzer 1941:139)

Figure 5. Dresden flood page 74 (drawing by J. A. Villacorta and C. A. Villacorta)

Figure 6. Dresden New Year page 25 (drawing by J. A. Villacorta and C. A. Villacorta)

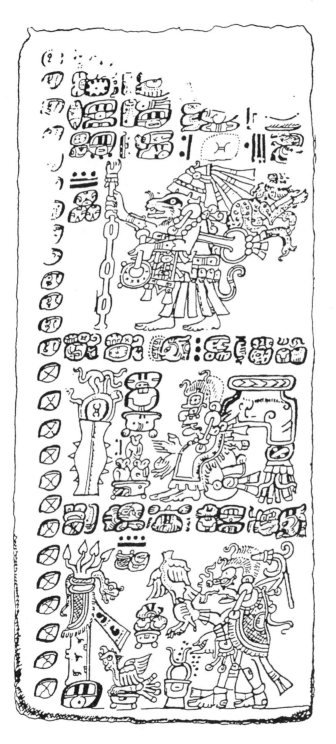

Figure 7. Dresden New Year page 26 (drawing by J. A. Villacorta and C. A. Villacorta)

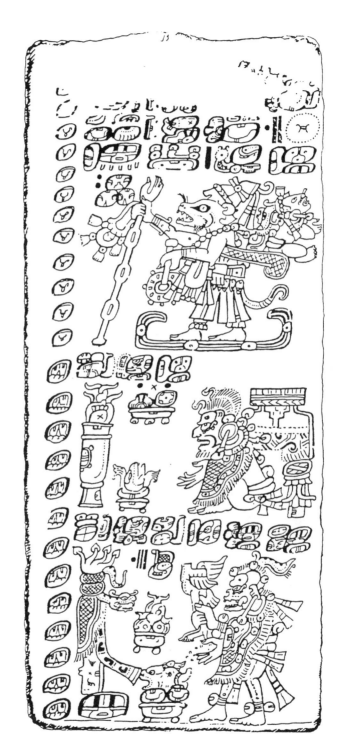

Figure 8. Dresden New Year page 27 (drawing by J. A. Villacorta and C. A. Villacorta)

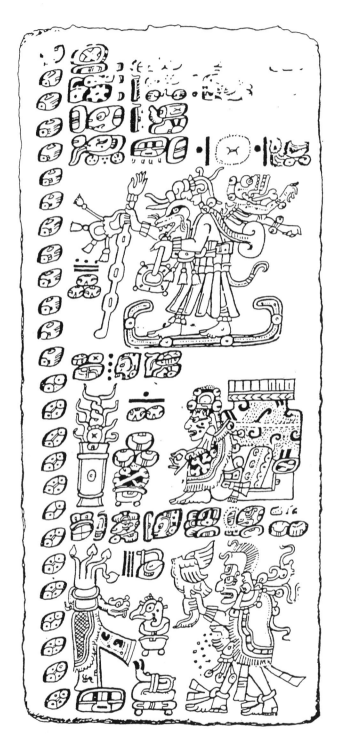

Figure 9. Dresden New Year page 28 (drawing by J. A. Villacorta and C. A. Villacorta)

A number of modern Maya groups retain the concept of a Mam deity associated with the New Year (Thompson 1930; Tedlock 1982). In various Maya languages Mam has the meaning grandfather, father, uncle, or older male relative.

The opossum actors are probably associated with the founding ancestors (the first father/grandfathers of the lineage) who in Quiche mythology carried their patron deities in backpacks and placed them at the borders of the community.

In the second scene the timeframe moves forward one day to the first day of the New Year. In each scene a different deity is illustrated sitting in a house with offerings and incense before him. These deities are God K (a lightning deity), God G (a sun deity), God D (Itzamna, the ancestral grandfather of the sea), and God A1 (a death deity).

The third scene illustrates some of these same deities making an offering of a headless turkey and incense/blood.[16] A partial paraphrase of the first sentence in each Dresden text reads: "The *chac* tree was set up, in the east. The *yax* tree was set up, in the south. The *yax* tree was set up, in the west. The *yax* tree was set up, in the north." We expect these trees to have color associations that reflect their direction, but, as Bruce Love (1991) points out, the meaning of *chac* and *yax* in this context is likely to be great and first rather than red and blue-green. In other words, these were not only great trees but the first trees of the world. The second sentence in each text makes a reference to the deity in the scene: God G, God K, God A, and God D, respectively. The image shows the event that happened following this action.

In the east scene an offering is made in front of a Chac idol. At the beginning of the Postclassic rituals, a guardian idol representing the Bacab/Chac/Pauahtun deity was taken from its location on a symbolic mountain (a pile of stones) at the midpoint on the side of the town and placed on a standard in the form of a tree. After an elaborate ritual, the idol and his tree/standard were then transported from the midpoint location to the center of town, where further rituals were conducted. At the end of these ceremonies, the guardian idol and his tree/standard were placed at the midpoint related to the upcoming year. The Dresden Chac wears a cape but lacks arms and legs. He is analogous to the guardian idol. In the remaining three Dresden locations (the south, west, and north) the

offerings are made in front of trees, which are analogous to the tree/
standards. Despite the fact that the tree/standard does not appear in the
first scene, the parallel positions of the idol and the tree/standards indicate that the first scene represents the guardian idol sitting on his tree/
standard.[17]

These last Dresden scenes are parallel not to the first actions of the
Postclassic New Year rituals but to the final action. In this ritual sequence
the tree/standard with the Chac idol sitting in it was set up in the ground
at the midpoint and an offering was made to the guardian idol. The idol
was then removed from the tree/standard and presumably placed on his
symbolic mountain. Finally, an offering was made to the tree/standard.[18]
These Dresden scenes tell us that the reordering of the world that followed
the flood involved setting up tree/standards and guardian deities at the
midpoints on the sides of the world.

This information is in agreement with Landa's statement that during
the last destruction and re-creation four guardian brothers were thought
to have been placed at the cardinal points:

> Among the multitudes of gods which this nation worshipped they worshipped
> four, each of them called Bacab. They said that they were four brothers whom
> god placed, when he created the world, at the four points of it, holding up
> the sky so that it should not fall. They also said of these Bacabs that they
> escaped when the world was destroyed by the deluge. (Tozzer 1941:135)

Landa stated that these guardian deities were also known by the names
Chac and Pauahtun.[19] Other sources indicate that these names refer to
related but distinct guardian deities. The Bacabs appear to have been the
senior of the three. The Chacs were directly related to lightning, thunder,
and rain, while the Pauahtuns were associated with wind and thunder
(see below).[20] The Dresden pages are also in agreement with the *Books
of Chilam Balam* of Chumayel, Tizimin, and Mani, which contain
passages concerning the reordering of the world after the flood. They refer
to the setting up of world trees in the four directions (Roys 1933:101). The
last four scenes in the Dresden codex illustrate the midpoints on the sides
of the world where the guardian idols and their tree/standards were placed
at the re-creation of the world. Those tree/standards were the world trees,
and the text refers to them as the *yax* "first" trees.[21] The Dresden scenes

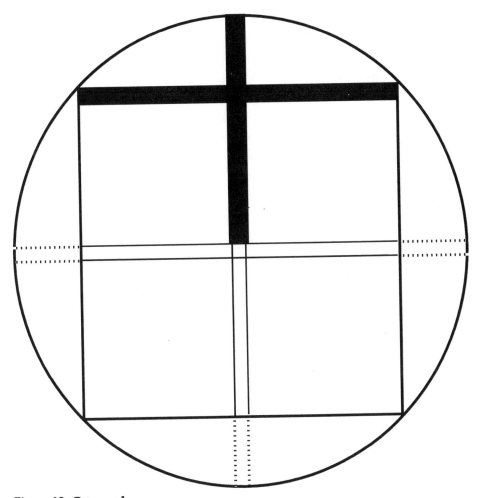

Figure 10. Crossroads

indicate that God G, God K, God A, and God D played important roles in the ordering of the world (see discussion below).

World Trees: The Dresden world trees each have four branches, referring to the four-part nature of the crossroads.[22] The world tree is illustrated as a cross on the Palenque Tablet of the Cross and in several pottery scenes (see fig. 48). The cross was a suitable symbol for the tree at the crossroads not just because it had the same shape (fig. 10), but because the tree transcended the layers of the universe with its branches reaching to the sky, its trunk on the surface, and its roots penetrating the earth, sea, and underworld. The tree/cross marked the midpoint as a location where access to these supernatural places was possible.

The concept of the world tree is evident in modern Maya worship of the tree/cross. This important symbol is not thought of as the Christian crucifix, but as a tree (La Farge and Byers 1931; Oakes 1951; Guiteras 1961). In the Chorti area the four town crosses and many of the house crosses are actually made out of living trees (Wisdom 1940:422; Fought 1972). Tree/crosses are often decorated with pine boughs and flowers that emphasize their tree aspect. This pattern is consistent across the highlands and even includes the same species of flowers (Sapper 1897).

In some areas the modern tree/cross is viewed neither as a deity nor as an idol. It does, however, always have protective powers and is employed in almost all ritual settings. Alfonso Villa Rojas (1945:43) described the practice of the Yucatec of Quintana Roo: "Around these two buildings, on small stone mounds, stand four crosses. . . . The quadrilateral area so bounded is protected by the crosses from evil winds and other dangerous influences."

The world trees are the clear antecedent for the tree/crosses that protect modern villages, such as those of the Chorti:

> Four important roads lead out of Jocotan toward the four cardinal points, and each of these has its cross at the point where it leaves the pueblo. The crosses are said to protect the pueblo from the entrance of evil spirits and apparitions, especially the Devil. They are stood up in the center of the trail so that the spirits, who theoretically could enter the pueblo only by way of the four trails, as people do, would be forced to pass over the crosses to gain entrance, and this would be impossible. (Wisdom 1940:421)

The protective quality of the tree/cross is found throughout the Maya area. In the Kekchi region there is a spirit of night/darkness who by its mere nature is the most malevolent of the spirits (Carlsen and Eachus 1977:52). Anyone who must sleep outside at night makes a tree/cross and stands it in the ground for protection from this spirit. The Tzeltal house is protected by a palm cross nailed to its door post (the midpoint on the side of the square house). This cross ensures the protection of San Pedro, the lord of lightning (Nash 1970:13). The tree/cross at the midpoint of the quadrilateral world is again the clear antecedent for this practice.

The tradition of erecting tree/crosses at crossroads is well documented: "At the crossing of the roads all the Indians of Guatemala and Chiapas belonging to tribes of the Maya family, erect crosses" (Sapper 1897:271). The intimate relationship between crossroads and trees is found at the cave of Esquipulas, an artificial tunnel some 42 meters long (Brady and Veni 1992:155). About 30 meters from the entrance a second tunnel crosses the main tunnel, transforming the cave passageway into the form of a cross. An altar marks this crossroads location as an important ritual space. The tree/cross of the famous Black Christ was said to be found at this crossroads.

In the Kekchi area, the tree/cross is particularly associated with mountains and caves:

> The crosses which are always found at the tops of mountains and at the entrances of caves are representations of Cu:l Taq'a [mountain valley deity]. . . . The cross is considered to be especially sacred and powerful because "It existed before the world was created. The cross was the first to see the light of day when the world was born." (Carlsen and Eachus 1977:41-42)

Villa Rojas (1947:579) noted the close association of caves with tree/crosses in the Tzeltal area:

> Each rural settlement is tied by religious bonds to a certain cave where a cross is kept as the main symbol of its sacred importance. . . . In addition to this main cave there are others of less importance, but also treated with respect and sanctified through one or more crosses.

The locations of cross shrines in Santa Eulalia are oriented to mountains:

> Wherever natural formation or culture emphasizes a particular spot, generally a union of the two—where trail crosses the top of a ridge, descends into the bottom of a valley [the foot of the mountain], passes close by a cliff, or the point on it from which one faces an important hill or cave—there is likely to be a cross. (La Farge 1947:112)

Charles Wagley (1949:55) noted the same pattern in Chimaltenango:

> Of equal importance as deities with the saints are the *Guardias de los Cerros* (Guardians of the Mountains). Wherever natural formation, or even cultivation, has emphasized a geographical spot—a peak of a mountain, a cluster of trees, a spring, or a promontory overlooking a valley—there is likely to be a shrine.

At these mountain shrines . . . one may pray and burn incense to the genus loci, the *Guardia*, of the mountain.

Oliver LaFarge (1947: 113) also noted that crosses are erected to mark locations that are inaccessible or invisible to the eye: "The placement of this cross in relation to the Holom Konop [an idol] illustrates the pattern of establishing a cross facing a particularly sacred spot, which is itself covered or otherwise inaccessible":

> One passes close to the cliff on the northern edge of the village, a point which is almost directly above the sacred cave of Yalan Na' and in a general way facing the sacred hill Yalan K'u across the valley. Here are three crosses in a group, known as *y-itc kanan* ("the lap of the cliff"), which seem to be definitely for communication with the sacred inhabitants of those spots. (La Farge 1947:113)

In many areas, tree/crosses that do not appear to be directly associated with a mountain or cave are still related by other features found in association with them. For example, at the Kanjobal village of San Miguel Acatan the circles of stones found in front of all the outside crosses are called *witz* "mountains." The ritual hole in front of the Chorti house cross is called a cave (Fought 1972).

In Zinacantan crosses that act as "doorways or entryways—as a means of communicating with sacred space or as boundary-markers between significant units of social space" are found in the patio outside the house, beside a waterhole, inside caves, at the foot and summit of mountain residences of the ancestral gods, and around the edges of parajes and the town center (Vogt 1969:388). The boundaries of modern Yucatec space— whether altars, houses, or communities—are thought to contain holes or doorways that function in a similar manner (Sosa 1985). These are often marked by tree/crosses. Ritual specialists focus their attention on these locations. They are symbolic cave entrances at the boundary from the safer tangible world to the dangerous dream world of the supernaturals, marked with tree/crosses that reflect the crossroads in their configuration.

The Road: Access to the supernatural space of the deities is not possible by simply following the cave passage into the interior. Caves, whether natural or constructed, merely provide a location for access. Through the use of ritual chants, incantations, or other ceremonies, the ritual specialist opens an imaginary door and summons the deities who come to this opening to receive their offerings.[23] In the modern Yucatec rain and thanksgiving ceremonies the evocation of the four directions and center called the *hé'ik bèel* "to open the road" (Hanks 1984:141). A title for the supernaturals that are the guardians of specific sites or areas is "guardian of the road or path" (Douglas 1969:71). Many Maya groups have such titles for the ritual specialists, who are responsible for the road between the supernatural and natural worlds and for the locations in their communities where these roads occur. In relation to the world model, these are the roads that radiate from the center of the world to the midpoints and into supernatural space. The creator deities brought order to the surface of the earth with the establishment of the quadrilateral space, the directional mountains, and the world roads. They also brought order to the sky.

THE SKY

The sky was ordered with some of the same mechanisms as the terrestrial plane. Like the earth, sea, and underworld, the sky appears to have been divided into four parts and, like the underworld, it was thought to be layered. The earliest sources refer to thirteen layers (Thompson 1950:10). The term used to describe these layers is also used to describe blankets laid one on top of the other or the layers of the *tutiwa*, a bread consisting of nine layers of tortillas (Thompson 1970:195; Roys 1933:128). When this layered form is combined with the domelike appearance of the sky the result is a series of concentric layers like an onion. What demarcated one layer from another is unknown, but there appears to be a hierarchy, with various celestial bodies and natural phenomena such as rain and lightning traveling in separate layers.

Celestial Bodies

After sunset, a panorama of constellations appear. As new constellations rise in the east, the old constellations move across the sky and set in the west. The path of a star across the sky appears to arc around the north celestial pole, which is closely marked by the star Polaris; stars that are very close to Polaris rotate around it and remain visible all night (Aveni 1980:50, 56). The faintly luminous band of the Milky Way also pivots around the north pole.

The surviving names for Maya constellations are few and inconsistent. Some examples demonstrate that the Maya, like most cultures, related these configurations to mythical events. For example, in an episode of the *Popol Vuh* a group of supernaturals called the Four Hundred Boys built a house near the western edge of the world. While they were inside ritually dedicating their home, the supernatural Zipacna flattened the house and killed them. In a later episode, when the hero twins assumed their roles as sun and full moon, the Four Hundred Boys became the Pleiades. The Pleiades' descent into the earth in the west is symbolic of their defeat by Zipacna (Tedlock 1985:336, 342).

The Motul dictionary indicates that the Maya constellation called *ac ek* "turtle stars" is Orion's belt, and a turtle with three stars on its back in the sky area of the Bonampak murals appears to be this constellation (Lounsbury 1982:167). A modern Quiche Maya constellation that shares one of the turtle's stars is called the Three Hearth Stones (Tedlock 1985:261). All Maya houses have three stones that form the fireplace. The stars Alnitak (the left star of Orion's belt when facing south), Saiph, and Rigel form the triangle, with the Great Nebula acting as the smoke of the fire. Madrid page 71a illustrates a turtle with three stacked *tun* "stone" signs above it. These three signs have been interpreted to be equivalent to the Quiche constellation of the Three Hearth Stones (Schele and Freidel, cited in Schele 1992).[24]

The moon and the planets are the wild cards in the sky. While the stars retain their relative positions night after night, the moon and the planets move along the ecliptic according to their own rhythms. It is clear from Classic and Postclassic inscriptions that the Maya were well aware of these cycles (Aveni 1980). The moon is intimately associated with agricultural practices and fertility. All over the Maya region planting is done according to the phases of the moon. The Maya personify the moon in different ways (such as the grandmother, mother, wife, or brother of the sun), depending on the phase. Venus, the most prominent of the planets, is closely related to the sun and is thought to be both younger and older brother of the sun. The Maya were particularly aware of the celestial bodies that rose and set at critical periods in their agricultural cycle.

Pathways

The Maya believed that the sky, like the surface of the earth, contained several different roads formed by the daily paths of the sun, moon, and stars across the heavens, by the ecliptic (the apparent annual path of the sun), by the Milky Way, and by rainbows. The serpent was often used to personify these paths in Maya art and in folktales. For example, the rainbow was thought to issue forth from a cave and to have the body of a serpent.

The zodiac is the imaginary belt of the heavens centered on the ecliptic, within which are the apparent paths of the sun, moon, and principal planets. The serpent and the skybands, which are often conflated with the body of the serpent, have been assumed to be symbols for the ecliptic and the zodiac by many authors. Attempts to correlate the signs found in skybands with planets, stars, constellations, and comets have met with varying degrees of success (Kelley 1976:45). Part of the problem rests in the fact that we do not know how the Maya grouped stars and what the names for their zodiac divisions were. The Paris codex illustrates a zodiac that includes a skeletal deity, a turtle, a serpent, a scorpion, a jaguar, and birds.[25]

The Milky Way appears as a faint arching band of white across the sky.[26] In one section the band divides into two, forming a cleft. The Quiche call this cleft the road of Xibalba (the underworld) or the black road. When the cleft is visible, the other end of the band, which is undivided, is referred to as the white road (Tedlock 1985:334). The black, rift road is marked as a crossroads by the modern constellation called the Northern Cross. The Maya name for this prominent cross-shape is unknown, but its location over a pathway to the supernatural world suggests that its crossroads shape would not have escaped them.

In the *Popol Vuh* the brothers Hun Hunahpu (Sun) and Vucub Hunahpu (Venus) are said to follow the rift road to the underworld. This event must take place when the rift road is in conjunction with the horizon, and this occurs during two important times in the yearly cycle: the summer and winter solstices. The rift road is at the east midpoint on winter solstice sunrise and summer solstice sunset. Conversely, it is over the west midpoint on winter solstice sunset and summer solstice sunrise.

The two areas of the sky where the ecliptic intersects the Milky Way were also crossroads. The first of these locations occurs near the modern constellations of Sagittarius and Scorpio. The black rift road of the Milky Way leads to this crossroads. The second crossroads is between the modern zodiac signs of Gemini and Taurus. The Gemini crossroads marks the center of the sky at sunrise on the autumn equinox and sunset on the spring equinox. Both of these crossroads come into conjunction with the terrestrial crossroads during the solstices. On the summer solstice, the Scorpio crossroads rises at the southeast corner at sunset, hovers over the south midpoint at midnight, and sets at the southwest corner at sunrise. The Gemini crossroads rises at the northeast corner on winter solstice, hovers over the center of the world at midnight, and sets in the northwest corner at sunrise.

The Milky Way also intersects the terrestrial crossroads on the solstices. At sunrise on the summer solstice and sunset on the winter solstice, the Milky Way arches across the sky from the northeast corner to the southwest corner. At these two important times for Maya calculations, the white road marks the exit of the sun from under the earth (summer solstice) and the setting sun appears to follow the black road into the underworld (winter solstice).[27] It is likely that the Maya used the movements in the night sky to order their world in the same manner that they used the day sun.

Illustrations of the Sky

A number of Period Ending ceremonies illustrate a bicephalic monster arching over the ruler.[28] In these contexts the bicephalic monster has been assumed to represent the arc of the sky. There are numerous variations of the creature that suggest that its role is more complex. The front head is usually infixed with Venus signs or crossed bands and has deer hooves or ears (fig. 11). The rear head is in skeletal form and wears the so-called Quadripartite Badge. The body has crocodilian form with cauac elements attached, but this can be replaced with skybands or cloud scrolls. The format of the creature suggests that it represents a pathway.

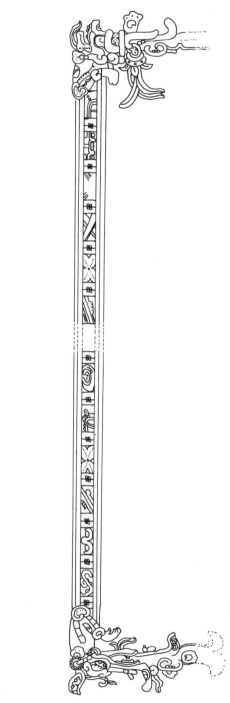

Figure 11. Bicephalic monster

This function as a celestial pathway is best demonstrated in Copan Structure 22, where the bicephalic monster arches from east to west, forming a path across the doorway of the inner room. The body of this monster is formed by scroll elements identified as clouds (Houston and Stuart, cited in Schele 1992:226). On each side of the doorway is a Bacab sitting beside or conflated with a cauac monster.[29] These actors are bent forward, giving the impression that they are bearing the weight of the bicephalic monster. The sun, the doorway, and this inner sculpture are aligned at noon on winter solstice. This bicephalic monster may represent the path of the sun on winter solstice, from the southeast corner to the southwest corner of the world.[30]

The terrestrial nature of the bicephalic monster is found on the hieroglyphic bench of Copan Group 9N-8, a replica of the quadrilateral world. The north edge of the bench is formed by a bicephalic monster whose body is replaced by a band of text. The front head of the monster is at the northeast corner of the bench. The legs at this corner illustrate a Bacab and Pauahtun deity, who appear to hold up this quadrilateral space. The northwest corner illustrates another Pauahtun in the same pose and a human Bacab imitator holding a cord, apparently the cord that is symbolically tied around the quadrilateral world. When the owner of the Structure 9N-8 bench sat on this seat, he was conceptually sitting on the surface of the earth. In the case of the Temple 22 doorway, the monster arches overhead from east to west, suggesting that it represents the celestial path. The direction of the bench monster is west to east, probably representing not the celestial path of the sun but the path of the sun under the earth. The celestial body most intimately associated with the path of the sun is Venus. It is likely that the Venus signs on the body of the bicephalic monster indicate that it can also represent the path of Venus under the earth.

The bicephalic monster also arches over eastern and western midpoints. For example, on Vessel 120 it is found over the western midpoint illustrated as Chac's west cave (see fig. 30 and chapter 2). In these contexts it would seem that the monster does not refer to the daily path of Venus and the sun but to their path along the horizon from the first appearance of Venus to its disappearance. In most cases, these paths arch over the midpoint (Aveni 1986:fig. 1).

THE UNDERWORLD

The *Popol Vuh* says that in the beginning there was only a calm sea and an empty sky. This is a direct reference to the location where the earth rose out of the sea, but it is not a description of the entire universe. Under the sea was another location known as the underworld.

The underworld was thought to be layered. During the contact period, some sources indicate that the underworld consisted of nine layers (Thompson 1950:10). The same term used to describe the layers of the sky is used here. This form can be directly related to the underworld if its basic shape is like the flat disk of the earth's surface. There is some evidence that the underworld was divided into four quadrants, each associated with a color and direction. One important aspect of the underworld is that it may have been dry, in contrast to the wet sea.[31]

In Postclassic Yucatan the souls of the departed who ended up in the underworld suffered "great extremities of hunger, cold, fatigue and grief" (Tozzer 1941:132). The *Popol Vuh* describes the underworld, Xibalba, as a place of death and disease. The root of this word seems to mean "fright" (Tedlock 1985:369). Although associated with death, the underworld does not appear to be the ultimate source of the destructive forces sent as retribution for inappropriate behavior.

The underworld is explained by the modern Maya in diverse ways. Even after five centuries, European Christian concepts of hell are not as evident as one might expect:

[Tzotzil—Chenalho]
'Osil-balamil is the world in which we live, the concept expressed by this world includes that of universe; therefore, the sun and the moon belong to *'osil-balamil*. *'Osil-balamil* is described as square-shaped, like the home and field, with the heaven supported by four pillars "like the posts of the home," and surrounded by water. Under this there is another square layer inhabited by the yohob, the dwarfs, the little people who have never "sinned." (Guiteras 1961:284)

[Tzotzil—Zinacantan]
Below the earth surface is another cube of approximately the same size called the "world below" (*'Olon Balamil*). Here lives a race of dwarfs known as Konchavetik, left over from the early creation of people described in the flood

myth. It is very hot there, since the sun in passing under the earth, comes very close the surface of the "world below," forcing the dwarfs to wear mud hats to protect themselves. (Vogt 1969:298)

[Tzotzil—Chamula]
The underworld is the dwelling place of the dead and is characterized by inversions of many kinds. When it is dark on earth, it is light in the underworld, while the sun is traveling that part of his circular path around the earth. (Gossen 1974:22)

[Tzeltal—Pinola]
On the other side of the earth, opposite to where man lives, are the 'ik'ales. They are little dark men who wear pottery hats to protect themselves from the heat of the sun, which travels closer to them than to people on this side of the world. The 'ik'ales used to be able to come out on this side of the world and do harm, but they were stopped. Now they just work. The only difference is that it is day in their place when it is night here, and vice versa. (Hermitte 1964:44)

Many authors assume that any deity from a cave is an underworld god. The cave was an access point to the underworld, but the two were separate locations. Furthermore, the cave, first and foremost, provided access to the sea on which the world floated and to the deities who inhabited this zone. Researchers have a bad habit of lumping together all skeletal deities and referring to them as underworld lords, but it must be kept in mind that although the ballcourt cave in the west where Vucub Hunahpu (Venus) was left as a skeletal being is the entrance to the underworld, Vucub Hunahpu was not a lord of death.[32] A skeletal head similar to the underworld God A appears in Classic contexts associated with Venus (Lounsbury 1982). I believe that some of the skeletal deities found in pottery scenes may refer to Venus deities.

The underworld was said to be inhabited by deities who were associated with death, stench, and disease. The principal underworld lords of the Popol Vuh were One Death and Seven Death. These lords had ten subordinates with names that referred to the methods by which they killed people, such as Pus Master and Jaundice Master. The Popol Vuh describes the adventures and conflicts of the ancestral couple's children (Hun Hunahpu and Vucub Hunahpu) and grandchildren (the hero twins Hunahpu and Xbalenque) as they encounter other supernaturals both on the surface of the earth and in the underworld.[33] Although they have been interpreted to represent astronomical cycles and the preparation of the earth for humans (Tedlock 1985), these episodes also established the hierarchy of Maya deities. Through their offspring, the creator deities battled these supernaturals and won. It is clear from these stories that the sky and sea deities were establishing and maintaining their positions.[34] The Quiche underworld deities were antagonists who attempted to defeat the hero twins. Had they succeeded, neither the cycle of the sun nor safe human space would have been established.

Two Yucatec underworld deities, God A and God A1, are illustrated in the Dresden New Year pages.[35] God A presents offerings in front of the west world tree on New Year's day and he is one of the patron deities carried by the opossum. In the second scene, God A1 sits in a temple receiving offerings. These illustrations suggest that the Yucatec underworld deities played a more proactive role in the ordering of the world than did the underworld deities of the Quiche.

THE DEITIES

A number of deities were associated with the creation and ordering of the world. In the Dresden New Year pages there are three categories of actors: the four ancestral figures who carry patron deities in their backpacks; the four patron deities (Chac, a jaguar, God E, and God A); and the four deities who order the world by setting up Chac guardian idols and world trees (Itzamna, God G, God K, God A). The *Popol Vuh* provides similar categories: creator deities who ordered the world, the first four lineage heads who placed the patron deities at the borders of the community, and the four patron deities (Tohil, Auilix, Hacauitz, and Middle of the Plain).

The Creator Grandparents

The Quiche creator couple of the sea (Xpiyacoc and Xmucane) have been described. The Yucatec Maya had a similar grandparent couple known as Itzamna and Ix Chel. In the *Ritual of the Bacabs* incantations they are said to be the parents of certain diseases that originate from the water of the four directional horizon caves. As sea deities, their association with the water of the cave is expected.[36]

In Yucatan Ix Chel "Lady Rainbow" was a goddess of medicine, sorcery, childbirth, and weaving. The attributes of Ix Chel are the same as those associated with the moon and she has been identified as such (Thompson 1939). The association of the moon goddess with bodies of water is frequently encountered. For the ancestral grandmother of the sea such an association is natural.[37] The Dresden goddess who floods the world is pictured as an old woman with a snake headdress and she is identified in the text as Chac Chel "Red Rainbow" (Ciaramella in press) (see fig. 5). She is shown with Itzamna on Madrid pages 106–7 and in some Madrid texts she is identified with the *sac cab* title used by other moon goddesses. Her red title associates her not only with the east but with the waning moon, which is predominantly found in the east. She shares this eastern orientation with the Quiche ancestral grandmother Xmucane, who also lived in the east.

Itzamna was an aged grandfather deity with a flower blossom and *akbal* mirror as a headdress. He was affiliated with calendar arts and the ability to perform divination. In many Classic period pottery scenes he is illustrated sitting on benches while other deities and supernaturals perform a variety of actions in front of him. His position on a jaguar mat bench indicates that he was a high-ranking member of the supernatural government. A quatrefoil cave opening usually appears behind the bench. In the Dresden New Year pages Itzamna played a key role in the ordering of the world when he set up the Chac guardian idol and his tree/standard (see chapter 4). Itzamna's association with Classic destruction and re-creation themes is demonstrated in the text of Quirigua Stela C, where he is said to have set up one of three guardian idols following the destruction of the world (see chapter 4).

We can conclude from this material that the ancestral grandparents played prominent roles in the destruction and re-creation of the world.

The Sun

The role of the sun in the ordering of the world has been described. In the *Popol Vuh* the deities who are identified with the sun are Hun Hunahpu (1 Ahau) and his son Hunahpu (Ahau). In the Dresden codex one of the deities associated with the ordering of the world is God G, known as K'inich Ahau "sun faced lord." Not all deities with the *k'inich* title are sun deities, but the head of God G is used in contexts where it is quite clear he had this association.

God K

The last deity associated with the ordering of the Postclassic Yucatec world is God K. Like the other three ordering deities, he makes offerings in front of the world tree and appears in one of the temple scenes. The close relationship between God K and Chac has been noted since the beginning of Maya studies. Both are lightning deities and both have attributes that are similar to the Quiche patron deity Tohil. As a lightning deity who participated in the ordering of the world, the Postclassic God K, however, is most directly related to the Quiche creator deities of the sky, who were also lightning deities.

The Postclassic God K is illustrated with a huge nose that resembles the shell of Chac's headdress. His name glyph is composed of a head with a smoking axe protruding from it. The phonetic rendering of God K's nominal glyph is K'awil, although the meaning of this name is unclear (Stuart 1987). In the Classic period both his name glyph and his illustration show a deity with an upturned nose and the axe head in the forehead. On Dos Pilas Panel 10 the axe head is marked with *cauac* "lightning" signs. God K can also have a dwarf form (Houston 1987).[38]

God K is most evident in Classic monuments as an effigy figure or scepter held during the Period Ending ceremony (see fig. 63). In some of these examples his leg has the form of a serpent's body with the foot terminating in a serpent head (see chapter 2 for a discussion of the serpent as an animal form of lightning).[39] These images of God K appear to indicate that he is the spirit of lightning (Chac's lightning axe), yet he appears in many scenes in the role of an independent deity. One of the earliest examples of God K appears on Tikal Stela 4 (circa A.D. 379). The deity's head is found hovering over the ruler in the same position as other deities such as GI.

On Yaxchilan Lintel 15 there is a phrase "na serpent, his animal counterpart, God K." On Palenque Temple 14 Tablet the animal counterpart of God K is said to be *sac bac na chan* "the white bone *na* serpent."[40]

These are possessive phrases meaning that the serpent is an animal counterpart belonging to God K. This raises a theological question: did God K have a personal soul like humans or was this serpent an animal counterpart that was owned and protected by God K? The explanation given for why the Tzeltal deity of Pinola does not have a soul is that he has no need for one. His function is to own or protect the souls and spirits of the world. If this was the case in the Classic, these phrases mean that God K owned the spirit of lightning that resided in the serpent. The alternative is that the lightning serpent was thought to contain the soul of God K. At the present we do not have enough evidence to choose between these interpretations.[41]

The Guardian Deities

I categorize lineage deities into two groups: patron deities of a specific lineage and the patron deity of the leading lineage, who also had the function of protecting not just the lineage but the community as a whole.

The *Popol Vuh* says very little about the Quiche patron deities with the exception of Tohil. Tohil provided the Quiche with fire, which they used for warmth in the darkness of the pre-sun world. Dennis Tedlock (1985) associates Tohil's fire aspect with lightning and suggests he was a deity of lightning. Like the Postclassic Chac of Yucatan, Tohil was the patron deity who guarded the Quiche community.[42]

The Yucatec guardian deity Chac was also intimately associated with the other guardian deities known as Bacab and Pauahtun.

Chac: The word *chac* is a cognate of *cauac* "lightning, thunder, storms." In Yucatan Chac was the deity associated with these phenomena. He was said to create lightning by throwing his axe or beating his drum. Some Mayan terms for lightning actually translate as the axe of the rain deity. Portraits of Chac swinging his axe are common in Maya art. The axe is often smoking in reference to its lightning/fire nature. The illustrations of Chac in the codices (God B) show a deity with a long nose and serpentlike elements at the mouth (see fig. 18). In five examples in Dresden pages 32, 36, and 37 Chac carries a nominal glyph, which is a portrait of his head.

a   b

Figure 12. a. and b.: Chac titles

Classic period images picture him quite differently with a bulbous nose and a cross-band headdress. A Classic period nominal glyph carried by rulers is composed of the bulbous-nosed Chac with his axe positioned over the ear (fig. 12a) (when an axe is thrown, the arm is drawn back over the shoulder; just before the pitch, the hand and the axe move past the ear). This title is an illustration of Chac throwing his lightning axe. A similar nominal glyph also appears in the Postclassic codices in reference to Chac (fig. 12b). The Postclassic version is highly stylized, with the hand conflated with the back of the head and the axe winging past the eye. As noted, the Postclassic Chac is named in some examples with a portrait of his head. This suggests that the axe-throwing second Chac name refers directly to his lightning aspect. Lightning was thought to be the most powerful spiritual weapon available, and it is likely that rulers were thought to have lightning/serpents as their animal counterparts (see chapter 7).

Pauahtun: Pauahtun was a wind deity: "These are the angles of the winds which were set up while he created the star, when the world was not yet lighted, when there was neither heaven nor earth: the Red Pauahtun, the White Pauahtun, the Black Pauahtun, the Yellow Pauahtun" (Roys 1933:110).

The *Ritual of the Bacabs* incantations indicate that certain diseases were believed to have originated at the houses of the Pauahtuns, which

a   b

Figure 13. a. Classic Pauahtun glyph; b. Classic Pauahtun illustration (after Coe 1873:#70)

were located at the four midpoint caves (Roys 1965:12-14; Bassie-Sweet 1991:172). Wind was thought to be created in the water of the cave and thus this water was the home of the Pauahtun. Many illustrations of Pauahtun (God N) show him to be an aged deity with a netted cloth headdress (fig. 13a). Often there is a headband nicknamed the "spankled turban" tied around this cloth (fig. 13b).[43] A waterlily is frequently tied to the headdress in reference to his watery home. In some examples Pauahtun emerges from a snail shell or carries one on his back. Occasionally these have waterlilies attached. The Pauahtun is also pictured wearing either a conch or turtle shell or emerging from one (fig. 13b). In the codices Pauahtun's name glyph is composed of the knot of his net bag (pauo) prefixed to either a conch or turtle shell main sign.[44] The Maya refer to the shell of the snail as its house (Hunn 1977:111). Pauahtun's snail shell and the conch and turtle shells represent his house in the water.[45] The most powerful forces of the wind deity were hurricanes, tornados, and whirlwinds. Snail and conch shells are also symbols for these winds; their coiled shape is reminiscent of the whirlwind's motion (Hunt 1977:75). Like the Chacs, the Pauahtuns had characteristics that related them to both sky and sea locations.

There are many contexts in which a supernatural appears with *cauac* elements on its body. Some researchers believe these elements are equivalent to the *tun* "stone" sign that uses the T528 *cauac* sign as its main sign, reasoning that these *cauac* elements are a partial spelling of the name Pauahtun and identify the deity as such. The notion that the T528 elements indicate stone is wrong. The T528 cauac "lightning" elements appear on objects to indicate the presence of the spirit of lightning. For example, flint and obsidian axe heads are so marked. The T528 tun sign represents a stone that contains the spirit of lightning (see chapter 5).

The God N head is used as a verb in contexts where it appears to refer to the dedication or preparation of a new space such as a house. The phonetic complements attached to the head in these contexts suggest a reading of *hoy* "ritual debut" (MacLeod 1990:338). The common feature in modern preparation ceremonies is a ritual circuit around the space with offerings usually left at the midpoints, corners, and center. These spaces are not safe for human occupation until the ceremony is performed. This can be compared to the creation of the world and its ordering. The deities created the earth, but it was not ordered and safe until the sun established the quadrilateral space and the guardian deities and trees were placed at the midpoints. God N was one of the guardian deities; hence the use of his portrait in a phrase that refers to the ordering of space is not unexpected.

Bacab: Numerous examples of both Pauahtuns and Chacs in immediate proximity to their respective name glyphs have been identified in the Classic and Postclassic corpus of art. The Bacab has yet to be securely identified in this way. The term *bacab* appears in the name phrases of rulers, where it is phonetically spelled in a number of ways. The most common one uses a waterlily variant with a value of *ba*. As noted, the waterlily also appears with the Pauahtun. Because of this association and their common function as "bearers of the sky," there has been much debate about whether the many actors illustrated with these traits are Bacabs or Pauahtuns. To add to the confusion, there are many illustrations of humans or ancestors imitating the role of these deities. Given that the ruler carries the *bacab* title, it is expected that he would have had such a role.

Although some authors view the Bacab and Pauahtun as different titles for the same deity, I am inclined to believe that they were related but distinct. There are some limited examples where a net bag deity is contrasted with a waterlily deity. The November Collection Vase 1 illustrates three Pauahtuns with their net bag headdresses (Robicsek and

Hales 1982:19). Above them are four deities with waterlily headdresses and *cauac* elements on their bodies. On the hieroglyphic bench from Copan Group 9N-8 two actors are illustrated at the northeast corner of the bench (Webster 1989:fig. 13). The main actor is an aged deity with a waterlily headdress and T528 *cauac* elements infixed on his body. He holds up the edge of this quadrilateral world with his right hand. Although his body faces the viewer, his head is turned to the left. Front-facing bodies are a standard Maya device used to indicate superior rank (Bassie-Sweet 1991:60). To the left is another actor with an upraised arm who shares in the load. This figure sits in profile, indicating his subordinate position, and wears the net bag headdress, which is only associated with the Pauahtun.[46] I believe it can be concluded that the waterlily deity is a Bacab. In the contact period sources Bacab is the dominant deity.

The specific role of the guardian Bacabs is far more elusive than their identification. An episode in the *Chilam Balam of Chumayel* that deals with the last destruction of the world states that the Bacabs sent a flood to cover the land (Roys 1933). Such an action indicates that they were either creator deities or subordinates carrying out their orders. In the *Popol Vuh* the children and grandchildren of the ancestral couple perform tasks for them. Bartolome de las Casas, Diego Lopez Cogolludo, and Juan de Torquemada indicate that Bacab was the son of the creator deity Itzamna (cited in Tozzer 1941:136). What can be said with certainty about the Bacabs is that they were intimately associated with the maintenance of the world order and that their waterlily motif linked them with the creator deities of the sea. One of the dominant motifs worn by rulers during the Period Ending event is the waterlily of the Bacab deities, and rulers are frequently named with the *bacab* title.

Many illustrations in Maya art show the Bacab and Pauahtun deities at the corners of the world shouldering a burden. According to Landa, one of the roles of the guardian deities was as sky bearers, holding up the sky at the midpoint of the quadrilateral world (Tozzer 1941:135). Modern sources have deities at both the corners and the midpoints that are said to support the sky and/or earth (Wisdom 1940:427; Vogt 1969; Gossen 1974:22). The cave passageways at the corners of the quadrilateral world were caves through which the sun passed on the solstice. This means that the passageway of the cave functioned as the sky of the night sun. I believe the role of the sky bearers was to hold open the cave entrance and allow the sun to pass but prevent the forces of destruction from leaving the cave. In this context they appear to be sky bearers but were, in fact, holding up the sky/cave passageway. The long debate over whether the guardian deities were at the midpoints or corners is not an either/or proposition but a case of deities having multiple functions.

SUMMARY

World view is an evolutionary process that changes in response to new information and conditions; continuity through time and space cannot be assumed. Regional variations indicate that we must proceed with caution when we analyze and compare different communities. What we are looking for is not standardization of detail but common themes. The Postclassic Quiche and Yucatec Maya shared common themes concerning the creation and ordering of the quadrilateral world and certain categories of deities such as the grandparents of the sea and lineage patron deities. They both believed that the lineage patron associated with lightning was also the guardian deity for the community.

In the culturally created universe of the precolumbian Maya there were at least five distinct areas: the domed sky, the flat surface of the earth (which was divided into two zones), the sea on which the earth floated, and the area beneath this sea called the underworld. At the horizon sky, earth, and sea met.

The deities created the earth by making it rise out of the sea. They created human space by placing a square on the flat disk of the earth. Within this square humans could safely live if they conducted themselves in the proper manner. The deities gave structure and order to time by creating the daily and annual passage of the sun. The sun defined not only time but human space as well. The corners of the world square were formed by the four solstice rise and set points; the center was defined by the zenith passage of the sun at noon. The human world was, therefore, also the domain of the sun. Each side of the world was associated with a specific color: east/red, north/white, west/black, and south/yellow.

The sun was thought to emerge from the earth through a cave as well as set into a cave. In addition to the caves located at each of the corners of the world square there was, centered at the cardinal midpoint on each side of the quadrilateral world, a mythological mountain and cave where the ancestors and certain deities lived. The last creation and preparation of the earth for human habitation involved the setting up of guardian idols and world trees at these locations.

Spiritual access to these mountains was along a road that radiated from the center of the world to each cardinal midpoint. The road did not end at the midpoint but continued along a cave passageway into the interior of the mountain, the sea beyond the mountain, and the underworld beyond that. Each cave opening represented the location where the road crossed the side of the square world, leaving the human world and entering the domain of the supernaturals. It was a crossroads, as reflected in the cross-shape of its tree. Like the crossroads on the face of the earth, the starry roads of the sky led to the corners and midpoints on certain critical days in the Maya calendar.

The guardian deities and world trees stood at the midpoints guarding the transition zone from the tangible, quadrilateral human world to the intangible world of the supernaturals. They kept the forces of destruction that existed beyond the quadrilateral world at bay.

The surface of the world was demarcated into two spaces, the human quadrilateral area and the supernatural mountains. This is reflected in the phrase "mountain/plain" used by the Maya to describe the surface of the world. Although it appears to be a simple combination of the earth's two most prominent features, the contrast is between wilderness (mountain) and cultivated land (plain). Because cultivated land is always a replication of the quadrilateral human world, the plain in mountain/plain refers to human space while the mountain refers to the wild, supernatural space. When the Maya replicated the quadrilateral world in the creation of human spaces, they were repeating the original act in which human space was distinctly separated from the wild.

The Maya illustrated the mythological caves of the horizon and the caves in the community that represented these sacred locations in diverse ways, as the following chapter shows.

2

ILLUSTRATIONS OF HORIZON CAVES

Maya illustrations tell us a great deal about the nature of caves and their role in Maya culture. This chapter focuses on depictions of the mythological horizon caves and the locations in the local landscape that replicated these sites.

T526 HORIZON CAVES

One of the representations of the caves at the horizon is the T526 day sign Caban "honey, beehive, earth," which is a profile view of a cave opening with a beehive hanging from its roof (Bassie-Sweet 1991:98–99) (fig. 14a). The T526 sign appears in compounds that represent sunrise or sunset, where a sun sign is seen between a sky sign and the T526 sign (fig. 14b). This is clearly a picture of the horizon, but the use of the T526 sign in this context goes beyond its phonetic value of *cab* "earth." In Maya thought the sun emerged from the earth at sunrise through a cave opening at the horizon and reentered the earth at sunset through another cave opening:

> [Yucatan]
> The explanation given for the setting of the sun and the moon is that when they arrive in the west, they enter a subterranean passage through which they pass to the point from which they started. (Villa Rojas 1945:156)

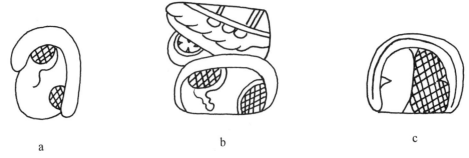

a   b   c

Figure 14. a. Caban cave sign; b. horizon sign; c. horizon cave with sun

> As for the horizon, the hmen believes Hahal Dios provides a hole in the form
> of a 'aaktun, a "cave," and that there is one for traversing the earth in *lak'in*
> and one in *cik'in*. (Sosa 1989:140)

The west-facing bench from Copan 10K-2 group also illustrates this
concept (fig. 15). The corners of this quadrilateral world model are each
formed by a cauac monster head (a symbol for a mountain cave—see
below). The two heads are joined by a band of hieroglyphic text. The legs
of the bench, which represent the rise points of the solstice sun, illustrate
the head variant of the sun sign emerging between a skyband and the
cab cave.

Some of the Distance Number Introductory Glyphs (DNIGs) that are
used in the hieroglyphic texts to indicate a change in time are pictographs
of the horizon. This is appropriate, for the basic unit of time (one day)
is marked by the rising and setting of the sun on the horizon. One of
these signs that refers to dawn and dusk is composed of the sun sign inside
the cave cartouche (fig. 14c). The back half of the sun is marked with
crosshatching, which indicates black in Maya iconography.[1] Caves have
a zone of light near their openings. I interpret this crosshatching as a
reference to the darkness at the back of the cave. In modern ceremonies
the time of day that a ritual occurs is very important; dawn is the preferred
time. When a passage uses such a DNIG, it may indicate that the new
event occurred at dawn. If this is true, the DNIG functions not only to
indicate a change in the timeframe but to specify a particular time for
the event.

The T526 *cab* cave was only one way in which the horizon cave could
be illustrated. The surface of the earth was often represented in Maya

Figure 15. Copan Bench 10K-2 (after Barbara Fash)

art as the back of a turtle or caiman (Redfield and Villa Rojas 1934:207; Taube 1988b). The turtle is an appropriate symbol for the earth not just because it has the ability to float on the surface of the sea but because it has a cross on its shell that represents the crossroads leading from the center to the midpoints on the side. Many authors have noted that the caiman's back is like the ridged surface of the world. The head and tail of these animals represent two of the midpoints. Actors are often illustrated emerging from the head and tail, suggesting that they act as symbolic cave openings. In some examples, God K, a highly appropriate deity for the midpoint, is seen emerging at this location.[2]

MOUNTAINS AND CAVES

In Maya art there are zoomorphs labeled with the elements found in the Cauac day name sign. Cauac monsters represent mountains. As noted, there is a consistent belief among Maya groups that all mountains and hills contain caves whether or not the elevation actually has a cave opening. When the Maya refer to mountains there is, therefore, an assumption that they are also referring to caves. The quatrefoil cave opening (a well-established symbol for a cave mouth) often appears in the top of the cauac monster's head. This symbol can appear as a full frontal view into the mouth of the cave or as a profile view (fig. 16). The four-part form of the quatrefoil is a direct reference to the four sacred caves on the horizon. *Cauac* has the meaning lightning, thunder, and storms and is a cognate of *chac*, the name of the Yucatec lightning and rain deity. The cauac monster is so labeled to indicate that it contains the spirit of lightning and that it represents Chac's mountains, the mythological mountains of the horizon.

Cauac monsters and their corresponding glyphs are often labeled or conflated with other symbols to specify certain aspects of these mountain caves. At Copan cauac monsters are conflated with benches, jaguars, and macaws. As later chapters indicate, all these elements are intimately associated with the cave.

In many cases the ruler stands or sits inside the cauac monster's mouth or on top of its head performing accession and Period Ending rituals. For example, on Copan Stela B the ruler is illustrated standing inside a cauac

Figure 16. Quatrefoil openings

monster that has been elongated to conform to the shaft shape of the
stela. These cauac monsters function to indicate the location of the
illustrated action.

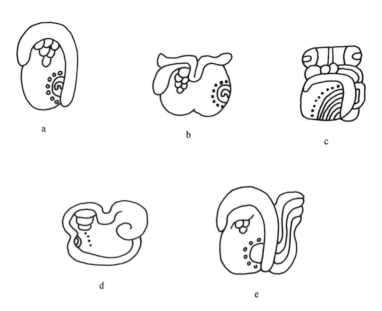

Figure 17. a. *cauac* sign; b. split variant of *cauac* sign; c. early variant;
d. split variant of *cauac* sign; e. *tun* variant

The Cauac day sign is a pictograph of the rain god's cave (Bassie-Sweet 1991:102–20) (fig. 17a). It represents a profile of the cave entrance with water and/or a dripwater formation hanging from its roof. In the literature, these hanging elements in the *cauac* sign have often been described as resembling a cluster of grapes. It is interesting that the nickname for speleothems with this configuration is cave grapes.

Cauac monsters frequently have corn foliage emerging from the quatrefoil opening. The association of corn with mountains and caves is found in the myth that the gods made humans with corn and water from a mountain cave. Furthermore, humans first obtained corn, the foundation of Maya life, from a mountain cave. In many myths the corn was found hidden under a rock (quite likely a stalagmite).[3] In some myths the rain god assisted in the procurement by splitting open the rock or the cave. Some examples of the cauac sign have a split (fig. 17b).[4] I have interpreted the hooked element on the side of the *cauac* sign as a symbol for corn based on Taube's interpretation of this element as corn in other contexts (Bassie-Sweet 1991:109–10). I think this hooked element represents the sacred corn with the water drops of the speleothem encasing it.[5]

The split in some *cauac* signs (T529) resembles the shape of the quatrefoil opening (fig. 17d). The phonetic rendering for *witz* "mountain" appears to substitute for these *cauac* variations, and it has been suggested that T529 is read as *witz* (Stuart 1987). By examining T528, T529, and the cauac monster elements for pictographic value, it becomes apparent that these signs are pictographs of mountains and their caves (Bassie-Sweet 1991:102–16), which, as noted, were inseparable for the Maya.

In certain contexts the T528 *cauac* sign has phonetic complements attached to indicate a reading of *tun* "stone" (Justeson and Mathews 1983) (fig. 17e). I have argued that this sign is a direct reference to the dripwater formation stone from which corn was obtained (Bassie-Sweet 1991:110–24).[6] The T528 *tun* stone was a receptacle for the spirits of water, corn, lightning, and fire and therefore this stone and other objects that replicated it such as stelae could function as idols.[7] These *tun* idols are further discussed in chapter 5. The mountain and its cave were a source of water, but the Maya believed that the ultimate origin was the great sea on which the world floated. The mythological mountains and their local counterparts provided access to the sea and its water.

THE SEA AND WATER SHRINES

There is a large corpus of Maya art that illustrates a layered body of water filled with waterlilies, aquatic animals, and supernaturals.[8] These waters contain both freshwater and saltwater attributes. Although many authors have identified this location as the underworld or the surface of the underworld, the more likely interpretation is that it represents the mythological sea, from which all the water of the world originated.

Water shrines, whether springs, lakes, pools of water within caves, or cenotes, were thought to be representations of that sea. In the highlands mountain shrines are classified as low shrines located near the foot of a mountain (often associated with a spring or water seepage) and high shrines located on steep slopes, ridges, and mountain tops (Vogt 1969:388; Tedlock 1982).[9]

Paja', one of the three main Momostenango community shrines, is a low water-place shrine with a spring of pure water nearby. When diviners call upon Paja' in their prayers, they do not refer to it by name: "rather, it is called upon as representing all the springs, lakes, and oceans" (Tedlock 1982:158). Water-place shrines on the side of the mountain are metaphorically represented in dreams as a lake under a mountain (Tedlock 1982:54).[10] The sea at the edge of the world is a lake under a mountain.

In the Quiche area the four seas of the horizon appear in the local landscape as four sacred lakes, each located in one of the cardinal directions. After returning from a pilgrimage to the sacred lakes, the ritual specialist deposits water from these locations into the streams at their low watery shrines. "This water both purifies the spring and adds information from the cardinal directions, which are called upon in divinations and prayers on behalf of clients with illness" (Tedlock 1982:139). This information provides direct links between the watery shrines, the sacred lakes of the community, and the four seas at the horizon.

Detailed descriptions of the actual acts performed during modern cave rituals are scarce. The most extensive documentation is found in the report on the excavation of Balankanche cave near Chichen Itza (Andrews 1970). The local ritual specialist performed a ceremony to appease the rain gods of the cave, believing that they were annoyed by the intrusion of the archaeological investigation. The ritual specialist chose two locations in the cave to perform his ceremonies that can be related to a high-mountain and a low-water site. Access to these locations was through "tiny and tortuous" passageways and included scaling a rock face with a rope. The first location was a chamber with a small hill in the center. On top of this domed floor was a dripwater column joining the floor and ceiling. A mass of stalactites hanging from the ceiling gave the formation the appearance of a yaxche tree; both natives and archaeologists remarked on the similarity. The second location was a lower chamber that contained an elongated lake. In reference to the world model, this represents the sea. Both locations, as well as other sites in the cave, contained the remains of ancient pottery vessels and offerings indicating a long history of ritual use.

With the help of thirteen assistants, seven young boys, and the archaeologists, the ritual specialist performed a series of acts in front of the dripwater column, including the offering of chickens and a turkey. Fifteen cups of a ritual drink were placed before the column; then the participants moved down the passage to the pool of water. After offerings and prayers were made at this location, another fifteen cups of ritual drink were placed in front of the water and left. The ceremony continued back at the column with more prayers. The fifteen cups were drunk and refilled. Leaving the refilled cups at the column, the entourage returned to the pool of water for another prayer round. There the fifteen cups were drunk and replaced again. These repetitive prayer rounds continued for nineteen hours as participants moved from the dripwater column (high location) to the pool of water (low location) and back again.

Some Classic place names contrast mountain and water qualities, such as the Mountains Place and the Mountains Water Place signs found at Caracol (Stuart 1987; Stuart and Houston in press). These two Classic place names echo modern naming practices.

The surface of the sea is characterized by waterlily plants (Thompson 1970:20). The T501 *naab* sign, which is a pictograph of a waterlily, carries the meaning of both waterlily and sea. In certain contexts the T501 sign can carry the phonetic value *ha* "water." This sign is a direct reference to the sea and is used in place names for water shrines that represent the great sea. On Dresden page 44a the *naab* sign appears as a place name on which Chac sits (fig. 18a). This place name appears in the text on Dresden page 34c, 40c, and 67c and is illustrated as a layered body of water in the image (figs. 18b, 18c, 18d). On page 39c Chac sits on the symbol for the cenote cave with layered water within it (fig. 18e). The text refers to this location using the cenote cave sign with a *naab* prefix. In Yucatan the cenotes, which are water shrines, are said to be the doors to the sea (Redfield and Villa Rojas 1934:265).

Watery shrines are illustrated on Machaquila Stela 4, Stela 7, and Stela 8. These stelae are lined up along the north side of a quadrilateral plaza in a position that relates them to the north midpoint. Each stela illustrates a ruler on the occasion of a Period Ending event wearing a headdress tied with a waterlily blossom. The ruler stands on a quatrefoil opening that is labeled with the T501 *naab* element (figs. 19, 20, 21). At Seibal Stela 8 is situated on the south side of a quadrilateral model (see chapter 3). It illustrates a Period Ending event that the text states occurred at a *naab*

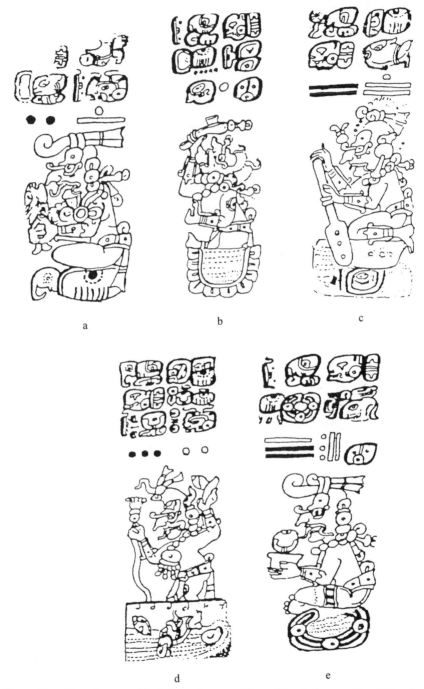

Figure 18. a. Dresden page 44a; b. Dresden page 34c; c. Dresden page 40c; d. Dresden page 67c; e. Dresden page 39c (drawing by J. A. Villacorta and C. A .Villacorta)

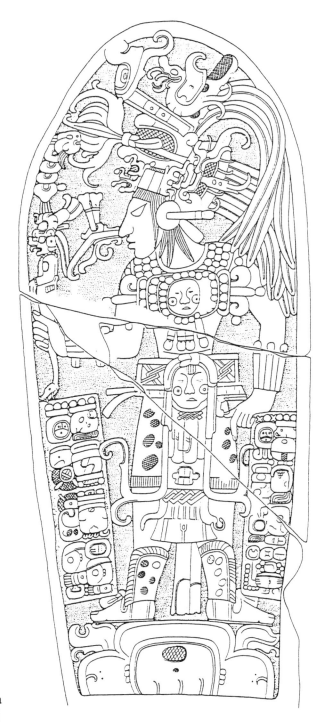

Figure 19. Machaquila Stela
4 (drawing by Ian Graham)

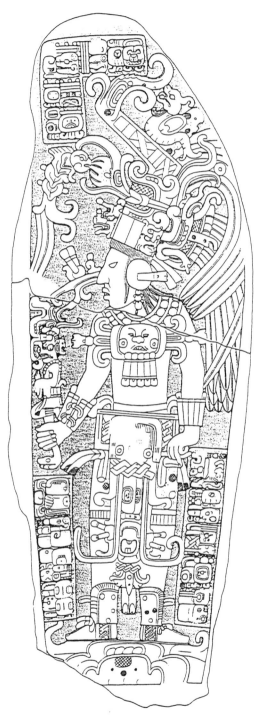

Figure 20. Machaquila Stela 7 (drawing by Ian Graham)

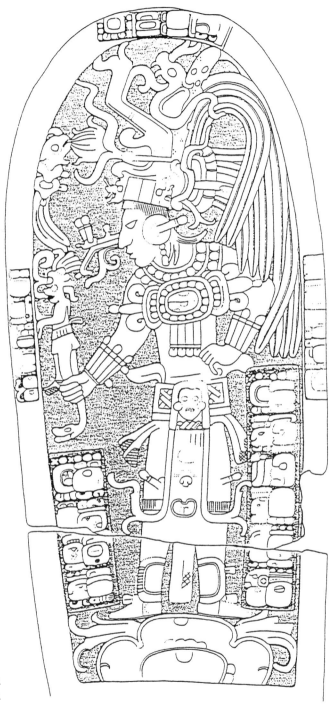

Figure 21. Machaquila
Stela 8 (drawing by Ian
Graham)

a   b

Figure 22. Seibal Stela 8 place name sign; Copan
Stela M place name sign

place. This water place name has the shape of the quatrefoil cave opening
(fig. 22a). On Copan Stela M the *naab* sign occurs in a place name phrase
"at the south *naab* place" (fig. 22b). These *naab* quatrefoils are evidence
for watery cave shrines associated with the directions during the Classic
period.[11]

Each of the four midpoint mountains had the potential of having at
least one low watery shrine at the base and one high shrine on or near
the summit. Both high mountain and low watery shrines could be aligned
with the midpoint. In the case of the Tikal twin pyramid complexes, the
east and west crossroads (the midpoints) are represented by the top of the
pyramid where the four staircases converge. This suggests that these
midpoint crossroads were high shrines.

The Corners as Water Shrines

In addition to low watery shrines aligned with the midpoint, watery
shrines were also found at the corners of the world. The corners of the
quadrilateral world joined the four sacred mountains together. The corners
had ceremonial importance not just as the entrance and exit place of the
solstice sun but as low shrines of the mountain deities. This is reflected
in Uaxactun Group E, where the corners were manifested as low shrines

(see fig. 3). As low shrine locations, these corners would be associated with water.

The watery nature of these low corner shrines is illustrated at Palenque. Temple 14 is located in the northwest corner of the cosmogram formed by the Cross Group plaza (see chapter 3). Its sanctuary tablet illustrates the young Chan Bahlum performing a pre-accession ritual with his mother (Bassie-Sweet 1991:223) (fig. 23). He dances beside a layered surface labeled with *naab* "waterlily/sea" signs.[12] The caption text explains what is happening in the scene, and this event is also repeated in the narrative of the main text. Three glyphs appear in the layers of the water. The right glyph is prefixed with *sac* "white" and the main text passage states the location of the event using this undeciphered compound. The other two glyphs can be directly related to caves. The main sign of the middle glyph appears in the layers of the water in the west mythological cave illustrated on Robicsek and Hales Vessel 120 (see below). David Stuart and Stephen Houston (in press) read this main sign as *k'ak' nab*, which means "sea" but translates directly as "fiery sea." This is an appropriate description for the location where the fiery sun rises and sets into the sea.

The left glyph is composed of a *nicte* "flower" and a place name used on Dresden pages 37, 40, and 69. In these Dresden scenes Chac sits on this place name. Nikolai Grube (cited in Schele 1992) has suggested the value of *hemnal* "valley place," which would fit with the interpretation that this is a low watery shrine location. Given the clear parallels between modern water shrines and the obvious *naab* cave locations of various deities both in the codices and on Classic period vessels, it is highly likely that the Temple 14 Tablet location is a water shrine location.[13] The temple's position in the corner of a quadrilateral suggests that it is also a corner shrine.

The Rio Azul tombs are also cosmograms that illustrate water (Adams 1986:452). The walls of the tombs are decorated to represent the corners and sides of the quadrilateral world. Some tomb walls are decorated with cauac monster mountain caves. Tomb 1 contains both cauac monsters and layered water indicating the sea on the edge of the Maya world. The corners of Tomb 12 are labeled with place name glyphs (Stuart and Houston in press). The northeast place name is the *naab* sign of the Palenque Temple 14 water shrine.

Figure 23. Palenque Temple 14 Tablet (drawing by Merle Greene Robertson)

Naab corner shrines also appear at Copan. As noted, each of the four panels of Copan Structure 18 illustrates the ruler Yax Pac performing a dance associated with one corner of the quadrilateral model. In each scene he stands on a cave symbol that represents his location (fig. 24). The southeast and southwest location symbols both contain *naab* and *cauac* elements.[14]

The concept that the corners were water shrines is reflected in the images used to represent the earth, such as the turtle and caiman. The

Figure 24. Place name symbols from Copan Temple 18 jambs (after Anne Dowd)

feet or flippers of the turtle are immersed in the sea at the edge of the world and represent the corners of the world. This arrangement is in accord with these locations as low watery shrines. The same pattern is found on Copan Altar T, where the world caiman has waterlilies tied to his feet to indicate the four water shrines of the corners (see fig. 55).

These mythological and historical examples provide evidence that the four horizon areas were thought to contain low watery shrine locations. This accords with the horizon's function as a gateway to the great sea on which the earth floats. The corners of the square as low mountain shrines explain why there are references to rain deities at the corners of the quadrilateral world. There has been a long-standing argument among researchers over whether these deities were situated at the corners or the midpoints of the world. It was not a case of one or the other.

In the *Popol Vuh* there are two categories of creator deities: sky and sea. It seems likely that the categorizing of mountain shrines into high and low reflects this. The low watery shrines were associated with the sides and slopes of mountains, waterholes, and the sea of the horizon; the high mountain shrines were physically associated with the tops of the mountains, ridges, and the sky. The midpoint contained both high and low shrines, while the corners were low shrines. One low watery shrine illustrated in Maya art is specifically related to the moon goddess.

The Home of the Moon Goddess

In the Dresden codex the ancestral grandmother (who is also a moon goddess) is pictured flooding the world. The moon is associated with rain throughout Mesoamerica. The moon goddess is most often said to live in certain bodies of water, in a cave, or in water in a cave. The so-called moon cartouche or lunar sign is a pictograph of her watery cave home, and the young moon goddess is the patron of the month Ch'en, which means "cave" (Bassie-Sweet 1991:95) (fig. 25). On a Chenes style capstone the moon cartouche cave is illustrated with rectangular elements that are found in the water of Chac's cave (see below). One of the animals frequently associated with the water of the cave was the serpent, which plays an important and complex role in the symbolism of the cave.

Figure 25. Moon goddess's cave

THE SERPENT

Snakes often live in caves. The snakes are not restricted to the ground of the cave, for many are at home in water and zigzag across the surface with great speed. Tales of encountering deadly supernatural snakes within caves are common; they are said to guard the entrance to the cave and its inner recess. In Yalcoba the four guardians who come at night to protect the entrances to the village are believed to live during the day in a cave that has an opening in the form of a snake (Sosa 1985:414). Snake imagery occurs at cave locations such as the Lacandon deity cave beside Lake Petha. The wall of the cliff next to the cave is carved with the figure of a two-headed serpent.

The Serpent and Water

In the Chorti area the Chicchan serpents are said to live in both caves and water. In addition to being lightning, they are said to be the "spirit or essence" of water (Wisdom 1940:394). No one would kill a snake found near or in a stream for fear that it is the spirit of the stream. Death of the spirit would result in the stream drying up. Yucatec priests scattered dew (pure virgin water) from an object in the form of a serpent (Taube 1992:34). The portraits of Chac often have a serpent hanging from the mouth. The association of these serpents with the mouth (one of the sources of moisture in the body) may indicate these serpents contain the spirit of water.

Copan Altar G is carved in the shape of a serpent. Its text contains a proper name composed of a serpent followed by the quatrefoil cave

Figure 26. Copan Altar G text (after Alfred Maudslay)

opening (fig. 26). Inside this quatrefoil is the dripwater element of the *cauac* cave sign. The corners of the quatrefoil are marked with *naab* "waterlily/sea" elements. Many of the serpents in Classic period art have waterlilies attached to their bodies or headdresses. They also have fish fins or tails or have fish nibbling at their bodies. I believe these traits identify such serpents as containing the spirit of water. Altar G has two companion pieces adjacent to it that take the form of feathered serpents. The three sculptures form a quadrilateral space, with Altar G representing the west midpoint and the other two replicating the north and south midpoints. Robicsek and Hales Vessel 120 also represents a west cave (see below). On this vase a serpent similar to Altar G has waterlily motifs on its body and is conflated with the Chac (fig. 27). The rear head of the serpent appears in the water below.

Figure 27. Robicsek and Hales Vessel 120 (after Justin Kerr)

A serpent with the same rear head appears arching over the ruler's head on Tikal Temple IV Lintel 2. This serpent is feathered and is marked with *yax* signs. In the *Popol Vuh* one of the creator sea deities is called Sovereign Plumed Serpent; as noted, the creator sea deities were intimately associated with the color *yax*. It seems likely that the Tikal serpent contains the spirit of water, which was ultimately controlled or owned by the *naab* sea deities.[15]

There is a serpent zoomorph that is frequently found in sea locations. The head of this serpent wears a headdress composed of a waterlily pad tied by a water flower stem. On occasion a fish nibbles on the blossom and the Shell Wing Dragon appears above.[16] In some scenes the body of the serpent actually replaces the layered water. In one Late Classic pottery scene the serpent's body is represented as the *naab* sign surrounded by rectangular elements often found in water. In some examples the snake may be feathered (Kerr 1989:#162), again suggesting an identification with the sea deities. The Waterlily Serpent is clearly related to the serpent that contains the spirit of water.

The Spirits of the Serpent and the Cave Passage

Many Maya groups believe that lightning takes the form of a serpent. A snake makes an ideal form for lightning: they both move in a zigzag pattern and kill with intense speed. As the animal manifestation of lightning, the lightning serpent must contain the spirit of lightning. Lightning is also said to be created when the rain god throws his axe. On the Dumbarton Oaks Tablet the young Kan Xul, who is dressed as Chac, is illustrated throwing such an axe (Bassie-Sweet 1991:220) (fig. 28).[17] The stone blade is marked with cauac "lightning" elements and the handle has the form of a serpent.

Lightning has two qualities that made it essential to the Maya elite: it is a natural source of fire and it has the ability to kill with alarming speed. The individuals who could command this force of nature were in unique positions of power.

In the *Popol Vuh* the creator deities of the sky are called Heart of Sky, Hurricane, Thunderbolt Hurricane, New Born Thunderbolt, and Raw Thunderbolt. The most powerful manifestation of wind is the hurricane. Associated winds such as cyclones and tornados are viewed by the Maya as similar forces. Such storms sweep across the landscape with terrifying destructive power. They are invariably accompanied by lightning. Although not as destructive as the other storms, whirlwinds are also much feared by the Maya. Great care is taken not to step across the path of a whirlwind, and amulets are worn to fend off its harmful effects. All of these whirling bodies of wind are symbolically related to objects that share their shape such as spiral shells, horns, and serpents. In the serpent two of the most powerful forces (lightning and wind) are united.[18]

The Tzeltal have a mythological horned snake that is said to make the cave passageways for rivers by smashing through the rock.[19] This ability is reminiscent of the way in which lightning was used to smash the rock that concealed corn. Some Chorti myths tell of horned snakes who also carve riverbeds with their bodies, and this motion is described as being directly related to lightning (Fought 1972:110–13). In the *Popol Vuh* the lightning sky deities formed rivers by "twisting along among the hills" (Edmonson 1971:13). The winding paths of springs, streams, rivers, and cave passageways are visually reminiscent of the erratic path of lightning.[20]

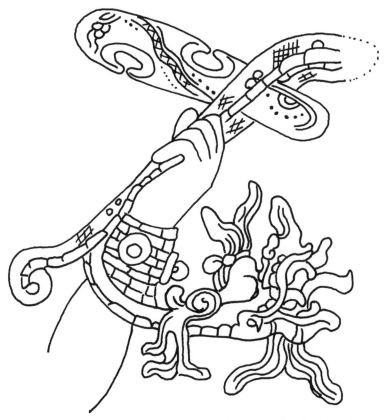

Figure 28. Axe from Dumbarton Oaks Tablet (after Linda Schele)

Figure 29. Cauac monster from Lords of the Underworld Vase 4 (after Coe 1978)

The lightning/whirlwind serpent moves through the earth and in doing so creates a river or cave passageway in its own image.

On Lords of the Underworld Vase 4 and several other vessels the mouth of the cauac monster/mountain cave is lined with serpent scales (fig. 29). The conflation of the cauac monster/mountain cave and the serpent/cave passage is logical.

Precolumbian, colonial, and modern sources freely substitute the terms and symbols for sky and serpent. These substitutions are based on the concept that the serpent/cave passage is the sky that the sun and celestial bodies travel through on their nightly voyage under the earth (Bassie-Sweet 1991:137).[21] In parallel Classic phrases, the glyphs for sky (*chan* or *caan*) and serpent (*chan* or *can*) alternate with each other.[22] The *Na Ho Chan* "na five sky" location illustrated on the Quirarte vase is depicted as a conflation of a cauac monster and a serpent (fig. 30). The deities sit on intertwined serpent bodies. The text states that it is a sky location, and the image illustrates this to be a serpent/cave passage (Bassie-Sweet 1991:139).[23]

The Serpent and the World Roads

There are numerous examples in the corpus of Maya art in which an actor

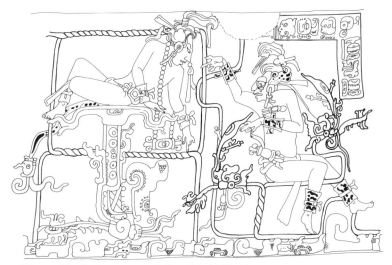

Figure 30. Quirarte vase (after Justin Kerr)

is illustrated standing or sitting on or being enclosed by a skyband. These skybands can be conflated with a serpent. Many authors have interpreted these skybands as symbols of the ecliptic. I have argued that in certain contexts they do not represent the sun's path across the sky but the sky of the cave passage (Bassie-Sweet 1991:149). The ecliptic is the apparent annual path of the sun in the heavens, while the cave passage represents the nightly path of the sun under the world. It is quite logical that the Maya would choose to use the same imagery to depict the sun's path whether it was across the sky or under the earth. The serpent was used as a symbol for the ecliptic, the cave passage, and lightning. It is a case of multivocal symbols that are intrinsically related.

A consistent feature of many modern and Postclassic lightning, thunder, and hurricane deities is that they do not live in the layers of the sky but inside mountains or at the horizon. They merely travel across the sky to do their work. The shrines for these deities are invariably high mountain shrines located at the tops or ridges of elevations. This is in contrast to the low watery shrines of the sea deities. I suggest that if a location is illustrated as a sky without cave associations it is likely to be the sky above, but if the location includes cave imagery it probably represents the terrestrial home of the sky deity.

There are numerous examples where the caves and shrines associated with the center are thought to be connected by subterranean passages to the caves on the edge of the community or the horizon (La Farge 1947; Hermitte 1964; Tedlock 1982:109). Deities and the souls of ritual specialists are thought to travel these passageways; these roads provide spiritual access from the center to the caves on the border of the community and the horizon. The four crossroads of the quadrilateral world that radiate to the horizon represent this concept, as do the staircases of the radial pyramids that emulate this form.

The Castillo at Chichen Itza illustrates the relationship of world roads, cave passages, and serpents. The two principal cenotes at Chichen form the north/south axis of the site (Carlson 1981). Midway between these two points is the Castillo. This radial temple/pyramid with a staircase on each side is a cosmogram of the world. In the early years of this century, the natives of the area believed that the two cenotes were connected by a cave passage (Tozzer 1941:182). Given that there is a cave under the Temple of the High Priest's Grave, which was modeled after the Castillo, it is not unreasonable to suggest that there is also one under the Castillo. What is perhaps more important is that the Maya believe there is a cave passage.[24] The base of the Castillo's north staircase is decorated with serpent heads. In the hour before equinox sunset the corner of each of the nine layers of the pyramid casts a shadow on the side of the staircase. This zigzag shadow creates the illusion of a serpent's body of light on the side of the stairs (Rivard 1971). This alignment turns the stairway/road into a serpent's body, that is, a cave passage. The symbolism may be carried further, for across the plaza from the Castillo serpent is the raised road that leads to the great cenote to the north. Rivard (1971:23) suggested that "if the serpent of light issuing from the temple is descending the stairway we could assume that he is going to the cenote."

This overview demonstrates that serpents can represent lightning, water, and wind; the path of a celestial body such as the path of the sun; and a cave passage. The representations often have directional associations because they replicate one of the horizon midpoints or some aspect of it. These are by no means the only roles and attributes of the serpent. The complexity of serpent symbolism illustrates the enigmatic nature of Maya symbolism; many of our interpretations address only a small part of complicated concepts.

THE SKELETAL JAW AS A CAVE OPENING

Another symbol for the entrance to a cave is a skeletal jaw that is found in diverse contexts. The Temple of the Inscriptions sarcophagus lid is a cosmogram that illustrates Pacal falling into these jaws (fig. 31). The upper jaw is fleshed, while the lower jaw is skeletal. The sarcophagus mouth is oriented to the south and represents the south midpoint cave.[25] The mouth of the cauac monster often takes the form of the upper jaw of the skeletal monster.

On Robicsek and Hales Vessel 120 the skeletal jaws form the mouth of a cave with layered water inside (see fig. 27). Chac is wading in this pool of water with rectangular elements on its surface and glyphs in the layers. A scroll shape emerges from the head of the Chac and branches into a plant on the right and a serpent on the left. A bicephalic monster arches overhead and the Principal Bird Deity hovers over the opening.[26] The upper text refers to the first appearance of Venus as evening star in the west, when it briefly appears on the horizon and then disappears back into the horizon cave. One of the place names of this event is composed of the skeletal jaws with a black prefix, the appropriate color for west. On Kuna Lacanja Lintel 1 a lord sits on a cauac monster (Bassie-Sweet 1991:168). The inscribed text associated with this location names it using the same skeletal cave jaws with the black prefix used on Vessel 120. In other words, this lord is at a local version of Chac's west cave.

A stylized version of the skeletal jaw cave symbol is used to denote a cenote cave in the codices (fig. 32a). In this type of cave Chac is seen performing an act on the mythological period ending of 12.9.0.0.0 (3331 B.C.) (fig. 32b). In other examples Chac sits or stands in the layered water

Figure 31. Palenque sarcophagus lid detail (after Merle Greene Robertson)

of this cave (see fig. 18e). On page 29 the Chac sitting in a cenote is painted black (the color of the west) and the text identifies him as a west Chac. On Naranjo Altar 1 the skeletal jaws take the form of the quatrefoil cave opening (fig. 32c). On Dresden New Year pages 27a and 28a the journey of the opossum on the last day of Uayeb is illustrated as taking place inside the cenote cartouche (see figs. 8, 9).

The sign for the day Uayeb is composed of the skeletal jaws over the *tun* "drum" sign (fig. 32d). On the Pomona Panel the Uayeb day sign has the moon goddess cartouche, but with the bone element of the skeletal jaw (fig. 32e). It is highly appropriate for the Uayeb sign to have the form of a cave, given that the climax of the Uayeb rituals is at the midpoint

Figure 32. a. cenote sign; b. Madrid page 73; c. Naranjo Altar 1; d. Palace Tablet Uayeb sign; e. Pomona panel Uayeb sign

on the side of the quadrilateral world (see chapter 4). The appearance of the *tun* "drum" in this sign is also appropriate, for this object is a key component at the midpoint. In the Dresden New Year pages it appears at the base of the Chac idol and the tree/standards. Another important ritual item found at mipoint is the seat or bench of the deity.

BENCHES

Since the beginning of their culture, the Maya have slept on benches constructed of wood and/or stone. In the small confines of a Maya house, these benches were also used for a wide variety of activities, including writing and painting, bloodletting, divinations, and the more mundane endeavors of everyday life. The stone bench was a large slab of stone often suspended by four corner supports. Wooden benches consisted of four forked poles thrust into the ground. The sides of the bed were supported by cross beams suspended by the forked poles. The surface of the bed was often formed by reeds or canes. Both wooden and stone beds were frequently covered with a woven mat and/or a mattress of plant fiber, presumably for comfort.

The surface of both stone and wooden bench beds represented the quadrilateral space of the world. As the quadrilateral world model was a culturally created human space in which the individual could safely live, the quadrilateral bed was a replication of that space in which the individual could safely sleep. This belief was extremely important, for the soul was most vulnerable to attack when the individual was asleep.

Thrones

When a bench appears in a structure we view as residential, we refer to it as a bed bench. When it is located in a more public than private space or when it is decorated in some way, we call it a throne. For example, there was a bench located in the front room of Palenque House E. Each of the front legs of the bench is carved with the image of a Bacab imitator holding up a waterlily in the air. The edge of the bench is inscribed with a text that relates the accession of Pacal II (A.D. 615), Chan Bahlum (A.D. 684), and Kan Xul (A.D. 702). The bench was positioned in front of the Oval Palace Tablet, which illustrates Pacal sitting on a double-headed jaguar bench receiving a headdress from his mother. A painted text on the wall around the tablet refers to the accession of Chaacal III (A.D. 722). The context of the House E bench has led many authors to view it as the throne of the Palenque rulers. Some authors regard plaza sculptures like Copan Altar Q and Altar U as outdoor benches or thrones. Such interpretations are difficult to prove or disprove. Perhaps it is more pertinent to ask in what circumstances a lord required a throne.

I define a throne as a seat that represents the office of the official. Because we do not have a clear understanding of the political and religious offices held by Classic elite, it is impossible to say with complete certainty what kinds of symbols we should find on Classic thrones. The jaguar mat seat that refers to the highest level of office is illustrated as a movable object that the lord was able to carry (see chapter 7). This suggests that although there may have been a council house with a stone bench used by the lord what made this bench a throne was the placement of the jaguar mat. Although some authors (myself included) have referred to the benches illustrated in Maya art as thrones, we have placed a connotation on these pieces of furniture that in many instances is clearly not applicable. Therefore, I refer to them all as benches here.

Altars

An altar is an object where offerings can be left for the deities, spirits, and ancestors. Many modern and precolumbian altars represent the bench of the deity.[27] This means that form alone cannot be used to distinguish between a bench and an altar. In precolumbian settings the primary factors used by archaeologists are the size, associated paraphernalia, and context of the object. For example, when benches are small, inside a shrine, or covered with residue from incense they are labeled altars. Large benches inside a residential building are assumed to be sleeping benches. It is the objects that fall in the middle of these two extremes that are hardest to identify. I believe that each example must be individually assessed.

Smaller sculptures often found on plazas, inside buildings, and in front of stelae have been called altars or pedestals. Both terms imply a function for these sculptures that may or may not be applicable. Not wishing to add yet another term to the literature I use the term altar here with the caveat that I do not necessarily attach that meaning to the sculpture.

Midpoint Seats

The Maya believed that existence inside the cave was structured much like the outside world. The deities were thought to live in houses and have possessions and needs similar to humans. The Postclassic Madrid cosmogram illustrates the midpoints as thatched houses. There are a number of examples that illustrate a bench at the midpoint.[28] In four Dresden scenes (pages 29b and 30b) a Chac is illustrated in association with a particular direction. In the south he sits in his tree. In the other three directions (east, north, and west) he sits on benches. These include a skyband bench, a *cauac* bench, and a bench marked with the *be* "footprint."

In the cave setting natural or modified rock ledges or flat stones are often called the bench of the deity. For example, the rock ledge at the entrance to the Yum Balam's cave is referred to as his bench (Sosa 1985:248). As the cave is the home of the deity, it is clear that these stone slabs represent his bed or seat. The majority of modern altars (places where offerings are left) are flat slab stones or tables that represent the bench of the supernatural. In Chamula an altar is actually called "the saint's bench" (Deal 1988:78). In other areas the altar found at the mountain shrine (on the slope of the mountain or near a spring) is referred to as the bench or the seat of the deity. In Momostenango some of the lineage shrines found on the sides of mountains are called *warabalja* "sleeping place (bed) of the house" (Tedlock 1982).

Like the bench, a table is often used as the surface for ritual acts. These tables are directly related in function and design to the precolumbian bench. In the Chorti area the altar table is built specifically like a bed and is "covered with a bed covering of thin reeds" (Wisdom 1940:383). In the sacred cave of Santa Eulalia each ritual specialist has his own flat ledge in the rock called a *mesa* "table" (La Farge 1947:128), which again relates the table altar to the bench of the deity.

The rock ledges and formations at the entrance to the cave are described not only as the deity's bench but also as details of a snake's mouth (Sosa 1985:414). In Chenalho a serpent is also said to be the seat of the rain deity. The words for altar such as Yucatec *canche* "serpent of the tree" and Tzeltal *ya canan cruz* "serpent of the cross" (Calnek 1988:79) appear to be references to the rock ledge of the serpent/cave passage located at the tree/cross of the midpoint.

Lineage shrines and stones act as altars because that is where the deities come to receive offerings. They are called sleeping and resting places because they function as symbolic representations of the cave bench of the deity. Given that the bench of the deity is located at the midpoint on the side of the square, it makes good sense that the modern house altar is most often placed at the center post of the rear wall (Deal 1988).[29]

Many of the ritual altars were also designed to represent the quadrilateral world. Offerings placed at the corners, midpoints, and center of the bench were symbolically being offered to those locations. The vessels used to contain offerings were symbolic cave locations as well. The Lacandon have vessels in which they burn incense to a particular deity (Bruce 1975:80). The

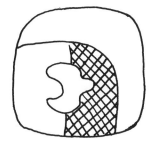

Figure 33. Seat signs

outside of the pot is decorated with the supernatural's face, while the inside contains a small stone that was originally obtained from some shrine belonging to the deity. It is referred to as the "seat of the god" in the same way that a stone within a cave is viewed as the seat of a deity. The Lacandon believe the deity comes and sits on this stone during the burning of the incense.[30]

The Seat Sign

A sign nicknamed the "impinged bone" has been associated with place names (Stuart and Houston in press). This sign has been read *kun* "seat" by Barbara MacLeod (cited in Schele 1992:232–34). Two 819 Day Count texts contain passages that refer to south and north as "south sky seat" and "north sky seat," respectively. This sign also appears in place name phrases in conjunction with a sky sign, a sky sign over *cab* cave sign (pictograph of the horizon), or just the *cab* cave sign. Thus, these places are sky seats, horizon seats, and *cab* cave seats, all appropriate descriptions of the midpoints on the sides of the world.

The reflexes for *kun* carry such meanings as seat, residence, place, origin, base, and trunk (MacLeod, cited in Schele 1992:232), which can all be associated with the midpoints on the side. The midpoints are the seats and residences of the deities and the cave is the ultimate place of origin. The Mayan word for horizon means trunk or origin of the sky.

In some examples the impinged bone of the seat sign clearly represents a skeletal lower jaw similar to the skeletal jaw opening that is used in Classic imagery to depict a cave opening (fig. 33). The connection between

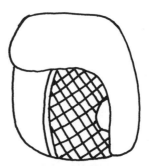

Figure 34. Seat sign

a seat and the skeletal jaw of the cave opening is reminiscent of the Yalcoba deity cave. The rock ledge of the cave is described as a serpent's mouth and as the bench of the deity.[31]

Bundled bones are used as benches in many Classic scenes. For example, on the Palace Tablet Kan Xul is flanked by his parents on the occasion of a pre-accession event; all three actors sit on bone thrones (Bassie-Sweet 1991:214) (see fig. 65 and chapter 7, note 7).[32]

The shape of the seat sign is the profile view of the cave. Often a line is drawn down the middle with the inner section cross-hatched to indicate black (fig. 34). As noted, I interpret this to represent the dark at the back of the cave.

The seat sign appears in the text on Dresden page 38b with a locative prefix "at the *cab* seat, the yellow Chac" (the verb is the same as the 819 Day Count, which refers to the setting up of a God K at the midpoint) (fig. 35a). In the image Chac stands on this location sign (the yellow prefix suggests this is a south seat). On Dresden page 42b Chac again appears with the same location sign (fig. 35b). On Dresden pages 30a and 67b Chac sits inside the *cab* cave (figs. 35c, 35d). On Dresden page 40c the text refers to the *cab* seat place, but in the location symbol in the image

a b c d

Figure 35. a. Dresden page 38b; Dresden page 42b; c. Dresden page 30a; d. Dresden page 67b (drawing by J. A. Villacorta and C. A. Villacorta)

a   b

Figure 36. a. and b. Dresden page 40c (drawing by J. A. Villacorta and C. A. Villacorta)

the bone is replaced with a head associated with the skeletal God A (fig. 36a). In the next scene the text says that Chac is at the sky and the image illustrates him sitting on a skyband with the same skeletal head, that is, at a sky seat (fig. 36b). On Dresden pages 33b, 34b, and 35b Chac is seen emerging from the serpent cave passage (figs. 37a, 37b, 37c). The body of the serpent forms an enclosure with water in it. The *cab* seat is again the place name in the text. The *cab* place name shows up on

Figure 37. a. Dresden page 33b; b. Dresden page 34b; c. Dresden page 35b; d. Dresden page 35b (drawing by J. A. Villacorta and C. A. Villacorta)

b

Figure 38. a. Madrid page 95b; b. Madrid page 51b (drawing by J. A. Villacorta and C. A. Villacorta)

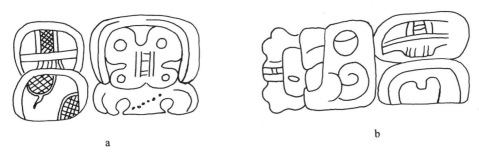

a   b

Figure 39. a. Tikal Stela 31 seat sign; b. Yaxha Stela 3 seat sign

Dresden page 35b, where Chac in the form of a serpent is seen in the
layered water of the cave (fig. 37d). On Madrid pages 95b and 51b a corn
deity sits in his house on a bench that is marked with *cauac* elements
(figs. 38a, 38b). The scene is related to each direction. The house is labeled
with the compound glyph "in the *cab* cave" suggesting that this too is
a *cab* seat location. From these varied examples from the codices, it can
be concluded that there were seats at each of the four directions and that
these seats were called *cab* seats and sky seats.

On Tikal Stela 31 several of the place names for Period Ending events
incorporate both the *cab* and sky seat signs. The 8.18.0.0.0 Period Ending
event location is a pictograph of the horizon followed by the seat sign
(fig. 39a). On Yaxha Stela 3 the location indicator includes the place name
expression "the Yaxha sky seat" (fig. 39b). In the Palenque Cross Group
several texts state that a fish-in-hand event is performed by Chan Bahlum
(A.D. 690). The Tablet of the Sun text states that Chan Bahlum performed
a "fish-in-hand" event at a location or locations named as the Lakam Naab
"Tree of the Sea," the Sky Seat, and the K'uk Lakam Witz "Quetzal Tree
of the Mountain."[33] On the Foliated Cross Tablet a "fish-in-hand" event
is said to have occurred at the Tree of the Sea, the Sky Seat, and the Seat
of the Six Sky Great Nine Chacs. The narratives on the Cross Group
Alfardas and Jambs state that two years later Chan Bahlum again performed rituals at the Tree of the Sea and the Sky Seat. On the Temple
18 jambs, which are later than the Cross Group, the accession rituals of
Chaacal III (A.D. 722) are said to have also occurred at the Quetzel Tree
of the Mountain, the Tree of the Sea, and the Sky Seat.[34] These examples

Figure 40. Dresden page 46a (drawing by J. A. Villacorta and C. A. Villacorta)

demonstrate that many rituals were structured according to the quadrilateral world model and that these ceremonies took place at the local versions of the horizon seats, that is, the midpoints on the side of the quadrilateral world.

Skybands often form benches on which both deities and humans sit. Many of these skybands are decorated with owl heads. On Dresden page 46a a deity sits on a skyband bench with an owl head (fig. 40). Itzamna is seated on a skyband with owl heads in many pottery scenes. On Lords of the Underworld Vase 11 a Chac sits in the jaws of a cauac monster decorated with an owl bird (Coe 1978). On Naranjo Stela 32 a ruler sits on a bench that is largely eroded (fig. 41). Under the bench is a reptilian figure. The base of the bench is composed of layered sky and *naab* bands. The skybands terminate with owl heads, which substitute for the seat sign (MacLeod, cited in Schele 1992); thus all these locations are also seats.

When precolumbian locations are labeled as seats with directional associations, they are being designated as a local variation of one of the four sky seats on the horizon. The precise location of these sky seats is discussed in chapter 6.

THE SIDE GLYPH

There is a set of signs with the value "side" that appear in midpoint contexts to indicate their direct association with the side of the quadrilateral model. In some contexts the sign T559 that is used in the day sign Kankin can have a phonetic value of *tzu* (Kelley 1976:171). Because *tzu* means "gourd" and *tzul* means "backbone," the pictographic value of this sign has been interpreted to be either a gourd or skeletal backbone. *Tzul* also means "dog," and the head variant has been interpreted as a dog. Although the Postclassic form of the sign resembles a backbone, the Classic form appears to be a tree with a sun sign or black circle beside it (Thompson 1972:46) (fig. 42).[35] Some examples of this glyph carry a phonetic *ku* sign to indicate *tzuk*. The T559 sign can be replaced by a T1017 head that has characteristics similar to those of God C (Grube and Schele 1991) (fig. 43a). The T559 sign and *tzuk* head also substitute for a variant of the mirror sign (Grube and Schele 1991) (fig. 43b). *Tzuk* can have the meaning of partition !Grube and Schele 1991), but Dennis Tedlock (1985) interprets this verb root to mean side. I believe the Classic *tzuk* signs indicate a location on the side of the world where the world tree occurs, that is, the midpoint on the side.[36] The mouth of the T1017 *tzuk* head has the shape of the cave quatrefoil, reinforcing its association with the

Figure 41. Naranjo Stela 32 (drawing by Ian Graham, courtesy of Peabody Museum)

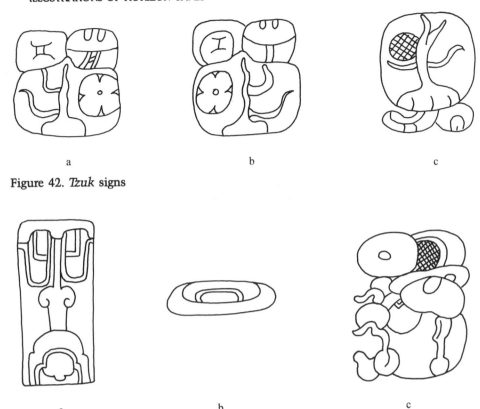

a   b   c

Figure 42. *Tzuk* signs

a   b   c

Figure 43. a. T1017 *tzuk* signs; b. mirror signs; c. Site Q Panel Ch'en sign

midpoint (fig. 43c). On the Site Q panel from the Saenz collection the T1017 head replaces the T528 cave sign in the context of the Ch'en month sign, again indicating its association with the midpoint cave.[37]

The *tzuk* head appears on the Chac illustrated at the west/black cave on Robicsek and Hales Vessel 120 (see fig. 27). Cauac monsters are invariably marked with *tzuk* signs, indicating their association with the mountains at the sides of the quadrilateral model. Several Rio Azul tombs have cauac monsters and T529 *cauac* signs painted on their walls. On the north wall of Tomb 6 the T529 *cauac* mountain cave is prefixed with the *tzuk* "side" sign, indicating its association with the midpoint on the side of the quadrilateral world model (fig. 44).

On the west-oriented Tablet of the Sun the cave passage on which Chan Bahlum stands is composed of alternating *cab* and *tzuk* signs, indicating its association with the side (see fig. 50). Likewise, the east-oriented Tablet

Figure 44. Rio Azul Tomb 6 glyph (after Richard Adams)

of the Foliated Cross (which illustrates the Cave of GII) displays a maize plant labeled with *Tzuk* heads (see fig. 49). The directional association of the Cross Group is discussed in the next chapter.

The Classic Period Ending ceremonies were structured using the quadrilateral model and oriented to the midpoints on the sides of the square (see chapter 4). The predominant motif on the loincloth of rulers performing Period Ending events is the *tzuk* head. Although this has been interpreted to mean the ruler is dressed like a tree, I suggest that it indicates the ruler's role as a Bacab and Chac, that is, a god of the side of the world.[38]

On Copan Stela B the *tzuk* head is illustrated on the back of the monument. Like the cauac monster on the front, it has been elongated to conform to the shape of the stela (fig. 45). Infixed in the *tzuk* head are *cauac* elements, indicating its conflation with the cauac monster. The *tzuk* head indicates that the Period Ending illustrated on this monument was oriented to the side, that is, it was a midpoint ceremony. In the Period Ending scene on Piedras Negras Stela 6 the niche within which the ruler sits is framed by a bicephalic monster with a skyband body that includes *tzuk* signs (fig. 46). Beneath the niche is a structure similar to the layered

Figure 45. Copan Stela B, back

Figure 46. Piedras Negras Stela 6
(after Teobert Maler)

shows the cave of GII, and the cave of GIII is feature on the Tablet of the Sun (figs. 48, 49, 50).[2] Chan Bahlum is pictured at each of these caves performing rituals on the occasion of a pre-accession event at age six (the small actor) and his accession at age forty-eight (the tall actor) (see introduction, note 6).

I have argued that the Cross Group buildings with their illustrated cave locations replicate three mountain caves in the vicinity of Palenque (Bassie-Sweet 1991:157-68).[3] This is a logical conclusion when we consider that supernaturals were thought to be born and to live in natural caves.[4] These mountain caves are in turn replications of the sacred mountains of the horizon. As a model of the quadrilateral world, the Temple of the Sun is associated with the west, the Temple of the Foliated Cross with the east, and the Temple of the Cross with the north.[5] The Cross Group tells us that the Palenque Triad of deities appeared for the first time on the surface of the world through the directional mountains.[6] Chan Bahlum performed a ritual circuit to the local versions of these caves during pre-accession and accession rituals, from north, to west, to east.

The quadrilateral world was used as a model for ordering many other Classic plaza/pyramid groups. The vast majority of these groups are not aligned with either the equinox or solstice points. For example, there are numerous Group E-type buildings in the vicinity of Uaxactun that are not precisely aligned (Ruppert 1940). The Maya were not building solar observatories; they were creating sacred space by duplicating the original creation of the world. The eastern buildings of Uaxactun Group E, in fact, have two stelae commemorating the successful re-creation of the world on 8.16.0.0.0 (see chapter 4).

In addition to these plaza groups, pyramids and temples were also built on top of or near natural caves.[7] Frans Blom and Oliver La Farge (1927:252) discovered that several mountain spurs around the Ocosingo valley had been modified into terraces to form a pyramid shape. A key feature of these precolumbian locations was the presence of several caves that were still being used:

We had heard that there were caves in the mountainside, and that every year, on the 3rd of May, the Indians come here to worship the god of the mountain. Soon we reached a small cave, or rock shelter, and upon entering saw that

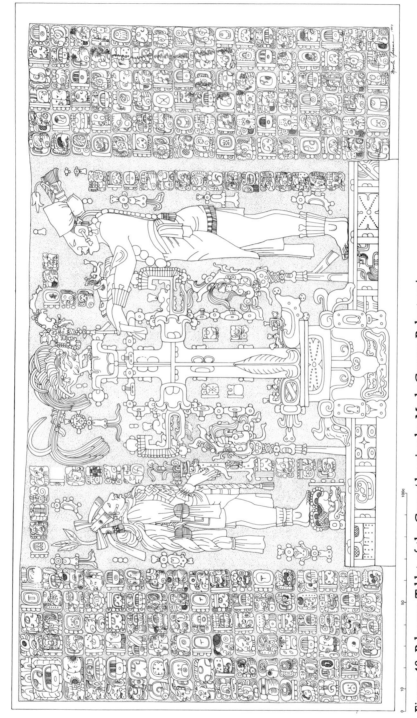

Figure 48. Palenque Tablet of the Cross (drawing by Merle Greene Robertson)

Figure 49. Palenque Tablet of the Foliated Cross (drawing by Merle Greene Robertson)

Figure 50. Palenque Tablet of the Sun (drawing by Merle Greene Robertson)

a tunnel led into the dark. This we followed, with lighted candles, into a small cave, and then on the floor we found signs of a small altar. . . . We then climbed to the top of the pyramid, and found a large level area in the center of which stood a small mound. On top of the mound Indians had erected a wooden cross and at its foot we found bunches of pine needles, also remnants of burnt copal incense. (Blom and La Farge 1927:252)

At Dos Pilas the major feature of the complex called El Duende is a large hill that has been modified into a pyramid/temple. The door of the temple is oriented to a spring of water to the north, and an important ritual cave is located to the southwest (Houston, cited in Brady 1991).

La Farge (1947:112) made pertinent observations regarding the reasons for constructing buildings in relation to caves:

The tendency of the Mayas to ascribe sacred nature to such points [mountain spurs], as well as to caves and the dramatic bottoms of gorges, is well known and probably goes back far into ancient times. The placement of the prehistoric temples upon outstanding heights of land may have been partly so as to secure prominence and a wide outlook for them, but it was probably partly due also to the previous existence of sacred power at those places. Other governing influences, such as boundary lines and roads, unquestionably did and still do affect the locations, so that many elements influenced the placement and importance of a given shrine or a modern cross; but the nature of these influences has not changed essentially since remote antiquity.

When the Maya built a temple or pyramid near or on a cave site or water shrine, they were creating a house that replicated the deity's home at the mythological mountain, thus duplicating a cosmological concept.[8]

It has been argued that the lowland Maya built pyramids as substitutes for the highland mountain and its cave (Vogt 1969:595). Vogt correctly suggested that the concept of ancient Maya pyramids with their dark chambered temples and elite tombs was based on the mountain/cave with its resident ancestors. He speculated that the modern tree/crosses and their altars were equivalent to stelae and the altarlike sculptures in front of them and that the ancient Maya came from their hamlets to these locations to pay homage just as the modern Maya go to the mountain. He also suggested that the pyramids in the flat Maya lowlands became the residences for the deities. In this interpretation the pyramid "became the dwelling places of the ancestral gods."

I do not believe this is true. The fact that the body was buried or entombed in a structure does not mean that its soul was thought to live at that location. The lowland Maya had numerous caves (including caves located on high points of land) in which their ancestors and deities could have resided; thus they did not need a substitute location. Whether specifically located near a real cave or oriented to represent one of the horizon mountains, temples functioned in much the same manner as modern shrines; they were sites where the deities and ancestors came and received their offerings. These houses were replicas of the supernaturals' home, but the supernaturals lived elsewhere—in the inner recesses of the mountains surrounding the community and in the four directions beyond the natural human world.

Temple of the Inscriptions

It is important to note that most pyramids and temple/pyramids found at Maya sites are not located at the center of the plaza but on the edges of quadrilateral spaces. These kinds of structures replicate one of the sacred mountains at the edge of the Maya world. When their function was funerary, the ruler was being symbolically buried at one of the mountain caves of the horizon.[9] Such a temple/pyramid is the Palenque Temple of the Inscriptions.

The motivation for the construction of the Temple of Inscriptions was discovered when the tomb of Pacal was found in the bowels of the pyramid. The excavation of the structure demonstrated that it was a single-stage construction built around a vaulted tomb. An inner staircase provided access, although this staircase was later sealed. Three panels inside the temple form a long narrative that begins with an early ruler nicknamed Chaacal I (circa A.D. 514) and proceeds through five generations of rulers. After relating numerous important events in the life of Pacal II, it climaxes with his death in A.D. 683. The final event records the accession of his son Chan Bahlum II four months later and some event on this day that remains undeciphered.

To gain access to the tomb, an observer follows a steep inner staircase oriented to the west. Two-thirds of the way down, the staircase reaches a landing and makes an abrupt turn. The stairs continue to descend toward

Figure 51. Palenque sarcophagus side (after Merle Greene Robertson)

the east and end at the doorway to the tomb. The sarcophagus contained
in the tomb is conceptually a bench (the final resting place of Pacal's body),
which in turn is a replication of the sky and earth. The box is the earth
and the lid is the sky. The sides of the box illustrate the ancestors of Pacal
sitting in *cab* cave openings on the sides of the quadrilateral world, precisely where the Maya believed ancestors lived (fig. 51).

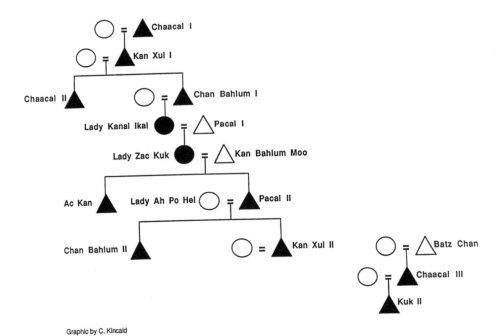

Graphic by C. Kincaid

Genealogy of Palenque rulers

The sarcophagus text that runs around the lip edge above these ancestors continues the story that was begun on the temple tablets. The story backs up in time to the death of Chaacal I (A.D. 524), the first character introduced on the temple text. The story proceeds through several episodes relating the deaths of all the previously mentioned rulers plus those of Pacal's father and maternal grandfather (table). The climax of the story is the death of Pacal.[10] The translation of the verb in these texts is "he entered the road" (Stuart, cited in Schele 1992). This verb does not appear to be related directly to the death of these individuals but to the moment when their souls entered either the road that leads to the horizon or the road into the ancestral cave.

The top of the lid is horizontal, so we must imagine the image lying flat rather than upright as the illustration shows (fig. 52). The borders of the lid represent the horizon area where sky meets earth. The edges of this quadrilateral sky are defined by skybands and quatrefoil cave openings.[11]

Two mirror-image skeletal jaws form a gaping cave opening on the south side of the sky. Pacal, or rather his soul, plunges toward this cave.[12] The directional orientation of the lid situates this world cave on the south

MERLE GREENE '75

Figure 52. Palenque sarcophagus lid (drawing by Merle Greene Robertson)

side of the quadrilateral world, but this is at odds with the ethnohistorical material that states that the dead travel with the sun to the west. If, however, Pacal is following the same road to the underworld as Hun Hunahpu and Vucub Hunahpu, he is traveling down the dark rift or black road of the Milky Way (Matthew Looper, cited in Schele 1992:133). In the *Popol Vuh* the brothers journey to the underworld by following this road (Tedlock 1985:334). At sunset on the night of Pacal's death the Milky Way arched across the sky from the northeast and terminated at the south midpoint. The rift road was slightly to the east of zenith, pointing to the south horizon. The Scorpio crossroads aligned with the southern terrestrial crossroads.

Behind Pacal is a tree. It has been suggested that this tree is a representation of the Milky Way (Looper, cited in Schele 1992:133). This concept has merit given that the Milky Way was viewed as a road, but the Inscriptions tree does not stretch across the entire sky like the Milky Way. A far better candidate for this cross motif is the Northern Cross, which marks the black rift of the Milky Way.

The Temple of the Inscriptions is situated on the south side of a plaza, butted up against the ridge of hills that define the south side of the site. Thus it is a replica of the south mountain of the horizon. The principal function of the temple was to house the body of Pacal, but the purpose of its orientation and artwork was to commemorate the life of Pacal and the journey of his soul to the other world. The only difference between this commemorative monument and a commemorative single sculpture such as a stela is our failure to recognize it as a whole statement. Within this statement the quadrilateral model is manifested on numerous levels.

As a replicated sacred location, the Temple of the Inscriptions probably became a site for ritual activity directed toward Pacal and his ancestors. The Cross Group did function as a ritual site, as the numerous incensarios found there attest. At these sites replicating GI's, GII's, and GIII's caves, ceremonies in honor of those supernaturals were surely performed.

As noted, some tombs such as Rio Azul Tomb 12 were also designed to represent cosmological models. The inscription on the eastern wall of Rio Azul Tomb 12 can be paraphrased as "On 8 Ben 16 Kayab, Lord X of Rio Azul was buried at 6 Cloud Sky" (Stuart and Houston in press). It is obvious that 6 Cloud Sky names Tomb 12, but what does Tomb 12 represent? Structure AIV, which houses Tomb 12, is located on the east side of a quadrilateral plaza. It represents the mythological eastern mountain cave and the local eastern cave that replicated this place. 6 Cloud Sky probably names all three places.

COPAN WORLD MODELS

The Temple of the Inscriptions sarcophagus illustrates the ancestors of Pacal living on the sides of the Palenque world in caves. The concept of ancestors living in the four directions is also found on Copan Altar Q. This square sculpture represents the quadrilateral world, with each side illustrating four Copan rulers. They sit on glyphs that state either their names or their titles. Yax Pac, the sixteenth successor, is portrayed on the west side facing the oldest of his predecessors, Yax K'uk' Mo' (fig. 53). The calendar round date of Yax Pac's accession appears between them. To Yax Pac's left is the fifteenth successor. As the viewer moves in this direction and follows the illustrations on the south, east, and north sides (the correct direction of a ritual circuit), the portraits of the deceased Copan rulers continue in descending order until the viewer returns to the west side again. By viewing the sculpture, the observer is led on a symbolic circuit around the borders of the Copan world where the ancestors lived, protecting the community.

Altar Q commemorates Yax Pac's validation by the heads of the ancestral government. It illustrates him as a member of that government and as a replacement for all those who preceded him. This validation is specifically depicted to have occurred at the borders of the Copan world. I interpret Altar Q to be the commemoration of a ritual circuit taken by Yax Pac on the occasion of his accession. This circuit culminated in the ritual illustrated on the west side, presumably at a west cave where Yax K'uk' Mo' resided.

Altar T also presents a model of the quadrilateral world on the occasion of the first katun of Yax Pac's accession.[13] The top of this square sculpture is a caimanlike monster that represents the surface of the earth (fig. 54). At the south midpoint on the side four human actors face a text naming a subordinate of Yax Pac. Each actor sits on place name glyphs that can be related to caves. The east and west sides are inhabited by both human actors and zoomorphs of fantastic form. Many of these have attributes that suggest they are the animal counterparts of the ancestors (fig. 55).[14] Unlike

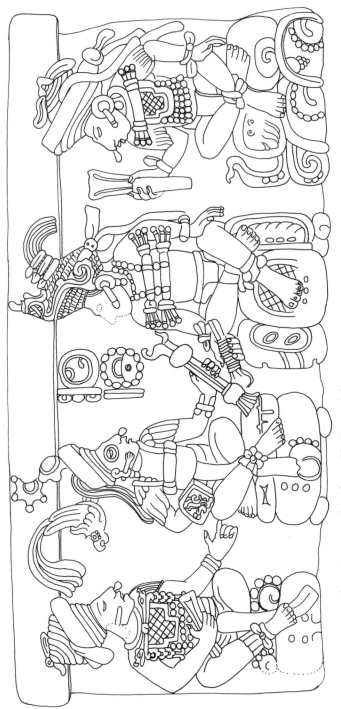

Figure 53. Copan Altar Q west side (after Alfred Maudslay)

Figure 54. Copan Altar T top (after Alfred Maudslay)

those of an ordinary person, the animal counterparts of the modern elite
are thought to live on in the ancestral cave and to protect the community.
Altar T probably illustrates this concept.

One point concerning ancestral caves needs to emphasized. In modern
Zinacantan the ancestors live inside the mountains surrounding the center.
While there may have been one principal cave to which ritual was directed
and in which the most senior ancestors resided, the ancestors were not
restricted to one location.

STELAE AND ALTARS AS COSMOGRAMS

We have seen many examples where Period Ending stelae are related to a
direction. The most comprehensive examples are those of Seibal Structure

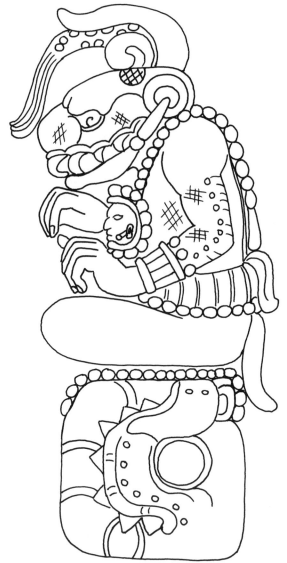

Figure 55. Copan Altar T side figure (after Alfred Maudslay)

A-3 (see fig. 47). These stelae demonstrate that at least five Period Ending rituals were performed on the 10.1.0.0.0 Period Ending: one in the center of Seibal and one for each direction. The north-oriented Period Ending event is said to have occurred in front of or in the middle of the Seibal ancestral cave and to have been witnessed by three foreign lords (see chapter 6 for a discussion of emblem glyphs and ancestral caves).[15] This information suggests that the other three Period Ending events performed at west, south, and east midpoint locations were also conducted at natural geographic features surrounding the community.

A similar situation is observed in the 9.11.0.0.0 Period Ending stelae of Copan's Smoke Imix God K. Four stelae and altars were set up on mountains and outlooks in the Copan valley.[16] Stela 13 is located on an eastern bluff next to the Copan River. The mountain directly east of this is the site of Stela 12. Stela 10 is situated on a mountain spur to the west, while Stela 19 is in a side valley a short distance away. A known ritual cave is in the vicinity of these last two monuments. Although the narratives on these monuments are eroded, there are midpoint references. The altar of Stela 13 contains the phrase "the East Sky Seat," while Stela 10 mentions the "Copan ancestral cave Sky Seat." This west-oriented stela also refers to Smoke Imix God K as a West Chac. The positions of the stelae indicate more than just the directional nature of the Period Ending events; they suggest that rituals were conducted in the hills surrounding Copan. It can be argued that the stelae mark the exact location of the rituals described in their texts, but it is just as likely that the stelae commemorate rituals performed in the vicinity at natural cave locations. I stress that these locations did not have to be impressive. The specific sites of many modern rituals are often no more than a crack in a rock or cliff face.

The stelae in the Great Plaza of Copan that were erected to commemorate the Period Ending events of 18 Jog reflect the quadrilateral world model as well. The Great Plaza itself is a quadrilateral space bounded on the east, north, and west by staircases and small structures and on the south by a pyramid with four staircases. The earliest stela (Stela C) was set up in the middle of the plaza, but subsequent stelae were lined up more toward the east (Stelae F and H), the north (Stela D), and the west (Stelae B, 4, and A). Five of the stelae have an altar in front of them. Many of these altars have been interpreted to be a representation of the earth (Baudez 1985) or a mountain (Stuart 1987; Bassie-Sweet 1991). By viewing the monuments in the context of the world model, new meanings emerge.

The first sculptures erected were Stela C and its turtle altar (9.14.0.0.0). This stela has an actor on both the east and west sides.[17] The rope of the world drapes down the sides of the stela. The altar is a three-dimensional turtle with deities emerging from the head and tail. The turtle as a representation of the quadrilateral world has been discussed. I have emphasized that it is important to analyze Maya art from the perspective of the viewer (Bassie-Sweet 1991). By standing in front of the turtle world model to view the image of the ruler on the stela, the observer is symbolically at the west midpoint, while the ruler is at the east midpoint. The viewer stands facing east in order to view this east ritual.

Stela H and its altar were erected on the east side of the plaza facing the plaza. The east and west sides of the altar are cauac monsters with the bone bench infixed in their heads. In other words, the east and west midpoints are illustrated as seats, as would be expected. Deities emerge from mouths on the north and south sides. The text refers to the setting up of a tree/standard by 18 Jog, which occurred 260 days prior to the 9.15.0.0.0 Period Ending. The text also refers to 18 Jog as a "lord of the side." The position of Stela H suggests this event occurred at the east seat.

The altars of two other plaza stelae also employ cauac monsters. The west and east sides of Stela C's altar are cauac monsters with knotted bloodletting elements infixed in the foreheads. Full figure jaguars drape over the north and south sides. The stela is positioned on the east side of the altar, suggesting it represents an east ritual. Stela D is located at the north midpoint of the plaza. 18 Jog is illustrated facing the plaza performing a north 9.15.5.0.0 Period Ending ritual. The altar in front of him has a cauac monster on the north side and skeletal head on the south.

Stela B records the 9.15.0.0.0 Period Ending. It has no altar, but instead is conflated with a cauac monster. This sculpture has the standard elongated shape of a stela, but the ruler is portrayed on the east side standing in the mouth of a cauac monster decorated with macaw heads. Stacked cauac monsters form the sides of the monument and surround the text. The rear has the form of a *tzuk* "side" head with cauac markings (see fig. 45). An actor who appears to be an ancestor sits in the quatrefoil in the forehead. The eyes are labeled "Macaw Mountain, 4 serpent/sky."[18] The position of

Stela B on the plaza suggests it represents a west-oriented Period Ending ritual.

The quadrilateral world model was applied to virtually everything in the community, including the boundaries, the town, the plazas, the buildings, the sculptures, the benches, and the ritual altars. Each of these sites had locations that represented the horizon caves and it is likely that they were all referred to using the name of the corresponding horizon name. This may cause considerable confusion when we attempt to ascertain specifically where a particular ritual is occurring. The layout of the Copan plaza and its monuments demonstrates the quadripartite nature of Maya rituals, but it is difficult to determine precisely where these illustrated events occurred. The Period Ending sculptures of 18 Jog's predecessor suggest that they were at natural cave locations in the hills and mountains surrounding Copan. As noted, the west-oriented Stela 10 mentions the "Copan ancestral cave Sky Seat," apparently indicating that Copan's ancestral cave was located in the west. Altar Q indicates that Yax K'uk' Mo', the founding lineage head, resided in the west. It seems likely that Macaw Mountain contained the senior ancestral cave of Copan.[19]

CEREMONIES AT THE CENTER

The layout of Seibal Structure A-3 suggests that in addition to the four directional Period Ending rituals a similar ritual was also performed in the center of Seibal. I propose that if a stela does not have directional associations it probably represents a center Period Ending event. The precise location of the center Period Ending event was likely to have been the place that the Maya perceived to be the center of the site. I speculate that center Period Ending events were rarely commemorated because the populace physically witnessed this particular part of the Period Ending ceremonies. The function of the stela as more than commemorative art is discussed in chapter 5.

SUMMARY

A number of architectural cosmograms depict some of the main features of the quadrilateral world. Some Maya temple/pyramids were oriented to represent the mountain caves of the horizon by being placed on the edge of a quadrilateral plaza or space. The review of the Temple of the Inscriptions provides insight into how the quadrilateral world model can be repeated on many levels. It also demonstrates that while the Maya produced single pieces of art as a commemoration of an event or person, they also created multiple works of art that were intended to be viewed together as a whole statement. The same can be said for the main plaza of Copan, where a series of stelae were placed over time to commemorate 18 Jog's sequential Period Ending events and related rituals. The stelae were not intended to be viewed as unrelated statements but as the lifetime accomplishments of a distinguished ruler.

At Palenque GI, GII, and GIII were intimately related to the north, east, and west caves, respectively; it was through these cave openings that the Triad was thought to have first manifested on the surface of the earth. The tablets of the Cross Group at Palenque illustrate pre-accession and accession rituals performed at the caves of the Palenque Triad. Recent archaeological excavations of the buildings indicate a single-stage construction on bedrock. The past and future tense events in the narrative of the tablets indicate that the Cross Group was built after the accession events; thus the Cross Group itself was not the site of these ceremonies. Given the physical evidence for ritual caves in the vicinity of Palenque and the Maya belief that deities and ancestors lived on the outskirts of the community, it is highly probable that the deity caves illustrated in the Cross Group represent natural caves. At Copan the placement of Smoke Imix God K's stelae in proximity to sacred geological formations in the surrounding hills suggests that the directional rituals illustrated on other Copan stelae are likely to have taken place at these natural sacred sites.

One point must be stressed here. Not all modern directional mountains are directly lined up in the appropriate direction (Hunt 1977:98). For example, in the Quiche area the four Year-bearer mountains are located to the east, south, southwest, and northwest (Tedlock 1983). Although I would argue in favor of the notion that the presence of caves in a particular region played a role in the original selection of a site, I do not expect to find four caves located in the four directions of every site or to find visually spectacular caves, given the mundane appearance of many modern sacred locations. I do, however, expect to find local variations of the general theme.

The Chichen Itza Castillo and Seibal Structure A-3 demonstrate that the quadrilateral world was conceived to be a mountain. In Eliade's generic world model for traditional societies the center of the world is an axis mundi where both heaven and hell can be accessed. Such a model meets the needs of any culture that believes in a three-part universe in which heaven is directly overhead and hell directly below. A mountain in the center of the community met the needs of the Maya, perhaps because its top (high shrine) provided access to the zenith sun, but ritual activity focused on the side midpoints that replicated the edges of the quadrilateral world. It must be kept in mind that the vast majority of Late Classic temple/pyramids and shrines were not oriented to the center but occurred at the edges of quadrilateral spaces. The Classic Maya did not look to the heavens for protection but to the borders of their community. Nonetheless, each mythological mountain had a center-oriented and vertical nature. The surface of the earth was divided into four quadrants. Each mythological mountain was the center of a quadrant, with high and low shrines. The next chapter discusses the ceremonies that provided the Maya with the means of maintaining the balance between order and destruction and the essential role the ruling elite played in that preservation.

4

THE RENEWAL OF THE WORLD

Although the deities created a quadrilateral world in which humans could live safely, the forces that existed beyond that world were constantly threatening its destruction. It was the duty of the guardian deities who inhabited the mythological caves to prevent the destructive forces from devastating the world. They acted as sentinels protecting the human world. At specific times dictated by the calendar (the end of the year and the end of the katun), the world was thought to be in particular danger. The Postclassic New Year and Classic Period Ending ceremonies performed at this time represented the symbolical destruction and re-creation of the world. The power of the elite rested in their ability to play the role of deities or to placate the deities and thus bring about this renewal of life. The rituals that reinforced and validated the structure of the universe are the focus of this chapter.

THE SOURCE OF DESTRUCTION

The four midpoint caves were openings where the destructive forces could enter and devastate the world. Wind was the vehicle in which the destructive forces traveled. Destructive wind is most often said to come from the four directions, a cave, or water within a cave.[1] The association between the forces of destruction and wind is natural, given the frequency of hurricanes and tropical storms in the Maya area.

The incantations recorded in the *Ritual of the Bacabs* describe the winds from the four directions that were thought to carry disease. The ritual specialist recites one of these incantations as part of the ceremony to cure a patient of a particular illness. The chant declares the names of the parents who gave birth to the illness, the method of its birth, and the birth location (a directional cave on the horizon). The four Bacabs of the midpoints are then commanded to take the "wind" back, and the cave birthplace of the "wind" is described further (Roys 1965). Modern beliefs echo this concept. There is a widespread notion that some illnesses are caused by an evil wind that appears to carry the spirit of illness (Wisdom 1940:317; Roys 1965). During Quintana Roo therapeutic ceremonies intended to purify the sick of evil winds, the ritual specialist recites a prayer that begins by invoking the winds of the four directions (Villa Rojas 1945:139).[2] He asks them what the nature of the illness is, which of the many winds has specifically caused it, and what will cure it. Branches are used to sweep everything in the house to remove the evil winds.

In the modern *loh* ceremonies of Yalcoba the ritual specialist asks the deities to send the offending evil sickness or wind back to the horizon cave (Sosa 1985:299). In the purification ceremony of the ritual specialist, the assistants use branches to sweep everything in the house with a motion toward the front door so that the evil winds will be swept from the house. The food offering made to the evil winds is then carried to a natural hillock on the outskirts of town and hung in a tree. The contaminated branches are also left there. The antecedent for this location is the tree at the midpoint mountain on the side of the quadrilateral world. As the source of retribution, the midpoints were the focus of ritual activity, such as the Postclassic Uayeb ceremonies.

THE POST CLASSIC RE-CREATION OF THE WORLD

The five days of Uayeb that ended the 365-day cycle were a time of intense ritual activity. Landa stated that the ceremonies conducted at this time were in honor of the guardian deities.[3] Taube (1988a) cogently argued that the Uayeb ceremonies were a reenactment of the destruction and re-creation of the world.

The Dresden New Year pages indicate that the following the destruction of the world four deities restored order by placing a guardian idol and world tree at each of the midpoints of the quadrilateral world. Landa's description of the Yucatec town layout indicates that it replicated the world model: the town had a formal ritual entrance on each of four sides. Four roads radiated from the center to these midpoints on the sides. Landa did not indicate what demarcated the corners, but each entrance was marked by two heaps of stones representing the mythological mountain. On each heap of stone was an idol representing a guardian deity and beside this his tree/standard.

In preparation for the Uayeb rituals a new idol representing the appropriate guardian deity for the current year was placed on the heap of stones.[4] A new statue of one of the four deities who ordered the world was placed in the house of a leading lord. This idol represented Bolon Dzacab, K'inich Ahau, Itzamna, or Uax Mitun Ahau, depending on the year of the ceremony. A pilgrimage was conducted from the center of the community to the entrance:

> The lords and the priest and the men of the town assembled together and having cleaned and adorned with arches and green the road leading to the place of heaps of stone where the statue [of the guardian deity] was, they went altogether to it with great devotion. And when they came there the priest incensed it. . . . The image having been incensed, they cut off the head of a hen and presented or offered it to him [the idol that represents the deity, in effect, the deity]. This having been done, they placed the statue upon a standard called *kante*. . . . And thus they carried it with much rejoicing and dancing, to the house of the *principa*. (Tozzer 1941:140-41)

The guardian idol was placed before the statue of the ordering deity, and everyone made offerings to both idols. Blood offerings were also made by those who were particularly devout to a stone belonging to a deity called the Acantun.[5] In other contexts the Acantun appears to be a stone representing the guardian deities (Roys 1933:114, 171) (see chapter 5).

There were four objects to which ritual offerings were made in these Uayeb ceremonies: an idol representing the guardian deity, his tree/standard, a stone related to the guardian deity, and an idol representing an ordering deity.

When the guardian idol and his standard (the world tree) were brought from the mountain into the community, the stability of the world was in jeopardy. The symbolic cord surrounding the town became untied and the destructive forces from the four directions threatened the world. A period of chaos, disorder, evil, and danger began in which the world was symbolically destroyed. A colonial song that refers to this period includes the phrase "Unbound is Cizin [god of the underworld], open is the underworld" (Taube 1988a:290).

Following much sacrifice, prayers, and purification on the part of the ritual specialists and the people, the statue of the ordering deity was placed in the temple and the guardian idol and his tree/standard were taken to the directional mountain for the upcoming year. The actions featured in the Dresden New Year scenes provide additional information about these final acts. Landa indicated that the idol of the ordering deity was placed in the temple at the end of Uayeb, and the second scene of the Dresden illustrates the deity sitting there the next day. The last act of the Uayeb ceremony was the placing of the guardian idol and his tree/standard at the midpoint. The Dresden indicates that the Chac idol was removed from the tree/standard and presumably replaced on the pile of stones and that both were given offerings.

The climax of the Uayeb ceremony was the replacing of the guardian idol at the border of the community.[6] The world was put in order again, and time was able to progress forward for another year.[7] The Maya world was thought to be in fragile balance. Only through proper ritual conduct could the balance between preservation and destruction be maintained. Regular ritual ceremonies on the part of the individual and the community were essential for the continued health and safety of all. Ritual activity reinforced and validated the order and structure of the world.

THE CLASSIC RE-CREATION OF THE WORLD

A similar theme of destruction and re-creation also occurred during the Classic period. This Classic event was tied not to the New Year ceremony but to the era event and Period Ending ceremonies. The zero base date of the current era (4 Ahau 8 Cumku) was not the beginning of time but the final katun of the previous era and the beginning of the first katun period of the current era.[8] The zero base date represented the destruction of the previous world and the creation of the new world.

There are a limited number of texts that refer to the era event. The most detailed written description occurs in a passage on Quirigua Stela C. The first phrase has been interpreted to mean "was manifested the image" (Schele 1992:122). On a looted panel that also refers to the era event the "image" is a turtle, which has been interpreted to refer to the Turtle constellation (Orion's belt) (Schele 1992:134). Given the likelihood that the era event represents the last destruction and re-creation of the world, it seems far more probable that the turtle here is a reference to the reappearance of the surface of the earth after the flood. The surface of the world is represented by a turtle in many scenes (Taube 1988b).

The verbs from the Quirigua texts that have been securely deciphered refer to the setting up of three T528 *tun* "stone" idols (fig. 56).[9] Paraphrased, the passages read:

> The Paddler deities set up the stone; it happened at *Na Ho Chan*, at the jaguar bench of the stone. The Black Great deity set up the stone; it happened at the *Cab* Side Place, at the serpent bench of the stone. *Na Itzam* placed the stone at the *naab* bench of the stone; it happened at the T128 Sky/the First Three Stones Place. His completion of the 13th cycle, *u cab* Six Sky Lord.

The narrative continues with the Period Ending ritual of an Early Classic ruler on 9.1.0.0.0 and the subsequent Period Ending of the ruler Cauac Sky on 9.17.5.0.0.

It has been argued that the placement of T528 stones on the era Period Ending was a model for human Period Ending ceremonies that also involved the setting up of T528 stones (Bassie-Sweet 1991:180-83). The *Cab* Side Place, *Na Ho Chan*, the T128 Sky/First Three Stones Place, and the *u cab* phrase were interpreted to refer to four separate ritual circuit locations, each associated with a different direction. I no longer find the interpretation of *u cab* as a place name viable, but the conclusion that these deities are providing the model for the ruler's Period Ending action is inescapable.

The first Quirigua location is at a jaguar bench at *Na Ho Chan* (fig. 57a). The stone is erected by the Paddler deities, who are consistently

Figure 56. Quirigua Stela C text (after Alfred Maudslay)

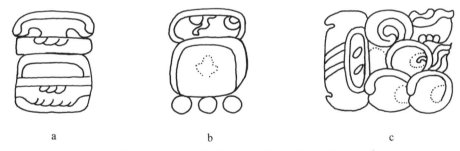

a   b   c

Figure 57. a. *Na Ho Chan;* b. *Cab* Side Place; c. First Three Stone Place

associated with this location in other inscriptions.[10] It seems highly likely
that *Na Ho Chan* is the name of the Paddlers' place of origin. On several
monuments the Paddler deities are called *Na Ho Chan* lords (Stuart and
Houston in press).

An illustration of *Na Ho Chan* is found on the Quirarte vase, where three deities are depicted sitting inside of Chac's cave, which is labeled with *tzuk* "side" signs (see fig. 30). The associated caption text states that the location is *Na Ho Chan*, the *witz xaman* "the mountain of the north."

The second Quirigua location is a serpent bench at the *Cab* Side Place (fig. 57b). I equate this place with the other *cab* locations that refer to the horizon area (see fig. 14). I believe the "side" sign indicates this is a midpoint. The *Ek Chac* "black great" deity who sets up this stone is an unknown supernatural, but the black prefix suggests that he is associated with the west.

The third location is a *naab* "sea" bench at the T128 Sky/*Yax* Three Stones Place (fig. 57c). This place name is associated with the end of era passages in several texts. It is composed of two compounds. The first is the *chan* "sky" sign prefixed with T128.[11] The second is composed of a *yax* "first, blue/green" sign and three stacked *cauac* signs. The top *cauac* sign is prefixed with signs that appear on *tun* "year" signs, and in some contexts *cauac* signs are read as *tun*. The T128 Sky/First Three Stones Place has been interpreted to be a location where all three stones of the Quirigua inscription were set up, as a reference to sky, earth, and underworld locations (MacLeod, cited in Schele 1992:125, 248), as a reference to the three hearth stones of the fire, and as the Three Hearth Stones constellation (Freidel and Schele, cited in Schele 1992).

The hearth area was the primary location for the preparation of corn. All Maya hearths consisted of three stones placed in a triangular arrangement. The hearth was an important source of fire and the hearth stones were likely receptacles for the spirit of fire.[12] I have suggested that the T528 *tun* sign is a reference to the stone from which corn was obtained by humans (Bassie-Sweet 1991). As noted, the stone that hid the first corn was struck by the lightning deity and thus also contained the spirit of lightning and fire. It seems a logical sequence of events that this *tun* sign would also be used to represent a hearth stone, with its intimate association with corn and fire.[13]

Although it is a reasonable argument that the Three Stones Place name was employed as a term for the Three Hearth Stones constellation, it does not necessarily follow that the T528 Sky/First Three Stones Place refers to this constellation or that the actions of the Quirigua deities occurred there. For example, it has been argued that the illustrations of an actor emerging from the cracked shell of a turtle represent the emergence of the corn from the earth (Taube 1988b). This is the location from which corn naturally emerges and is in accord with the belief that corn first came from the cave. Another interpretation is that the actor is a personification of the Milky Way as a corn plant "rising" out of the Turtle constellation (Schele 1992:135). This image may represent the Turtle constellation, but the configuration of the constellation represents the myth that corn was obtained from the earth. The Maya did order and name the parts of the sky using features of the earth, but corn was not found in the Turtle constellation—it was found on earth in a mountain cave.

There are several attributes of the ancestral couple that relate them to the *Yax* "first, blue/green" Three Stones Place and the concepts of the hearth. The ancestral couple Itzamna and Ix Chel were both closely associated with the color *yax*. As deities of the sea, the ancestral couple of the *Popol Vuh* are said to be enclosed in glittering *yax* light, metaphorically referred to as quetzal feathers. They are called "the maker of the *yax* plate, the maker of the *yax* bowl." These titles refer to the dishes in which ritual offerings were contained, indicating that the ancestral couple were the makers of the first ritual dishes. The use of the *yax* prefix in the Three Stones Place name suggests that it refers to the first or blue-green hearth. The first hearth would have been located in the home of the ancestral couple.[14]

This leads to the conclusion that the T128 Sky/First Three Stones Place is a name for the ancestral couple's home. Evidence for this is found in the Quirigua text, which states that Na Itzam (the first ancestral father of the sea) placed the stone on the *naab* "sea" bench. In the *Ritual of the Bacabs* the ancestral couple Itzamna and Ix Chel reside in the waters of the directional caves, which, in effect, represent the sea.[15] As noted in chapter 1, Ix Chel is associated with the east. In the *Popol Vuh* the ancestral grandmother also has an eastern association, for in later episodes she lives at the house of Hun Hunahpu, located near the eastern horizon and ballcourt.

Thus these three end of era ritual locations (*Na Ho Chan*, *Cab* Side Place, and the T128 Sky/First Three Stones Place) appear to have different directional associations. These deities set up a T528 *tun* stone at a bench first in the north, then in the west, and finally in the east—the direction of most precolumbian ritual circuits. This means that Classic period reordering of the world involved the setting up of T528 stone idols at three of the four directions. The benches at these locations likely refer to the seats of the midpoints.

Given the quadrilateral nature of the world, it is surprising that the Quirigua text refers to three stones rather than four. It may be important that in the *Popol Vuh* the Quiche start out with four lineage heads and their respective patron deities, but by the time the first community is founded only three of these deities are placed around the community and worshiped.

The metaphor or model that is used for the triadic ordering of the world appears to be the configuration of the three hearth stones of the house. The house of the ancestral couple has three hearth stones, and the quadrilateral world that is, in effect, the house of humans also has the same configuration.

The placing of three stones in front of benches on the surface of the earth is found in the rituals performed by Postclassic Yucatec travelers (Tozzer 1941:107). For protection from harmful forces at night, a traveler created a ritual space in which to burn incense to the guardian of travelers, known as Ek Chuah. This space consisted of a small dish, three small stones, and three flat stones. In the dish the traveler erected three stones with a few grains of incense on each then placed a flat stone in front of each stone. During petitioning, the traveler threw incense on these flat stones and burnt it. This ritual space replicates the cosmological model, with the dish representing the disk of the world and the stones and their altars representing three of the midpoint idols and their seats.

Classic Period Ending Rituals

The Maya believed in the cyclical nature of time. When a katun period ended the conditions that occurred on the zero base date were likely to occur again. The integrity of world order was threatened by the destructive forces from the four directions at each katun ending.[16]

Many Classic Period Ending narratives and scenes are associated with directions either through the text, which actually states the direction,

Figure 58. Tree of the stone phrases

or through the positioning of the monument. In some cases the directional orientation of the Period Ending ceremonies can be inferred, such as those of Palenque. Some Classic Period Ending phrases state that stone idols and tree/standards were set up at this time.

During these events, the ruler is said to set up a T528 *tun* "stone" and a "tree of the stone." In some examples the stone and tree are given proper names. The tree of the stone compound is composed of a pictograph of a tree prefixed to the T528 *tun* sign (fig. 58). In an example from Copan Stela D the *tun* is a full figure variant and the tree appears as a branch with *cab* "beehives" hanging from it. Based on phonetic complements, Stuart has suggested a reading of *lakam* for this tree sign. *Lakam* means "standard," which fits with the precolumbian concept of the tree/standard.

In other phrases the Period Ending event is called "the seating of the *tun*." This refers to both the establishment of the *tun* "year" and the placing of a *tun* "stone" idol.[17] These acts are parallel with New Year rituals, where the last day of Uayeb was the establishment of the New Year (the seating of Pop), and the time when the guardian idol was replaced at the midpoint (when the deity was seated) and the world trees were erected. The seating of the *tun* and its tree signified the completion of the ordering of the world.

The Temple of the Inscriptions passages that refer to the Period Ending events of Pacal indicate that he dressed in the costume of each member of the Palenque Triad and performed rituals.[18] The structure of the Cross

Group rituals suggests that these three ritual dressings occurred at the directional caves of the Palenque Triad. Thus part of the Period Ending ceremony may have involved the ruler imitating the role of a deity at three of the midpoint locations. This parallels the Dresden New Year ceremonies, where a different deity is illustrated performing a ritual at each of the midpoints.[19]

The three-event nature of the Palenque Period Ending ceremony is reminiscent of three rituals of the Quirigua narrative. The locations of the Quirigua actions are similar to at least two of the Palenque Triad caves. Both the era event and the Palenque rituals begin with actions oriented to the north. Although no direct parallels can be made between the north *Na Ho Chan* and GI's north cave of birth, the next location is the *Cab* Side Place. At this location a black deity sets up a stone on a serpent bench. The west cave of GIII, which is associated with black by color/ directionalism, is illustrated as a band of *cab* and side signs. The bench at GIII's cave is a bench with serpent heads at each end and a jaguar head in the middle (see fig. 50).[20] The final location (the T128 Sky/First Three Stones Place) is related to the ancestral couple and a *naab* bench, that is, a water shrine. In the *Popol Vuh* Hun Hunahpu's house in which the ancestral grandmother lives has a corn plant in its center. Water forms the baseline of the eastern cave of GII and a corn plant marks its center (see fig. 49).

The monuments of the Terminal Classic Structure A-3 at Seibal also document the directional orientation of Period Ending rituals, but in this case all four midpoints are sites of ritual activity (see fig. 47). As noted in chapter 3, this building is a four-doored pyramid/temple with its sides oriented to the four directions. Each side of the pyramid has a staircase running from its doorway down to the plaza. A stela was erected at the center of the temple and at the base of each staircase, marking the center and midpoints of the world. Each stela illustrates a different event from the ceremonies performed on the 10.1.0.0.0 Period Ending. I have interpreted the arrangement of Structure A-3 and its stelae to be a commemoration of a ritual circuit performed by the ruler on this occasion. The scene on each stela represents one of the locations where the ruler performed a ritual (Bassie-Sweet 1991:179). In the case of the midpoint stelae, these locations would be midpoints on the edge of the Seibal community. This kind of ritual circuit still exists in the Chorti region:

The movements of the participants in the pueblo rain-making ceremonies describe a square in that they march to each of the four cardinal points of the pueblo to pray to a Chicchan [rain deity], to a Working Man [rain deity], and to a saint [rain deity] at each of them. (Wisdom 1940:430)

A similar theme of the renewal of space and the preservation of order occurs in modern ceremonies. The Yucatec *loh* ceremony with its ritual circuit around the community purifies and makes the community safe again. The Zinacanteco house and field ceremonies that include ritual circuits create social order and emphasize the safety and civilized nature of these spaces (Vogt 1976:59). The description of the Zinacantan year renewal ceremony emphasizes this point:

A crucial aspect of the Year Renewal rituals is the drawing of a boundary around the municipio. By making offerings of all the tribal shrines and praying at Kalvaryo, the ritualists are symbolically defining Zinacantan, establishing ritual purity within, and setting the municipio apart from the disorder outside. By exaggerating the difference within and without, the rituals symbolically recreate order each year for all of Zinacantan. (Vogt 1976:187)

The concept of renewal is also found in the Period Ending scenes that illustrate a sacrificial captive lying at the feet of the ruler.[21] The purpose of sacrificial offerings during the Period Ending ceremony is not completely clear, but rebirth and renewal through death is a common theme in Mesoamerica. The most obvious model is corn, which is decapitated, placed in the earth, and reborn. In many modern sources the establishment of a quadrilateral space requires blood sacrifice. Most often this is the sacrifice of a chicken or turkey, but the concept of human sacrifice is still evident. The Chorti description regarding the construction of the shrine of Esquipulas states that several attempts to build the church failed until living men were placed in the mortar in the corners (Fought 1972).[22]

The cord that was thought to encase the world and protect it from the destructive forces is also found in a number of Classic Period Ending contexts. On Copan Stela F, which illustrates a Period Ending ritual (9.14.10.0.0), the cord is wrapped around the text, creating cartouches. A cord also loops around the ruler and encases him as well. On Stela 4, which illustrates the 9.14.15.0.0 Period Ending, the same cord also encircles the ruler. This cord appears between the ruler's legs, suggesting it may perforate his penis.[23] These contexts indicate that the ritual circuit of the ruler may have involved the untying and tying of space, that is, the destruction and re-creation of the world.[24]

Another feature that the Period Ending ceremonies share with both the Dresden New Year scenes and the *Popol Vuh* is the action of carrying lineage supernaturals. The *Popol Vuh* has the four lineage heads carrying the lineage deities from their sacred place of origin to locations in the vicinity of the future Quiche community. The Dresden illustrates four ancestral figures carrying supernaturals on their backs. Landa's account of the Postclassic Uayeb ceremonies describes how the guardian idol is placed on his tree/standard and carried into the town. This activity was accompanied by dancing. During the Classic period, lords and supernaturals are often illustrated carrying a backrack. In most examples these actors are dancing. The backrack assemblage is most clearly seen in pottery scenes, where it includes a cauac monster or emblem glyph with a supernatural sitting on it (Coe 1978:94; Reents 1985). A skyband usually arches overhead with a bird perched on top. Quatrefoil cave openings, *tzuk* "side" signs, and jaguar mat benches can also appear in the assemblage. All these motifs are associated with the midpoint and indicate that the backrack is a replication of the midpoint.

As discussed in chapter 6, emblem glyphs name the senior ancestral cave, which in turn is a replica of one of the mythological mountains (the cauac monster). The supernatural depicted varies in these scenes, but it has been shown that certain supernaturals are specifically associated with a particular emblem glyph (Coe 1978:96). The correlation between a specific supernatural and the ancestral cave suggests that these are either lineage patrons or animal counterparts that guard the community.

Some of the mythological backrack scenes have Ahau dates associated with them, suggesting they represent Period Ending actions. On stelae illustrations of Period Ending rituals often show the ruler wearing the backrack. I suggest that when the ruler is illustrated wearing the backrack he is in the process of carrying a lineage-related supernatural to the midpoint or is at the midpoint setting up this supernatural.

The Period Ending ritual act most commonly illustrated is the holding of a double-headed ceremonial bar with deities emerging from the ends. This object represented many interrelated concepts, including the cave passage. In these Period Ending events the ruler is illustrated at one of the midpoints controlling this opening into the supernatural world, precisely the role of the Bacab. The predominant title carried by Maya lords was *bacab*.[25] This title is often prefixed with a directional glyph. A frequent Period Ending costume element is the waterlily of the Bacab. It would appear that one of the ruler's duties during the Period Ending was to play the role of this supernatural.

The ruler also carried a title referring to the guardian deity Chac. As noted, this title is an illustration of Chac throwing his lightning axe. Lightning was the ultimate supernatural force used by the guardian deities to protect the community. The *chac* title indicates that the ruler was in command of this power.[26]

Tikal Stela 22 provides significant information regarding the importance of lightning to the Period Ending event. The text of this monument begins with the 9.17.0.0.0 Period Ending event of Ruler C and illustrates him hand-scattering on this date. The text continues with the statement that Ruler C was the son of Ruler B, a "4 katun Chac." This means that Ruler B had been a Chac during 4 Period Endings. The text backs up in time and says that it was 2 tuns (years) and 36 days since Ruler B was seated as Chac and then he hand-scattered on the Period Ending. The story indicates the importance of being a Chac in relation to the Period Ending. As the guardian of his community, Ruler B preserved the balance and order of the world during the Period Ending ceremony, using the same lightning/axe weapon that Chac did. He played the role of the guardian deities and commanded the forces of those deities.[27]

SUMMARY

The Maya are often portrayed in popular literature as worshipers of time, but their alleged fascination is nothing more than the basic human preoccupation with the control and continuation of time and thus human existence. The central power of the Maya elite was rooted in their ability to maintain the balance between order and destruction. The Period Ending ceremony reenacted the destruction and re-creation of the world. It represented the cyclical maintenance of order by the elite. These rituals were acts of renewal.

The Classic texts that refer to the last destruction and re-creation of the world suggest that certain deities who played key roles in that event set up guardian stone idols in the north, west, and east in front of bench altars. Like these deities, the ruler set up guardian stone idols at the borders of the community during the Period Ending event. The ruler also set up tree/standards. Although the very brief texts regarding the era event do not mention this act, a parallel can be drawn from Postclassic sources, where world trees were set up at the midpoints. In addition, the ruler carried to the midpoint a patron supernatural in his backrack. It is likely that these assemblages were set up at the midpoint. As the maintainer of the world, the ruler also appears to have functioned as a guardian. His *bacab* and *chac* titles attest to this role.

With this interpretation of Period Ending events in mind, commemorations of these events take on new meaning. The Temple of the Inscriptions contains three tablets that form a continuous narrative. The east tablet begins the story with the 9.4.0.0.0 Period Ending of Chaacal I and then relates the earlier accession of Chaacal I as background information about the Period Ending. The accessions and Period Endings of Kan Xul I, Chaacal II, Chan Bahlum I, Lady Kanal Ikal, Ac Kan, Lady Zac Kuk, and Pacal II are then presented. In each case the accession is given as background information and the Period Ending is the highlighted event. Several authors have suggested that the accessions are tied to the Period Ending in order to establish the timeframe. The narrative structure of the text indicates that this is not the case. This story is not about the accession of Palenque rulers, but about their ability to maintain the order of the world.

The conclusion of this narrative occurs on the sarcophagus. The last episode in this text gives the birth and death of Pacal, but it also includes the important statement that he participated in four katun ceremonies in his life. Although some researchers suggest that this statement was included as a distance number between the two dates, it actually summarizes the importance of this great ruler: he was able to protect and defend his community and maintain the order of the world. It is of no little interest that the subject matter of the majority of stelae is not accession events but the Period Ending event.

There were great regional variations in the Period Ending event. For example, the Palenque narratives indicate the importance of the deities GI, GII, and GIII, while many of the Period Ending events of other sites focus on the Paddler deities. These variations probably reflect the community's need to modify and transform the world model to meet local needs. How diverse these variations were remains unknown until we have better decipherment of the texts and a complete site-by-site analysis. What is certain is that the Late Classic Maya shared common beliefs concerning the nature and meaning of the Period Ending ceremony and the role of the ruling elite in that event.

The importance of the ruler in maintaining the order of the world suggests that his death would have placed the community in jeopardy. I speculate that the burying of a ruler at a symbolic mountain at the edge of a quadrilateral space (e.g., Pacal in the Temple of the Inscriptions, Tikal Ruler A in Temple 1) represented not only the soul's transfer to the mythological mountain but also the reestablishment of the community's safe space.

The final act of the Postclassic Uayeb/New Year ceremony was the placing of guardian idols and world trees at the perimeter of the town. During the Classic, the climax of the Period Ending ceremony was the placing of stone idols and trees at the perimeter of the community. These stones are the subject of the next chapter.

5

GUARDIAN IDOLS

The deities placed T528 *tun* stones at the midpoints during the Classic re-creation of the world. The ruling elite emulated these actions during the Period Ending ceremonies. This chapter discusses the nature and function of these stones as well as their Postclassic counterparts.

POSTCLASSIC STONES

Landa's reference to the courtyard of the temple describes what appear to be a tree/standard with an idol and a stone:

> In order to make these various sacrifices, there were in the courts of the temples several great beams [tree/standards] standing erect and ornamented with sculptures [the deity idol]; and near the staircase of the temple they had a round wide pedestal, and the center of it was a rather slender stone four or five palms high, standing erect. (Tozzer 1941:115)

This passage indicates that there were stone idols resembling small stelae. Four stone idols called Acantuns were part of the New Year ceremonies. After the guardian idol and his tree/standard were taken to the house of a chief and presented with offerings "others drew blood from themselves, cutting their ears, and anointing with it a stone which they had there of a god Kanal Acantun" (Tozzer 1941:141). The description of this ritual action during the next three years is similar:

> And those who were devout had to draw their blood and to anoint the stone of the idol Chac Acantun. . . . Others drew their own blood, and anointed with it the stone of the god Sac Acantun . . . and many drew blood from many parts of their bodies and anointed with it the stone of the god called Ekel Acantun. (Tozzer 1941:145-47)

The word *acantun* can be translated as thunder stone, set up stone, and stone shaft (Roys 1933). These translations are not mutually exclusive.

The color references to these idols indicate they had directional associations. In the *Ritual of the Bacabs* the acantuns are located at the directional caves: "overturned at the opening of his *acantun*, when his birth occurred, when his creation occurred" (Roys 1965:10):

> Four are the doors to his arbour; four are those to his *acantun*, where his birth occurred. Four splotches of blood, four splotches of clotted blood are behind the *acantun*, the *acante*. (Roys 1965:12)[1]

> Four are the doors to his arbour, four are the openings to his *acantun*. Four splotches of blood, four splotches of clotted blood were behind the *acantun*, behind the maxcal-plant, when his birth occurred. (Roys 1965:18)

> At one time there was the *acantun*, the *acante*, a great splotch of blood behind the *acantun-acante*. One time there was a great rainstorm, a great whirlwind with rain. (Roys 1965:31)

> There the *acantun* was cast down to break. (Roys 1965:39)

The four directional acantuns also appear in Landa's description of the making of wooden idols. A special fenced-in hut was constructed to house the priest, his four Chac assistants, and the craftsmen who would carve these statues. An Acantun was placed at each of the midpoints of the enclosure, and many blood offerings were made to them. The making of wooden idols was considered to be extremely dangerous and the craftsmen believed "a fainting sickness" would overcome them (Tozzer 1941:160). The Maya attribute unconsciousness to the loss of one's soul. The participants feared the loss or partial loss of their souls, which would result in insanity or death. The evil winds that attacked the soul came from the four midpoints. The Acantuns that were placed at the midpoints in this ceremony clearly had a protective function similar to the guardian deity idols and tree/standards.[2]

In the *Book of Chilam Balam of Chumayel* there are parallel passages that refer to the stone of a Mucencab guardian deity:

> The red flint stone is the stone of the red Mucencab. The red ceiba tree of abundance is his arbour which is set in the east. . . . The white flint stone is their stone in the north. The white ceiba tree of abundance is the arbour of the white Mucencab. . . . The black flint stone is their stone in the west. The black ceiba tree of abundance is their arbour. . . . The yellow flint stone is the stone of the south. The ceiba tree of abundance, the yellow ceiba tree of abundance, is their arbour. (Roys 1933:64)

This indicates that the stones of the Mucencab guardian deities were related to lightning, for flint was thought to contain the spirit of lightning. The modern Maya often place chips of flint and obsidian at their tree/ crosses and community entrances to act as protection from outside forces. It would seem that flint and obsidian can protect because they contain the spirit lightning. The primary lineage deities of the Quiche (Tohil) and the Yucatec Maya (Chac) were lightning deities. Lightning, the ultimate precolumbian weapon, was used by the guardian deities and the ruling elite to protect the community. Thus these Postclassic references indicate that the stones of the guardian deities had a protective function and probably contained the spirit of lightning.

CLASSIC STONES

As noted in the previous chapter, T528 *tun* stones were placed at the mid-points by the Classic ruling elite during the Period Ending event. These actions replicated the placement of T528 *tun* stones during the re-creation of the world by the deities. The *tun* sign is composed of the pictograph of the guardian deities' cave (the T528 *cauac* "lightning" sign) with phonetic complements to indicate a reading of *tun*. The word *tun* could also be represented by a personified sign that incorporates the T528 elements.[3] The employment of the T528 elements in both *tun* glyphs indicates that it was not just any old stone but one that contained the spirit of lightning.

The placing of these Period Ending stones at the borders of the community defined the space in which the community could safely live and provided spiritual protection from outside destructive forces. That protection included not just destructive forces of the deities but destructive supernatural forces sent by other communities as well (see chapter 6). The deities who were in charge of that protection were the guardian deities; thus, it is likely that the T528 *tun* stone represented them.

Speleothems

As noted, the main sign of the *tun* glyphs is a pictograph of Chac's cave. These guardian deities lived in the directional caves, which were thought to be the source of corn, water, and lightning. What better stones could there have been to contain the spirits of these elements and to represent the guardian deities than the speleothems of their caves?[4] The Yalcoba guardian deities associated with rain are known by the names *ah baalam* "the guardian," *ah k'at* "the clay dwarf," *ah kanan* "the protector," and *ah tunn* "the stone." The ritual specialist "indicated that a stone stalactite in the cave was *ah tunn*" (Sosa 1985:414). Here is evidence for the association of the guardian deities with dripwater formations.

Dripwater formations were a focus of ritual activity in ancient times and continue to be so today. They were often removed from their original position and reset somewhere else in the cave or on the surface. There is a growing body of archaeological evidence that this was an ancient and important practice.[5] Stalagmites, stalactites, and flowstones visually produce water and thus appear to be the ultimate source of the water in the cave. It was logical for the Maya to conclude that these speleothems contained the spirit of water. Corn was also associated with speleothems. A number of myths concerning the origin of corn say that corn was hidden under or in an immovable rock. The terms used to refer to this stone (stone pillar, uncontaminated stone, and great pointed stone) suggest it was a dripwater formation (Bassie-Sweet 1991:86).[6] A variety of methods were tried to split the rock, but eventually an aged rain deity struck it open with a lightning bolt. Many cultures share the belief that certain stones are infused with spirits through a divine or mythical act. It is likely that the Maya believed the spirit of lightning was embedded in the dripwater formation through this act of splitting the rock. As a receptacle for the spirits of water, corn, and lightning, the dripwater formation contained three of the most important spirits belonging to or protected by the guardian deity.

Speleothems were occasionally modified by carving. In the vicinity of Yaxchilan Teobert Maler (1901–3:202) visited a ritual cave with a pre-columbian stalagmite idol:

> The ascent was very steep and rocky. After reaching the summit of the mountain, we examined the slope on the other side and soon found the rather spacious open cave. . . . In the centre of the cave where the ground had been somewhat levelled, there was an almost vertical boulder about two and half meters high. On the wall back of this rock an oval stalactite had formed in the course of years. Into this two round holes for eyes, two quite small ones for the nose, and short line for the mouth had been cut. . . . A heap of stones near the cave seemed to me to be the remains of a building once standing in the vicinity.

The cave at Andasolos Chiapas contained a speleothem carved with a humanlike face (Navarrete and Martnez 1977). Similar speleothems have been found in Honduras, the Peten, and Belize (Gordon 1898; Pendergast 1970; Brady n.d.). What do the faces on speleothems represent? I suggest they are either the personification of the spirits in the rock or the guardian deity. Many of the dripwater idols are crudely carved or modified stones that have little in common with the grand public sculptures of the Classic plazas and temples. In discussing a cave idol in a remote section of Guatemala that was reported to be carved, J. E. S. Thompson (1975:xxxix) noted: "At the end of that long ride and perhaps in the face of Indian opposition, one might find only a strangely formed stalactite." We can now appreciate that the power of these speleothems rested not in the refinement of the carving but in their function as representations of the guardian deity and in their ability to contain the spirits of water, corn, and lightning.

Given the replication employed in Maya ritual, it is highly likely that the Maya created idols that represented the sacred speleothem. This may be the case with the incensario idols found at Copan and other sites that have the form of the personified *tun* sign. It is also probably the case with stelae.

Stelae

When the ruler placed the T528 stones and trees at the climax of the Period Ending ceremony, he was ordering the world and replicating the sacred model. Certain stelae replicate the community midpoint locations and commemorate the actions that took place there on the Period Ending (see chapter 3). I believe the stela functioned to commemorate the midpoint ceremonies performed in front of the speleothem guardian stone. The sculpture was shaped to represent the shaft form of the dripwater formation. The ruler's figure was never liberated from the stone to become a free-standing, three-dimensional sculpture because the stone's shaft-shape was intrinsic to the meaning of the monument (Bassie-Sweet 1991:110).[7]

Other authors have suggested the setting up of the *tun* stone or the tree of the stone recorded on a stela actually refers to the erection of the stela itself on that date. In this interpretation both the stone and tree of the stone describe the stela. One of my objections to the Period Ending stelae being part of the actual Period Ending event is the fact that the artist would have had to create these narratives and illustrations in advance of the actual event. The Period Ending was the symbolic destruction and re-creation of the world. These kinds of ceremonies were probably a time of intense fear for the entire community during the Classic period as they were for the Postclassic people. The power of the ruler rested in his ability to keep the forces of destruction at bay. The successful completion of the ceremony resulted in the continuation of the world; that success may have been anticipated by divination, but it was not assumed. Producing a piece of commemorative sculpture in advance of the event would have detracted from the urgency and importance of the ceremony and thus would have eroded the power of the ruler.

Regarding the sculptures found in plazas, Landa said that it was the custom to erect a commemorative stone every twenty years (Tozzer 1941:38). Fray Diego Lopez de Cogolludo wrote that at the end of a katun they "placed a carved stone on another carved one, fixed with quicklime and sand in the walls of their temples and houses of the priests" (Tozzer 1941:38). Neither of these sources suggests that these commemorative sculptures were the purpose or focus of the Period Ending rituals.

The use of the stela as a commemorative sculpture may be one of the reasons why many sites do not have stelae for every Period Ending and why some communities have none at all. The Period Ending was likely performed at each community, but not all communities had the necessary resources to erect these kinds of public monuments.

If the stela was a representation of the dripwater formation, it contained the spirits of water, corn, and lightning. As such it would have been viewed as a particularly sacred stone and as a place where offerings could be left for these spirits and for the deity responsible for these spirits.[8] There is evidence in the shape of some stela altars to suggest that they were intended to be used as offering sites. For example, the round altar of Copan Stela 4 has a bowl-shaped indentation in its top suitable for holding liquid offerings.[9] I think it is highly likely that a Period Ending stela within the community had at least two functions. As a commemorative piece of art, the Period Ending stela documented the successful completion of a ceremony that guaranteed the continuation of life. The stela also replicated the midpoint location and provided a place for future ritual activity. The stela did not, however, replace the midpoint; it simply provided another sacred location.[10]

SUMMARY

The guardian deities of the Postclassic Quiche and Yucatec Maya were lightning deities who used this powerful weapon to protect the community. Idols that represented these deities or contained the spirit of lightning were thought to be located at the midpoints on the sides of the world. These idols were replicated at the midpoints of the community as well as the midpoints of quadrilateral ritual spaces.

A similar configuration is found in the Classic period, where T528 *tun* stones that contained the spirit of lightning were placed at the midpoints of the world by creator deities. The midpoint was the house of a guardian deity. According to the Quirigua text, these stone idols were specifically placed at or on benches, suggesting that this action represented the establishment of the guardian deities in their homes at the borders of the human world. The sun established the quadrilateral space on the surface of the earth, but until the creator deities placed the guardian deities at the midpoints it was not a safe human space. The ruling elite repeated this action when they placed the T528 stones at the borders of the community during the Period Ending ceremonies.

The midpoint caves were thought to be the source of rain, corn, and lightning. The stone that embodied the spirits of these essential elements was the stalagmite of the guardian deity's cave. It is highly like that the T528 *tun* stone was such a stone. I believe that stelae replicate the stalagmites of the cave.

It is apparent that the Maya had a variety of stones that were thought to contain the spirit of lightning. In addition to the stalagmites and the stones that replicated them, they also believed that flint and obsidian had protective value. Chips and flakes of these materials are commonly found in caches and covering tombs. These practices appear to be directly related to the belief that they contained the spirit of lightning and therefore had the ability to protect. Through the manipulation of the spirit of lightning, the ancestors and ruling elite also had the ability to protect the community, as the next chapter shows.

6

THE RULING ELITE

The rulers played central and multifaceted roles in the renewal rituals that maintained the order of the world. This chapter discusses the spiritual power of these ruling elite and the ancestral caves where this power originated. The beliefs of the modern Maya illuminate these Classic period concepts.

THE MODERN MAYA

Modern Maya groups perceive, define, explain, and categorize souls, spirits, and ancestral caves in diverse ways. As would be expected, there are many gray areas and contradictions. This section concentrates on modern perspectives that can be directly related to Classic views.

The Soul

Many Maya believe that humans consist of three parts: a soul, a human body, and an animal counterpart. The body exists in the world of the conscious mind, while the soul and animal counterpart belong in the world of the dream state. The most important aspect of the soul is that it simultaneously exists in both the human body and the animal counterpart.

In many areas an individual is thought to have up to thirteen different animal counterparts.

The soul in the body is said to be specifically located in the blood or heart. This soul leaves the body at times of sleep, fright, excitement, illness, and injury. When the individual is asleep, a Zinacantan soul can sit on the tip of its owner's nose or wander (Karasik 1988:5). The soul can be visualized as having the form of a human body or being just air, breath, or wind. Wind is an ideal metaphor for the concept of a soul because of wind's ability to move through space in an invisible and almost imperceptible form. Animal counterparts live in a sacred cave, which is often located on a mountain to the east of the village.[1] In many areas the supernaturals of the sacred cave are the protectors of the animal counterparts. These supernaturals are also said to place the soul in the body of the newborn.[2]

For the people of San Miguel Acatan in western Guatemala, the animal counterparts are such things as snakes, scorpions, fish, buzzards, rabbits, birds, and sheep (Siegel 1941:70). A ritual specialist can have up to thirteen of these animal counterparts. The animal counterparts at Quiche Chichicastenango take the form of "some animal or sacred object—some snake, or bird or wild beast that wanders in the forest, or some stone idol that is buried in the earth" (Bunzel 1952:275).

This concept of an animal counterpart having the form of a stone idol is one of the exceptions to an animal form, as is the dwarf dressed as a Catholic clergyman. Other exceptions are the animal counterparts of extremely powerful individuals that take the form of a natural phenomenon such as lightning, whirlwind, or a meteor, although it should be kept in mind that lightning and whirlwind can be manifested as a serpent.

A person is supposed to be able to distinguish an animal counterpart from a real animal because the animal counterpart does not behave in a typical or proper way or has some unusual physical attribute. There are, however, cases where a hunter shoots an animal and later learns that someone in the village has died. Only then does he realize that he shot an animal counterpart. There are also tales of an encounter with an animal counterpart in which the animal disappears from the view of the observer because it is just wind.

The strength of an animal counterpart is often rated according to the strength of its associated phenomena or animal form. The animals that appear to be viewed most often as at the top of the hierarchy are the jaguar and the serpent. Animals such as the hummingbird, which are not ordinarily associated with strength, are also highly rated. This may be based on the aggressive behavior of the hummingbird in defending its territory. In Pinola the animal counterparts are structured into a hierarchy, with thunderbolt, whirlwind, and meteor being the most powerful. Thunderbolt and meteor both have three manifestations distinguished by colors; black is the strongest (Hermitte 1964).[3]

Unlike the soul in the body, the animal counterpart soul always remains in the body of the animal while the individual is alive. When a person is asleep, the animal counterparts leave the protective confines of the cave. The animal counterparts of an ordinary person simply roam the woods, but those of a sorcerer go out and do evil. Dreams are said to be the scenes the soul or the animal counterparts encounter in their wanderings or portents of future events. The association of dreaming and sleeping with the soul and the animal counterpart is reflected in the Tzotzil term for animal counterpart, *wayhel*. The root of the word *way* means "dream or sleep." It refers to the other plane of existence, the dream world.

The deities may expel an animal counterpart from the cave due to a transgression by the individual. A consistent belief is that loss of the protection of the guardians will result in great harm to the soul and hence to the individual. Although it can be attacked by evil forces at any time, the soul is particularly vulnerable when it leaves the protective confines of its domicile (i.e., the body or the cave). Soul loss generally occurs after misbehavior on the part of the individual, the spiritual leaders, or the community; therefore, proper conduct is of paramount importance. To regain the protection of the guardians, lengthy and expensive rituals must be performed at mountain shrines. The deities, the ancestors, or the souls of the ritual specialists may intervene and restore the soul if proper petitions are made; otherwise the person will die or be permanently damaged.

There are also ritual occasions when the soul leaves the body. For example, the souls of the people from various Kanjobal towns are said to travel to the sacred cave of Santa Eulalia during the New Year ceremonies and then return to their bodies after the ceremonies (La Farge and Byers 1931; Siegel 1941:72; La Farge 1947). The theme of renewal is associated with precolumbian New Year ceremonies. The departure of the souls to the cave and their return may symbolize the destruction and re-creation of humans.

Death results when the soul permanently leaves the body of a person. At San Miguel Acatan the soul is thought to leave the body at death as a tiny, invisible butterfly (Siegel 1941:70). In Tzeltal and Tzotzil areas the departing soul has the form of an invisible fly.

There is a common belief that certain individuals can transform themselves into an animal form or phenomenon and use the strengths or characteristics of the animal/phenomenon to do some kind of physical or spiritual harm to another. Several authors have confused this transformation with the concept of the animal counterpart by suggesting that people can transform themselves into their animal counterparts. This misrepresents the concept of the animal counterpart; powerful people may direct their animal counterparts, but they have no need to transform themselves into these forms because they themselves are their animal counterparts.

A quote concerning the Tzeltal of Pinola illustrates their concept of an individual:

> Several *nahuals* [animal counterparts], one *ch'ulel* [the soul in the body], and the physical person are co-essential. A man, in good health and in possession of his faculties; unscathed because his *nahual* is healthy and protected in the caves by the supernatural guardians; unharmed by magic fright which causes the separation of body and *ch'ulel*; safe from the attacks of witches who devour his *ch'ulel*, is a total being. (Hermitte 1964:113)

The Ancestors

The concept that the ancestors reside in sacred caves in the neighborhood of the community is prevalent.[4] There is often more than one cave or mountain associated with the ancestors, but one location is frequently thought to be where the most senior and important ancestors reside. There are many tales in which an individual is magically transported into the mountain cave and encounters deceased relatives, who often have their natural human form.

The concepts surrounding the final destiny of the soul reflect the belief that the ancestors live in caves. Although the Christian concepts of heaven, hell, and purgatory have entered into the picture, the ultimate abode seems to be the cave. For example, the Kekchi describe how the soul must remove a large rock blocking the entrance to the mountain deity's cave by reciting the proper prayer (Carlsen and Eachus 1977:46). In some regions the soul returns to the cave permanently after death.[5] In other regions the soul returns to the cave at death, spends a certain time there, then is redeposited in the body of a newborn, and a new life cycle begins again. For certain Maya groups, only the souls of young children are redeposited in a new body. In some areas souls are said to travel with the sun after death. When the sun, moon, and stars rise or set it is said that they do so by means of a cave at the horizon. In this concept the soul again enters the cave after the death of the individual. All of this suggests that the cave is the ultimate source and final abode of the soul.

The Maya frequently go to the caves to petition and worship the deities and the ancestors. A model for this behavior is found in the *Popol Vuh*. The twins Hunahpu and Xbalenque attempt to revive the skeletal bodies of their father and uncle at the western ballcourt/cave. When the twins fail to give life to these bodies, they promise Hun Hunahpu and Vucub Hunahpu that humans will come to their remains (bones) to worship them. The twins then rise and become sun and full moon. Thus these two deities visit the remains of the ancestors (their father and uncle) when they enter the western ballcourt/cave at sunset, setting an example for humans to emulate. Like the twins who visit the cave of their ancestors on a regular calendric basis, humans must visit the caves of their ancestors.

In some areas in the Chiapas region the cave was used as the repository of ancestral bones, as this quote by Bishop F. Núñez de la Vega, who was stationed there in 1698, demonstrates: "The bones of these pagans have been venerated to this day, as though they had been saints, the people taking copal incense and flowers to the caves where they are set" (Butlar 1934:223).

Ancestral bones are still said to be worshiped in the cave of the Lacandon rain deity (Tozzer 1907). This practice is reminiscent of the treatment given the bones of Hun Hunahpu and Vucub Hunahpu.

The reverence for ancestors is partially reinforced by the custom of naming a child after an ancestor. For example, an Ixil child may be named

after a relative from the grandparent generation. The child is thought to
be the present and future replacement of this person. After the death of
the older person the namesake is expected to remember the departed in
prayers and rituals (Colby and Colby 1981:303).

Life inside the interior of the cave is structured like that of the natural
world. The ancestors who had political and religious power during their
life also retain this role in the ancestral community. They join with the
deities in monitoring and regulating the behavior of the people, forming
a supernatural government (Hermitte 1964:46-47).[6] "The powers whose
influence on human affairs is continuous and unremitting are the
ancestors, who represent the great moral force of the universe" (Bunzel
1952:269).

The Ancestral Cave

The name of San Andrés Larrainzar's most senior ancestral mountain and
cave is White Cave. This is also the indigenous name for this Tzotzil town.
Some other highland towns and hamlets were also named after their sacred
cave:

> In the municipio of Oxchuc [Tzeltal], best known to the writer, each rural
> settlement is tied by religious bonds to a certain cave where a cross is kept
> as the main symbol of its sacred importance. Usually the rancheria is known
> by the name of the cave to which it belongs; thus the rancheria of Dzajalchen
> (Red Cave) is connected with the cave of that name. (Villa Rojas 1947:580)

The name of the senior ancestral cave of Pinola is Muk' Nah "Senior
House," located on a hill called Sohktik to the east of the town. The other
three caves, each associated with a different direction, are Campanatón,
Tzawahunch'én, and Ch'en (Hermitte 1964). At Zinacantan the senior
ancestral mountain is called Senior Large Mountain, located to the east of
the village. It is the home of the most senior of the ancestors as well as
the animal counterparts. Although some of the other ancestral Zinacantan
mountains have obscure or undecipherable names, a number are clearly
related to precolumbian myths. For example, the mountain called House
of the Raven is thought to house both ancestors and ravens. This bird is
said to have brought the first corn to Zinacantecos (Laughlin 1975:199).

The two mountains bordering Senior Large Mountain are called White Cave and the Shoulder of the Mountain. White Cave is thought to be a doorway to the house inside of Senior Large Mountain, while Shoulder of the Mountain is said to be the corner of the house. In ritual speech these three peaks are called the Three Hearth Stones (Vogt 1976:107). This is an appropriate designation for the area that houses the oldest of the original ancestors, for the hearth is physically the center of home life and symbolizes the concepts of home and, by extension, origins. As discussed in chapter 4, the Classic Period place name T128 Sky/First Three Stones Place is associated with the east and with the ancestral couple.

The Ritual Specialists

What distinguishes ritual specialists from ordinary individuals is the spiritual strength of their souls. In many areas this strength is directly linked to the number and species of their animal counterparts. For example, the Pinola ritual specialists called *me'iltatiles* (the most spiritually powerful individuals in the village) have thirteen animal counterparts and only they can have the form of thunderbolt, whirlwind, and meteor (but just one of the three) (Hermitte 1964).

Lightning is one of the most powerful forces in nature. The ritual specialists' ability to control this phenomenon puts them in a unique position of power. The literature is full of accounts where lightning is used by ritual specialists, ancestors, and saints as a weapon to protect the village from outside forces. It was the ultimate precolumbian weapon of destruction. Many tales recount intercommunity conflicts not in terms of the actual physical battle but as struggles between the animal counterparts of the patron saint, ancestors, and ritual specialists of the two regions. The group with the stronger or smarter animal counterparts wins.

The deities are said to place the soul in the body at birth and decide what the animal counterparts will be; thus, it is believed that the supernaturals decide which individuals become powerful ritual specialists. Methods of ascertaining the identity of one's animal counterpart are diverse, but they include calendar associations and divinations.[7] The revelation often comes to the individual or the ritual specialist in a dream. The career of modern ritual specialists generally begins when they have a series of dreams indicating that the supernaturals want them to begin. Frequently, novices consult with an established ritual specialist who interprets these dreams for them. In many cases, they become the apprentices of this individual. Through this process, the ritual specialists control the membership and training of their group.

Some of the more malevolent supernaturals of the cave are intent on capturing the souls of humans. Ordinary people's intense fear of caves is partially based on the belief that such a supernatural may steal their soul and they will die. There are numerous tales of foolish people who go to the supernatural's cave and make "improper" requests or petitions. The result is that they die (lose their soul) or go mad (lose part of their soul). The damage to the soul that is caused by fright, illness, or witchcraft is often described as the soul being eaten by the deity or another soul. The belief that the ordinary individual cannot directly approach the supernaturals sets the stage for the ritual specialists to play the role of intermediator.

The ritual specialists physically fulfill this role by conducting pilgrimages to various mountain and cave shrines located some distance from the community as well as those in the immediate vicinity. The ritual specialists may do this individually, as a group, or in the company of other community members. In some cases, the majority of the community may be involved in the ceremony, but it is the ritual specialists who officiate and conduct these rituals. During their lives, the ritual specialists stand between the community and the supernaturals as the humans' representative. The ritual specialists in the highest levels of political office are, however, not merely intermediaries with the supernaturals: "The authorities do not act in their own name: each one represents or is the personification of all those who preceded him back to the 'beginning of the world'" (Guiteras 1961:78). In this statement is a concept that is basic to the underpinnings of precolumbian politics and class structure.

During their lives, the ritual specialists are considered members of the upper echelons of the ancestral community. In collaboration with the deities and ancestors, they are responsible for protecting the individuals' souls while they are within the boundaries of the community. It is also their duty to protect the village from harmful outside sources. At the same time, they punish individuals and the community for transgressions. In death, they permanently join the senior ancestors and continue their role as protectors and punishers of the people. When ordinary individuals die, so do their animal counterparts, but the most powerful animal counterparts of the ritual specialists also live on in the sacred cave. There is a practical reason for such a belief. The animal counterpart of an ordinary individual has no role to play in the afterlife. The ritual specialists' animal counterparts, however, are used to defend and protect the community. The ritual specialists continue this role after death and therefore still require their animal counterparts.

In many areas the ritual specialists and the ancestors are referred to as "mother/father" or "grandmother/grandfather." The term *balam*, which means "jaguar" (one of the most powerful animals of the animal counterparts) as well as "guardian" or "protector," is also employed. This title appears to stem directly from their animal counterpart and their ability to protect the individual and the community with this spiritual weapon.

Esther Hermitte (1964:124-25) provides a succinct description of the modern ritual specialist:

> Conscious knowledge is control over one's nahuals [animal counterparts], capacity to master one's animal co-essences at will, and to attack by supernatural means.
>
> Man, at the apex of metaphysical knowledge, which is supernatural might, is characterized by a cluster of attributes which enable him to communicate with other powerful beings, to sanction his fellow men, to foresee the future, to fight evil, and to perpetuate himself after death in an eternal after-life in the sacred cave of Muk' Nah.

THE PRECOLUMBIAN MAYA

Evidence for the concepts of the soul, the ancestral cave, and the status of the ruling lineage in regard to that cave can be found in Classic period art and inscriptions.

The Soul

One Classic period verbal phrase has been associated with the departure of the soul from the body since it was first suggested as a term for death

a

b

Figure 59. a. flower death sign; b. *way* sign

(Proskouriaoff 1963:163). This phrase is composed of a verb nicknamed "a serpent wing over a shell" and a possessed noun composed of the signs *sac* "white," T533 *nik* "flower," and *ik* "breath, spirit, wind." The verb has been read phonetically as *ch'ay* and related to the Colonial Tzeltal *ch'ay ik'* "extinguished breath" (Stuart, cited in Schele 1992:43). The white flower sign is in a possessive form indicating something owned by the deceased (fig. 59a).[8] What concerned both precolumbian and modern Maya at death was the transfer of the soul to the otherworld. For example, when the soul is jarred loose from the body due to fright or by falling down, the area around the person is often swept in the direction of the body to encourage the soul to reenter it. The same procedure is followed at death, but in this case the sweeping is away from body to encourage the soul to leave. It is highly likely that the white flower in this death phrase is a reference to the soul.

Certain Classic parentage statements include the *nik* "flower" sign. These phrases have been interpreted to mean that the child is the flower of his parent (Grube and Nahm, cited in Schele 1992:154).[9] There is some evidence that flowers can also represent sacrificial blood in Mesoamerican art. This seems to reflect the fact that the soul was thought to be housed in the blood and heart. The interpretation of the *ahau* sign as a flower and as a metaphor for the soul and blood is not contradictory. It is an example of the multiple and layered meanings inherent in Maya symbolism.[10]

The flower sign also appears in a compound glyph that represents an animal counterpart. This compound has been deciphered phonetically to read *way* (Houston and Stuart 1989; Grube 1989). *Way* means "lie flat," "sleep," and "dream" (Guiteras 1961:302; Fought 1972:130), and, as noted, the animal counterpart at Tzotzil Chenalho is *wayhel*. The animal counterpart sign may carry the value of "sleep, dream" because it is only during this time that the *way* animal counterparts of ordinary individuals were animated and active.

In contrast to the white flower sign of the death phrase and the flower sign of the parentage statement, the main sign of the *way* glyph is composed of the flower sign partially covered by jaguar skin (fig. 59b). Houston and Stuart (1989:14) suggest that the "face [the *ahau* flower sign] represents a human and the pelage a soul, with each depicted as part of an integral whole." I lean toward the interpretation that the flower sign in this context is a generic reference to the soul, while the jaguar skin specifies that this refers to the soul that resides in the animal counterpart. As noted, the jaguar is one of the most powerful of the animal counterparts and as such makes an excellent symbol for this concept. The jaguar's relationship with the cave (the home of the animal counterparts) is direct: caves are common domiciles for jaguars. The jaguar is primarily a nocturnal animal and its associations with the interior of the earth are pan-Mesoamerican.[11]

In Classic pottery scenes the *way* glyph often appears in a caption text that frames an actor. These actors frequently have the characteristics of an animal counterpart: they take the general form of a jaguar or other animal but have human or other characteristics that clearly indicate they are not real animals. The text begins with the name of the actor, followed by *u way* "his animal counterpart," and an emblem glyph title "the lord of X." The structure of this phrase indicates that the animal is the animal counterpart of the lord of X. As an example, Robicsek and Hales Vessel 138 illustrates a waterlily jaguar with the penis and testicles of a human. The text states that this animal is the *way* of a Seibal lord.[12]

Many of the animal counterparts illustrated in Maya pottery scenes are composites of cave animals. On Lords of the Underworld Vase 3 (Coe 1973) three such *way* animals are illustrated: a *uinal* toad with a reptilian belly, a waterlily jaguar with a *kin* infixed in its belly, and a serpent with a deer ear.

Each species of animal counterpart was divided into several types, which seem to have individual names. For example, the waterlily jaguar

could be named using the headless body of a jaguar with a *te* subfix. This
suggests that each Classic species of animal counterpart was divided into
a hierarchy similar to modern animal counterparts.

Many of the ruling elite incorporate animal counterparts in their
names. For example, the name of the first ruler in the Yaxchilan succession
narrative is composed of a jaguar head prefixed with a penis and testicles,
much like the animal counterpart illustrated on Robicsek and Hales Vessel
138. Chan Bahlum's name "serpent jaguar" contains a reference to the
two most powerful animal counterparts.

In many contemporary communities the guardian deity is the owner
of lightning. Modern ritual specialists use their lightning animal counterpart, bestowed on them by the guardian deity, to defend their community. As noted in previous chapters, the Classic period *chac* title
represents the ability to use lightning in the defense of the community
in the same manner as the guardian deities. This lightning takes the form
of a serpent. Although the evidence is circumstantial, there is a very good
chance not only that elite members used lightning to protect the
community but that the lightning serpent was one of their animal
counterparts.[13]

During the seventeenth century in the Chiapas highlands, boys
were personally introduced to their animal counterparts at the age of
seven (Calnek 1988:56). Similar ceremonies may have also occurred
for the young men of the Classic period. This would have been an initial
step in preparing these children for more complex and difficult adult
roles.

Descent from the World Tree

Landa's statements regarding the afterlife provide evidence that the souls
of the deceased were thought to reside either at one of the four mytho-
ogical mountains on the horizon or in the underworld:

> They believed that there was another and better life, which the soul enjoyed
> when it separated from the body. They said that this future life was divided

into a good and a bad life—into a painful one and one full of rest. . . . The delights which they said they were to obtain, if they were good, were to go to a delightful place, where nothing would give them pain and where they would have an abundance of foods and drinks of great sweetness, and a tree which they call there yaxche, very cool and giving great shade, which is the ceiba [yaxche], under the branches and the shadow of which they would rest and forever cease from labor. The penalties of a bad life, which they said that the bad would suffer, were to go to a place lower that the other, which they called Metnal [underworld], which means "hell," and be tormented in it by the devils and by great extremities of hunger, cold, fatigue and grief. They maintained that there was in this place a devil, the prince of all the devils, whom all obeyed, and they call him in their language Hunhau [Hun Ahau]. (Tozzer 1941:132)

Despite the overtones of Christian heaven and hell, this reference suggests that souls reside at one of the world trees or in the underworld, which is described only as being "lower than the other." This is the relationship between the horizon area and the underworld.[14] We can infer from Landa's comments and the Maya belief in ancestral caves that the soul of a good person would live on in one of the directional caves under the protection of the yaxche, the world tree.

A picture of the ancestral cave of the Postclassic Xiu illustrates that the ruling elite identified themselves with that tree. In this image, a yaxche tree is seen growing from the loins of the lord Hun Uitzil Chac (fig. 60). Each descent line is represented by a branch, and the last descendants are illustrated as blossoms on the tree. Hun Uitzil Chac and his descent tree are illustrated emerging from the mouth of a mountain cave with other trees and mountains surrounding it. Landa noted that the yaxche protected the souls. The founding ancestor and his decedents may have been depicted as a yaxche because their job was also to protect the souls.

The *ahau* "lord" title carried by the Classic ruler and the other members of his lineage (both male and female) can be related to the Xiu image. The ahau title could be written in many ways, including the incorporation of the T533 nik "flower." The ruler and lineage members carried a title relating them to flowers because like the Xiu descendants they were thought to be flowers of the yaxche tree. I emphasize that this yaxche grew from the ancestral cave, and was one of the world trees.[15]

Figure 60. Xiu family tree (courtesy of Tozzer Library, Harvard University)

There is also another Classic period title read *ch'ok* "young child, sprout" that is related to the world tree (Grube and Stuart 1987; Ringle 1988; Schele 1992). This title is predominantly carried by young lords prior to accession. In several pottery scenes the world tree is illustrated not as a cross, which emphasizes its crossroads function, but as a stout trunk with many sprouts growing from it (see fig. 16). In relation to the Xiu tree, the young lord was a sprout; as the descent line grew, the sprout became a limb of the tree.

There are many Mesoamerican beliefs in which the ruling lineage is said to be descended from a tree, rock, or river:

> By advocating kinship to the land itself, Mixtec lords had permanently and irrefutably fixed their role as mediators with the supernaturals. By being literally descended from specific parts of the land they could establish a proprietary claim to it beyond the rules of inheritance of property. (Pohl and Byland 1990:116)

In addition to claiming descent from one of the mythological caves, the Maya ruling elite envisioned their senior ancestral cave to be a replication of this location.

The Senior Ancestral Cave

As noted in the introduction, I have interpreted the main sign of the emblem glyph to be the name of the senior ancestral cave. These emblem glyph main signs are often pictographic in nature, and some of these symbols can be directly related to cave imagery. For example, Xultun and Ucanal both incorporate the *witz* "mountain" pictograph, Ixtutz is the *cab* cave sign, Yaxchilan uses both the *cab* cave sign and a split sky sign, Calakmul is a serpent, and Copan is a bat. Seibal employs the Three Stones Place name, a logical choice for an ancestral cave given that the T128 Sky/First Three Stones Place names the domicile of the ancestral couple.[16] Water shrine names include Itzan, which uses a *naab* "sea" sign in a vase, and Yaxha, whose emblem glyph phonetically spells *yaxha* "blue/green water."[17]

The main signs of emblem glyphs are occasionally combined with seat signs or sky seat compounds that indicate their association with the midpoint of the world model.[18] In several cases the main sign of an emblem glyph is the location of a midpoint Period Ending event. For example, on Seibal Stela 10 the location of the north-oriented Period Ending event is said to be "within the Seibal emblem glyph place."[19] The emphasis on the ancestral cave as a site for Period Ending rituals points to the concept that the ancestors played a role in maintaining the order of the world. On many of the Yaxchilan Period Ending stelae the ruler's deceased parents are seen in cave cartouches above the action. This suggests that they played an active role in this event.

The use of emblem glyphs in *way* constructions indicates that the animal counterparts lived in the senior ancestral cave just as they do in some modern areas. In a number of pottery scenes the *way* animal counterpart sign is found in possessive constructions that read "A (is) the *way* of B." The name of the possessor can be an emblem glyph place name with the *ahau* "lord" prefix or just the emblem glyph place name. Using the Seibal example, the phrases can be translated as "the waterlily jaguar is the animal counterpart of the Seibal senior ancestral cave" or "the waterlily jaguar is the animal counterpart of the lord of the Seibal senior ancestral cave." When a text states that a person was an *ahau* of the emblem glyph place name it does not mean that individual was a lord from that community or polity but that he or she was of the senior ancestral cave, a descendant of the founding ancestors, a flower of the yaxche world tree.

The "star" event compounds that have been associated with hostile actions between communities are composed of a star sign over a shell, *cab* cave, or emblem glyph main sign. In these compounds the emblem glyph has been interpreted to indicate the community with which the home site was having conflict. While modern accounts of war are practical descriptions of the battles and strategies, native conflict descriptions often portray the encounter as a struggle between the animal counterparts of the two opposing forces. The ancestral cave where the animal counterparts lived appears in these war contexts because the ruler was fighting the supernatural forces of that community.

It is possible that the community was named after its senior ancestral cave, much as modern communities are named after their caves. When an emblem glyph is used as a place name, the context should indicate whether it refers to the cave or to the community. For example, on a local monument that commemorates a ruler performing a specific Period Ending ritual for the community the text may state that the illustrated ritual occurred at the emblem glyph place and the ruler may even stand on this place name in the image. "It happened at Seibal" does not tell the audience anything about the specific location of this event, because all of Seibal's Period Ending rituals occurred in the community. By contrast, "it happened at the Seibal ancestral cave" does.

The Tikal Ancestral Cave: Tikal is one of the earliest sites to document an ancestral cave in its inscriptions. There are seven Late Classic architectural groups known as twin pyramid complexes that provide information regarding the directional association of Tikal's ancestral cave. The seven twin pyramid complexes appear to have been built at twenty-year intervals ranging from 9.12.0.0.0 to 9.18.0.0.0. Whether the buildings were constructed before or after the Period Ending is unknown. We do know that the southern buildings underwent renovations over time, so they clearly did not have one single-purpose function. They did, however, have some limited usefulness, for three of the complexes (L, M, N) were altered to make way for new constructions.

The north enclosure of each complex replicates the north midpoint of the world (see fig. 4). Each of the stela/altar pairs located in the north enclosures of Twin Pyramid Complex P, Q, and N name and illustrate a location where north-oriented Period Ending events occurred. Several authors have suggested that the stelae mark the location of the rituals illustrated on them (Coggins 1980; Stuart and Houston in press). Although I do not believe this to be the case, what can be said with certainty is that all these scenes represent the north midpoint, wherever that might have been. By examining these scenes, we should be able to accumulate some information about this Tikal midpoint.

Stela 16 and Altar 5 of Twin Pyramid Complex N form a continuous storyline. The text of Stela 16 relates the 9.14.0.0.0 Period Ending event and states that the ruler placed a stone idol. This is followed by a proper name. In a standard transitive construction this would name the idol, but Stuart and Houston (in press) have suggested that this proper name refers to the location of the event. Place names following a verb are found in the burial phrases on Dos Pilas Stela 8 and Rio Azul Tomb 12 (Stuart and Houston in press). The Tikal name is a head and *yax* sign prefixed to the skeletal cave jaws (fig. 61a). The image illustrates Ruler A holding a ceremonial bar on this occasion.

The rim text of Altar 5 changes the timeframe and relates a series of background events that led up to the 9.14.0.0.0 Period Ending event;

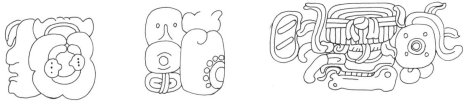

Figure 61. a. *Yax* Head cave name, Tikal Stela 16; b. Flower Mountain name, Tikal Stela 22; c. *Yax* Tikal Seat Place, Tikal Altar 8

Figure 62. Tikal Altar 5 (drawing by William Coe, courtesy University of Pennsylvania Museum, Philadelphia)

the final event of this series is just thirty-two days before the Period Ending (fig. 62). The altar illustrates two actors standing before a skull and pile of thigh bones. The actors carry implements that have been associated with blood offerings. The text that conveys the last pre-Period Ending event is directly above the two actors. The *u cab* phrase between the actors is a continuation of the rim text and draws the viewer into the scene. This device indicates that it is the last pre-Period Ending event illustrated on the altar. The caption text under the bones identifies the skull as that of a Lady *Yax* X Jaguar.[20]

The north enclosure of Twin Pyramid Complex Q contains Stela 22 and Altar 10. The stela illustrates Ruler C performing a ritual on the 9.17.0.0.0 Period Ending. The proper name is Flower Mountain (fig. 61b). Although eroded, the associated Altar 10 illustrates the location of the event as a quatrefoil cave opening with a captive sprawled before it. Twin Period Complex P contains Stela 20 and Altar 8 in its northern enclosure. Ruler B is illustrated on Stela 20 performing an action on the 9.16.0.0.0 Period Ending. The proper name is eroded, but the story continues on the altar. Here a captive sprawls on the place name *Yax* Tikal Seat Place (fig. 61c).[21]

The use of this emblem glyph on Altar 10 indicates that the north midpoint was associated with the senior Tikal ancestral cave.[22] This north orientation parallels Seibal, where the ancestral cave is also oriented to the north. The association of north with Tikal ancestors is also found on the main plaza, where elite tombs are primarily found on the north side in the North Acropolis.[23] The other two proper names associated with this north midpoint are both related to caves. We have seen the flower sign's use as a reference to the soul. It is, therefore, possible that Flower Mountain is a direct reference and alternate name for the ancestral mountain, the home of both the souls of the departed and the animal counterpart souls. The Head *Yax* Cave glyph of Stela 16 is obviously also related to a cave. The altar of Stela 16 illustrates a site where bones are the focus of ritual activity. The Maya are known to have venerated the bones of their ancestors in caves.

Stuart and Houston (in press) interpret the Head *Yax* Cave Place and the Flower Mountain as references to the twin pyramid complex in which they are found, Complex N and Complex Q, respectively. Following this line of reasoning, the *Yax* Tikal Seat Place must name Complex P, yet it is also found in several Early Classic contexts at Tikal (Stela 1, Stela 39). These Early Classic contexts cannot refer to the Twin Pyramid

Complex P or specifically to its north enclosure, for these are Late Classic constructions. Where, then, were these rituals actually performed? The obvious choice is the north midpoint of the Tikal community, which was also its ancestral cave.

The Dos Pilas Ancestral Cave: The relationship between Tikal and Dos Pilas also gives us some insight into ancestral caves. The Tikal emblem glyph is found in the name phrases of lords who ruled the site of Dos Pilas during the Late Classic. Recent work at Dos Pilas has uncovered epigraphic evidence that Dos Pilas Ruler 1 was probably the relative of a Tikal ruler (Demarest 1993:97). It has been suggested that he left Tikal to set up a "splinter kingdom" and that relations between the two sites were hostile.[24] A Tikal text that refers to Ruler 1's son (Dos Pilas Ruler 2) does not call him a lord of the Tikal emblem place as he is called in Dos Pilas inscriptions but a lord of the "Dragon Water Place."[25]

This Dos Pilas place name is composed of a Shell Wing Dragon and a cross-hatched *naab* sign.[26] It is illustrated as a band of *cab* and *cauac* signs, indicating its association with a midpoint, and is also called a seat. This is the place where Ruler 1 performed an undeciphered event on 9.12.5.10.1 and where one of Ruler 2's accession rituals took place. Ruler 2's subsequent 9.13.15.0.0 and 9.14.0.0.0 Period Ending events and his 9.14.10.4.0 ritual dance and setting of the *k'inich* stone (idol) also are stated to have occurred there.[27] The Dragon Water Place was the location of the 9.15.0.0.0 Period Ending by Ruler 3 and the 9.15.4.6.11 *nawah* act of the captive Jaguar Paw of Seibal.

The monuments that refer to the Dragon Water Place are found in the center of Dos Pilas and at a complex called El Duende approximately one mile to the east. The major feature of El Duende is a hill that was modified into a temple/pyramid. Stelae 14 and 15, which illustrate the Dragon Water Place, are located on a terrace of this structure. The temple/pyramid is oriented to a spring of water directly in front of it (Houston, cited in Brady 1991). An important ceremonial cave is located to the southwest of this temple/pyramid; it is part of a cave system that extends under the hill. When Dos Pilas came under siege from hostile forces this cave was ritually sealed to protect it (Brady 1991; Demarest 1993).

The Dos Pilas lords appear to be immigrants to this region and thus would choose a cave in the area in which they could access their ancestors.[28]

Although many of the caves in the Dos Pilas region show signs of ritual use, the special treatment of the El Duende cave indicates its importance. It is highly likely that the Dragon Water Place refers to this watery ritual cave.

The Dragon Water Place occurs in another context that reinforces its association with the ancestral cave. The main plaza of Dos Pilas is a quadrilateral area bounded on the east side by a ballcourt and Structure L5-1. Stela 8, which was erected during the reign of Ruler 3, is located in front of Structure L5-1. Its narrative includes a reference to the burial of Ruler 2 (Ruler 3's father) at the Dragon Water Place. In the belief that this was a reference to Structure L5-1, excavations were carried out in hopes of discovering an elite tomb (Demarest 1993). Although no confirming hieroglyphic text was associated with the discovered tomb, it was of suitable construction and date to be that of Ruler 2. I do not argue with the assumption that this is Ruler 2's tomb or that this tomb was called Dragon Water Place, but is it the site of the previous and subsequent Period Ending ceremonies and ritual dances of Ruler 2 and Ruler 3 (also said to have occurred at the Dragon Water Place) or does the tomb replicate the final resting place of Ruler 2's soul? The ritual importance of the El Duende cave to the east of this location suggests that the tomb replicates that ancestral cave.

If the Dragon Water Place was a replication of the Tikal ancestral cave, a north orientation would be expected. The east orientation of the Dragon Water Place appears to be at odds with that interpretation. Migration stories, however, often focus on the eastern nature of the migrating group. In Yucatan many of the elite groups are described as having arrived from the east, while the migrations and pilgrimages of the Quiche of the *Popol Vuh* also had this directional association.

SUMMARY

Several points need to be emphasized from this brief overview of the soul, the elite, ritual specialists, and ancestors. The human soul resided in both the body and the animal counterparts. The soul of the body was housed in the inner recess of the body at the heart, while the animal counterpart resided in the inner recess of the mountain at the senior ancestral cave. What set the senior ancestors and senior ruling elite apart from ordinary individuals was the nature of their animal counterparts. They were gifted with spiritually strong animal counterparts that represented the most potent powers of the deities, such as lightning, whirlwinds, and jaguars. The ruling elite used these weapons to keep not only the supernatural forces but the forces of neighboring rivals at bay.

It is apparent from the many examples of serpent and jaguar animal counterparts in Maya art that there were a variety of these supernaturals. It seems likely that each species was divided into a hierarchy similar to modern animal counterparts.

Although they acted as mediators between the supernaturals and humans, the ruling elite were more than agents; they were recognized as living members of the senior ancestral group. The authority of the lord rested in membership in the ancestral council. In life, the ruling elite joined with the deities and senior ancestors to protect and punish the individual and community. It was their duty to regulate and guide people in the hazards of everyday living. After death, they entered into the world of the supernatural and permanently joined the senior ancestors in the sacred cave. The directional orientation and seat sign designations of the senior ancestral cave indicate that this cave was a replication of one of the directional mountains. The ruling elite claimed descent from the world tree at this location. Tikal and Seibal both have senior ancestral caves oriented to the north, while Copan's cave seems to be situated in the west. The reason for these orientations is not clear.

Many of the symbols of power and authority used by the Maya elite refer to their ability to maintain the balance between destruction and order. The following chapter reviews some of those symbols, the concepts they represent, and the methods by which the lords acquired their power.

7

SYMBOLS OF POWER

There has been considerable discussion about what symbols in Maya art constitute emblems of power and authority. This chapter is a review of some of the symbols relating to the spiritual powers of the ruling elite and the training these lords underwent within the environment of the cave in order to obtain that power.

ACCESSION

Accession information is usually restricted to the text of a monument and is often only given as background leading to a Period Ending ceremony or other ritual event. Many of the verbs used in accession phrases refer to the seating of the ruler on a jaguar mat pillow or into an office. The same jaguar mat bench is often found in pottery scenes as the seat of a deity. The phonetic *po* sign infixed in the seat has been interpreted to be a reference to *pop* "mat" and some examples of this seat have a woven trim indicating a mat. On Kerr 1398 God G sits on such a jaguar mat seat, which in turn is located on top of a cauac monster. The jaguar mat seat of the lord replicates the seat of the deities, which was located at the midpoints of the world.

During Postclassic accession ceremonies, highland lords were seated on low benches covered with a mat. This mat has been interpreted to be the crown of the king and the symbol of his office (Miles 1955; Robicsek 1975). In the Classic these mat symbols were not, however, used exclusively by the ruler but also by lesser lords. For example, on La Pasadita Lintel 2 Bird Jaguar and the *sahal* both have mat headdresses. *Pop* has the meaning "mat" but it also means "council" (Tozzer 1941:63; Roys 1943:64). The mat consisted of many reeds woven together to create a strong, unified whole, which is reminiscent of the community council, consisting of the ruler, subordinate lords, the senior ancestors, and the deities, who joined together to govern and protect the community. I believe the mat was a reference to this council.

The notion that the ruler did not rule in a unilateral fashion is reflected in the creation myths, where the deities gather together as a council to create the world and humans. The destruction and re-creation of the world were not a singular feat either but a joint effort. The deities provide a model for the ruler and subordinate lords.

The jaguar was one of the most powerful animals of the animal counterparts, and a jaguar skin is employed in the animal counterpart glyph. I believe the jaguar skin of the mat is a generic reference to the animal counterparts that the deities, ancestors, ruler, and subordinate lords had at their command to protect and defend the community and its souls. It is a reference to *balam* "jaguar, guardian, protector."

Not surprisingly, jaguar skin is intimately associated with war iconography. Classic warriors commonly carry the jaguar-covered shield, most often illustrated with the face of the Twisted Cord Deity. The Tablet of the Sun central icon is composed of this shield and two crossed spears sitting on top of a bench. The jaguar's association with war iconography is also found in Postclassic depictions of shields. In the Dresden codex Chac is illustrated carrying a spear and a shield composed of an *ix* "jaguar" sign with death eyes in each corner. The Postclassic call to war was "to spread out a jaguar skin" (Roys 1931:331). The Motul dictionary lists *zin balam* "spread the jaguar" as a phrase that means to fight.

These two symbols, the jaguar and the mat, represented the basis for the elite's power and authority. The elite commanded the supernatural power of the animal counterparts and were vital members of the ancestral government.

The only actions illustrated at Palenque that can be clearly demonstrated to represent an accession are those of Chan Bahlum on the Cross

Group Tablets. The Cross Group cosmogram has been discussed in earlier chapters. As a model of the Palenque world, it demonstrates that the Palenque Triad were thought to have been born from three cave locations, each situated in a different direction. The narratives in the Cross Group tell us that Chan Bahlum performed pre-accession and accession rituals at the local versions of these locations.[1] The accession verb used in these passages refers to Chan Bahlum tying a white headband on his head (Schele, Mathews, and Lounsbury 1990). He performed this action at all three cave locations. To this cloth other elements were added, presumably relating to the offices or duties of the deity. The accession statements from other sites tend to be brief. The expanded documentation at Palenque allows us to appreciate how complex and involved these ceremonies were. It also helps us to understand the less elaborate accession scenes. For example, on Bonampak Sculptured Stone 1 a lord is pictured receiving the Jester God headdress of GIII. The text states that the occasion is his accession. The narrative ends with a reference to the future Period Ending on 9.13.0.0.0, which the text states will occur at the *cab* seat. In the Cross Group the west cave of GIII is the *cab* seat. In other words, this lord received at his accession a costume element he would require in order to perform this west Period Ending event.

PREPARATION AND TRAINING

The pre-accession rituals of the Cross Group tablets indicate that before accession the ruler underwent considerable preparation and training (Bassie-Sweet 1991:201–10). Direct interaction with supernaturals was considered dangerous and even life threatening; the participant had to be well prepared for such encounters. Modern ritual specialists undergo intense training and initiation rites. Training begins at an early age through observation. The future ritual specialist attains a basic knowledge and skill level by participating in the rituals of the family and community. Training through observations has been noted in Zinacantan:

> Experiences involving beliefs about the soul and animal spirit companion are shared in conversation. But even more learning appears to take place when a shaman comes to diagnose an illness or returns to perform a curing ceremony; small children hear and observe the proceedings as a matter of course. . . .

The boys are pressed into duty as assistants for the shaman—to help carry the candles or the pine boughs or to serve as drink-pourer. The girls are expected to make tortillas, and to help kill and cook the chicken for the ritual meals that accompany the ceremonies. The children are similarly involved during a k'in krus for a sna or waterhole group, and from an early age they are taken to ceremonies in the ceremonial center. (Vogt 1969:193)

The training of young boys occurred during the Balankanche cave rituals (Andrews 1970). Although their primary role was to imitate the croaking of frogs and toads during one of the offerings to the stalagmite column, the boys also prepared ritual offerings and were observers of the entire ceremony. The pre-accession events illustrated at Palenque show a series of rituals performed at caves (Bassie-Sweet 1991:201–28). Chan Bahlum performed cave rituals at age six, thirteen, and eighteen years, while his younger brother Kan Xul participated in his own rituals at age seven, nine, twelve, and twenty-six.

Gaining supernatural experiences through the use of a heightened or altered state of consciousness, ecstatic trance, or dream is a theme that appears in many areas of the Maya region (Furst 1976; MacLeod and Puleston 1978). As the domain of the deities, the cave provides an ideal location for such experiences; the environment of the cave impacts the ritual specialist both physically and psychologically.

Altered states can be achieved through a combination of techniques, including fasting, fatigue, drugs, and traumatic experiences. In addition to the prerequisite fasting of the ritual specialist and the long duration of the ceremony, the rarefied atmosphere of the cave produces fatigue, as this quote regarding the ritual conducted at Balankanche cave demonstrates:

The accessways were dangerous and were passable with only the utmost difficulty. Living conditions inside were made impossible by darkness, complete lack of ventilation, and 100 per cent humidity. . . . Even with less than 15 men in the large inner chambers, the oxygen became exhausted in an 8 hour day, leaving the workers panting, after a minimum of exertion, as if they were atop a tall mountain peak. (Andrews 1970:6)

During ancient rituals, the oxygen would be further depleted by the burning of pine pitch torches and incense.

At one point in the Balankanche ceremony the ritual specialist placed his assistant alone facing a pool of water in the dark while the rest of the group returned to the dripwater column to perform another round of the ceremony. Fear produces adrenaline and creates brain chemistry changes. To this agitated state, add the loss of sensory input, which is known to produce disorientation. In these conditions the senses are heightened and the mind strives to compensate. Sensory deprivation and traumatic experiences can alter the brain's chemistry for long periods, even permanently. Such altered states and their subsequent flashbacks were quite likely one of the goals of Maya cave experiences, although the Classic period monuments that deal with cave rituals provide no information regarding the lord's state of mind.[2]

It has also been demonstrated that early traumas make an individual more susceptible to the impact of later traumas. Thus indoctrination at a young age is desirable. The youngest age for cave rituals noted in Classic inscriptions are those of Chan Bahlum and Kan Xul when they were six and seven years old.

Pre-accession Rituals

Of the three pre-accession events shown on the Cross Group tablets, the GIII rituals illustrated on the Tablet of the Sun were highlighted and emphasized (Bassie-Sweet 1991:201–20). The Tablet of the Slaves, Palace Tablet, and Oval Palace also illustrate pre-accession rituals at the cave of GIII. The Temple 14 Tablet and the Dumbarton Oaks Tablet depict pre-accession cave events of a different nature. The following section reviews the symbols associated with these various cave rituals.

The Power of Lightning: The importance of lightning as the ultimate spiritual weapon has been discussed in the preceding chapters. I believe a succinct example of the ruling elite's relationship to lightning is found in a representation of the day Ahau. Although *ahau* means "lord," the day sign is most often represented by a pictograph of a stylized flower because the lord was a blossom of the world tree. On Machaquila Stela 13 Ahau is represented not by the flower, but by a young lord who carries the lightning axe of the rain deity.

The Dumbarton Oaks Tablet illustrates the twelve-year-old Kan Xul dancing in the costume of the guardian deity Chac (Bassie-Sweet 1991:220).[3]

He commands the lightning axe of the rain deity. The thirteen-year-old Chan Bahlum is seen on the Temple 14 Tablet receiving a God K idol (see fig. 23). On Yaxchilan Lintel 58 the young Shield Jaguar holds a shield and God K scepter, while his maternal uncle Great Skull displays a lightning axe.[4] As noted, God K is a lightning deity whose forehead often has the axe protruding from it, while his leg takes the form of the lightning/serpent (fig. 63). When a lord is seen grasping either the God K scepter axe or Chac's axe he is, in effect, commanding the spiritual power of lightning.[5] The scenes on the Palenque monuments and Yaxchilan Lintel 58 suggest that prior to his accession and his central participation in Period Ending events the lord was trained in the skills necessary to carry out the duties of his office, including the manipulation of the spirit of lightning.

The War Symbols of GIII: The Tablet of the Sun, Palace Tablet, Oval Palace Tablet, and Tablet of the Slaves all illustrate rituals conducted at the cave of GIII. Classic lords are often depicted battling individuals in hand-to-hand combat. The most common implements illustrated in such scenes are long spears and shields. The war association of GIII is obvious: the central icon of the Tablet of the Sun prominently displays spears and the Twisted Cord Deity shield. The other two icons shown in these scenes, the flint/shield and the Jester God headdress, are also associated with war.

The narrative on the Temple of the Inscriptions indicates that the Jester God was the headdress of GIII. On the Oval Palace Tablet the young Pacal (age twelve) receives GIII's Jester God headdress from his mother prior to his accession (fig. 64).[6] On the Palace Tablet Kan Xul (age nine) is handed GIII's helmet by his father Pacal (fig. 65).[7] A similar action is repeated on the Tablet of the Slaves, where the *sahal* Chac Zotz also receives the helmet (fig. 66). Although it has been suggested that the Jester God distinguished the ruler from subordinate lords, it must be concluded from this evidence that the Jester God was not a symbol of supreme authority but a symbol of some attribute of GIII. The Tonina portrait of Kan Xul as a captive illustrates him wearing GIII's Jester God headdress, apparently not as a sign of rulership but as a representation of his war powers (although it did not seem to do him much good).

On the Palace Tablet and Tablet of the Slaves the female on the right hands the lord a personified flint and shield (figs. 65, 66). The left side

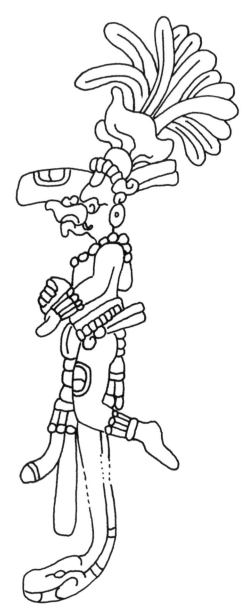

Figure 63. God K

of the Tablet of the Sun pictures the young Chan Bahlum holding up the shield, which he has apparently just received (see fig. 50).[8] The flint and shield have been phonetically deciphered in other contexts as *tok pacal*, which literally means "flint shield" (Houston 1983). In the Tikal inscriptions

Figure 64. Palenque Oval Palace Tablet (drawing by Merle Greene Robertson)

Figure 65. Palenque Palace Tablet (drawing by Merle Greene Robertson)

the flint and shield appear to be objects that could be captured during a battle? Chac Zotz was forty-three years old at the time of his flint shield event. The Tablet of the Slaves storyline moves forward from his GIII event and relates a series of his capture and war events. This GIII ceremony does not appear to have been about learning to fight, but about receiving enhanced spiritual power and knowledge from the ancestors and deities (in this case, GIII) that allowed one to overcome opponents and destructive forces. The contexts of the flint and shield seem to indicate that they represent the lord's ability to conduct war: one is a weapon of offense (the lightning

Figure 66. Palenque Tablet of the Slaves (drawing by Merle Greene Robertson)

flint) and the other is more for defense (the shield).[10] The personal ability of the lord to do battle was centered in the strength of his animal counterpart. If lightning was his animal counterpart, the flint and shield may have been one representation of this concept.

In many examples of Period Ending events the ruler wears the costume or attributes related to GIII. For example, the Jester God headdress and the Twisted Cord Deity shield are very common Period Ending attire. In the same regard, symbols and costume elements related to the other two members of the triad also appear in Period Ending contexts. We are left with the conclusion that the lord was trained or prepared at an early age to imitate these very important Period Ending deities or at the very least to interact with or petition them. God L, who was one of the deities involved with the destruction and reordering of the world, is pictured holding up the Tablet of the Sun bench on which the spears and shield rest. This suggests to me that these power objects do not relate simply to fighting petty wars with neighboring foes but also to the sacred task of maintaining the world.

Tlaloc Symbols: A number of war-related motifs are associated with Tlaloc. During the central Mexican Postclassic, Tlaloc was known as the directional god of rain, thunder, and lightning. He lived in a mountain and his lightning took the form of serpents. Unlike Chac, he had jaguar characteristics. The association of Tlaloc and caves is dramatically demonstrated at Balankanche, where Tlaloc imagery is the predominant motif on the pottery. The source of Tlaloc belief appears to be the great central Mexican city of Teotihuacan, whose power was at its highest in the Early and Middle Classic periods.

An early event in the life of a young Piedras Negras lord is documented on Piedras Negras Lintel 2. In this scene six youths kneel before Ruler 2 and a seventh youth stands beside him (Bassie-Sweet 1991:229). The caption text identifies the kneeling youths as lords of the Yaxchilan, Lacanha, and Bonampak lineages.[11] Each holds a spear and square shield. Their headdresses are composed of "trapeze and ray" elements associated with Tlaloc. Although the meaning of the scene is unclear, it is apparent that these youths possessed helmets related to Tlaloc and warfare. This is parallel to the Palenque youths who possessed the headdress of GIII.

Another motif associated with Tlaloc is composed of a spearthrower and shield. The shield in these contexts is T583 or has T528 elements in it. In some examples the shield is replaced by an owl (Schele and Freidel 1990:449). This shield appears in Pacal's nominal phrase as a title (Bassie-Sweet 1991:251). In some substitutions of Pacal's name this shield is replaced by an owl with the T583 shield infixed in its eye. Spearthrowers allow the user to throw the spear or dart farther and with greater velocity. The predatory owl, who flies with great speed, would naturally be associated with such a weapon for fighting an enemy at a distance. The nocturnal owl would also be a great spiritual weapon against the animal counterparts, who were also thought to be active at night. The T583 shield appears to be related to GIII; in the context of Pacal's name, this shield is consistently prefixed with GIII's *k'inich* title.

These Tlaloc-related emblems appear in Period Ending scenes such as Piedras Negras Stela 9, where the ruler wears the owl in his headdress and the "trapeze and ray" motif appears above it. On Aguateca Stela 2, which illustrates a Period Ending event, Ruler 3 is pictured wearing an owl pendant, "trapeze and ray" headdress, goggle-eyed mask, and Tlaloc deity apron (fig. 67).[12] He also carries the Twisted Cord Deity shield from GIII's cave. We can conclude from this information that some lords acquired Tlaloc-related emblems in their youth and that these symbols of power were prominent in the Period Ending event.

Tlaloc-related motifs appear on some of the earliest Maya monuments. The significance of these foreign motifs has been hotly debated for many years and will continue to be so. Although the implications of this foreign imagery are beyond the scope of this book, a parallel can be drawn with the *Popol Vuh*. The second generation of lineage heads traveled to a foreign citadel a great distance away, where they were given symbols of lordship. Given the prominence of Teotihuacan, it is feasible that Early Classic Maya lords traveled to this great pilgrimage location and brought back symbols of power and/or patron deities that were incorporated into the local structure.

SUMMARY

The inventory of pre-accession events in the art of Palenque demonstrates that the acquisition of power required a great deal of ritual preparation and training, which began very early in the young lord's life and continued

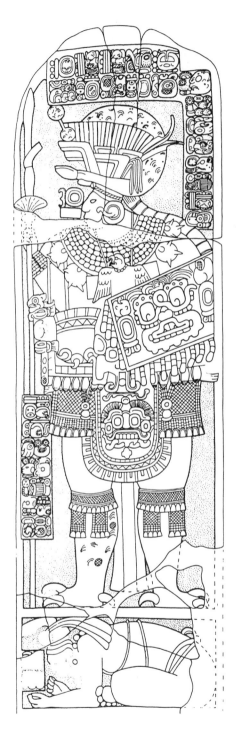

Figure 67. Aguateca Stela 2 (drawing by Ian Graham)

throughout his pre-accession career. The pre-accession scenes illustrated on the Cross Group, Oval Palace Tablet, Palace Tablet, and Tablet of the Slaves indicate that these ceremonies were directly related to the Palenque Triad, who in turn played key roles in the Palenque Period Ending ceremonies. In addition to these cave ceremonies, other pre-accession rituals such as those on the Temple 14 Tablet and Dumbarton Oaks Tablet involved the manipulation of lightning. Lightning was the primary weapon of the guardian deities, who were also directly involved in the Period Ending ceremonies. Like the guardian deities, the ruling elite apparently used lightning to protect the community and its members. It seems clear that the same spiritual powers that allowed the lord to maintain the order of the world and the community's position in that world were also used in conflicts with rival neighbors and lineages.

Pacal and his wife Lady Ahpo Hel may appear in several of the pre-accession scenes, not as the father and mother of the protagonist, but as the living representatives of the ancestral government. In other words, the young lord received his validation from both the deities and the ancestors during these cave ceremonies. It must be emphasized that the young lords were not just shamans-in-training who were learning to access the ancestral wisdom, but the living replications of the ancestors.

A pre-accession event was but one step in a sequence of rituals that prepared the future ruler for rulership and for the Period Ending ceremonies. As the seat of the supernatural government, the cave was an ideal location for pre-accession and accession ceremonies.

CONCLUSION

Despite the tremendous amount of variation from site to site in the rituals performed by the Classic Maya, there was standardization regarding such concepts as the vertical layering of the universe into sky, earth, sea, and underworld; a quadrilateral space on the surface of the earth formed by the path of the sun; four directional mountains containing the caves of the guardian deities and ancestors; and the general nature of the guardian deities. Belief in the ruling elite's descent from one of the directional world trees was also shared.

During the Postclassic, it was thought that the creator deities caused the surface of the world to be formed. They sent their children and grand-children to establish the cycles and rhythms of life in order to prepare the world for humans. In order to perfect their creations, they destroyed and re-created the world and humans a number of times. Humans' obligation to the deities was to honor them through offerings and sacrifice. Although the texts of the Classic period are brief, a similar theme appears.

The creator deities demarcated the surface of the earth into two zones: a square in which humans lived and the horizon area of the supernaturals. The need to separate human space from the wild or from supernatural space is fundamental to all cultures. The corners of the world square were defined by the rise and set points of the solstice sun. At these points the sun was thought to emerge from the earth through a cave. The center of the quadrilateral world was established by the zenith passage of the sun at noon. In the solstice-based world model, the sun delineated the maximum borders of human space.

The four mythological mountains were particularly sacred locations because they were located where the sky visually met the earth. These mountains were the homes of the ancestors, the animal counterparts, and the guardian deities. A road radiated from the center of the world to each of the midpoint caves. At these midpoints the world roads crossed the perimeter road that ran around the edge of the quadrilateral world forming a crossroads location. The cave opening allowed the world road to continue into the mountain, to the sea beyond the mountain, and to the underworld beyond that.

The cave was the doorway not just to the guardian deities and ancestors but to the supernatural world of the sea, sky, and underworld deities as well. The cave opening was marked with a tree/cross in the shape of the crossroads and a seat that represented the bench of the guardians. Through these doorways certain deities first manifested themselves on the surface of the earth. From these caves the deities sent the essential elements of life to humans. Through these same gates destructive forces could be unleashed to punish. The guardian deities acted as sentinels at the cave openings to prevent the forces of destruction from entering the world and destroying it.

On progressively smaller scales, the quadrilateral world model was used to create other human spaces: communities, towns, milpas, houses, altars, and ritual spaces. It can be concluded that the Maya ordered their world and the parts in it according to their culturally formed concept of the universe. By structuring their world in this manner, they created a safe and ordered place in which to live. When they placed objects and performed rituals at the midpoint and corners of a quadrilateral space, they were symbolically performing rituals at the threshold to the supernatural world.

The concepts that structured and ordered Maya life were intimately related to natural cycles and observations. The recurring cycles of sun, moon, and stars reinforced and validated the structure of the world on a daily, annual, and synodic basis. The rituals of the Period Ending ceremonies provided the Late Classic Maya with a cyclical human counterpart to those cycles and gave the ruling elite a means of reinforcing and controlling universal order.

The Period Ending ceremony was a ritual of renewal in which the world was destroyed and re-created. The creator deities and their children played important roles in the preparation of the world for humans and were evoked during the Period Ending events. The ritual action included a ceremonial circuit around the community to reestablish its borders and the placing of guardian idols and tree/standards on the sides of the community. These idols protected and defended the community because they contained the spirit of lightning as well as the spirits of the two most essential elements for Maya existence, corn and water. The climax of the Period Ending ceremony was the establishment of a safe and ordered world.

The ruling elite of the Classic Period shared in the belief that their senior ancestral cave was located at one of the directional mountains and that they were senior members of the ancestral council that resided there. They also believed they had spiritually strong animal counterparts. Because the rulers were in command of lightning, they were able use this spiritual weapon to protect their communities just as the guardian deities did.

Many metaphors were used to describe the ruling elite's descent from one of the directional mountains, the most prevalent being the concept that they were flowers or sprouts of a world tree. The Postclassic Xiu illustrated their founding lineage head as the trunk of a world tree. His descendants are pictured as both limbs and flowers of this tree. One of the reasons the ruling elite identified themselves with the world tree was that both had the responsibility of protecting the world and maintaining order. The ruling elite's descent from the founding ancestors and the world mountain gave them proprietary rights to the land and its people.

At least some of the rituals illustrated in Maya art occurred at cave locations related to the world model, and many other ritual locations were symbolic representations of those sites. The Maya were not divorced from their landscape but intimately connected to it. Caves played a fundamental role in their world view and, therefore, in their life.

Appendix
DIRECTIONAL TERMS

Two questions concerning directional terms have created considerable debate. First, do the Maya directional terms refer to the cardinal points?

The directional glyphs for east and west have been phonetically deciphered as *lakin* and *chikin*, respectively. Nicholas Hopkins and Terrence Kaufman (cited in Josserand and Hopkins 1991:163-64) have demonstrated that these terms are reduced forms of **elab k'in* "the exit of the sun" (from the earth) and **ochib k'in* "the entrance of the sun" (into the earth).[1] The modern terms for east and west echo the ancient terms. The Chul word for east is *tz-'el k'uh* "the sun comes out"; the Tzotzil *lok'eb k'ak'al* "where the sun rises"; and the Quiche *chirelabal k'ij* "at the rising of the sun." The corresponding words for west are *tz-'och k'uk* "the sun goes in"; *maleb k'ak'al* "where the sun sets"; and *chukajibal k'ij* "at the setting of the sun," respectively.

By definition, the terms for east "the exit of the sun (out of the earth)" and west "the entrance of the sun (into the earth)" can be applied to any point between the solstice rise and set points, including the cardinal directions of east and west. Terms and glyphs for north and south (*na*, *xaman*, and *nohol*) are attested as early as the Postclassic.[2] In some modern sources north and south are called "the sides of heaven" or "the side of the sky on the right hand, the side of the sky on the left hand" (Guiteras

1961:36; Gossen 1974; Sosa 1989). North is on the right hand of the sun and south is on the left if the sun is perceived as a personified being who rises facing the west.[3] Other modern expressions for north and south can be related to the midpoint cave. As an example, the Kekchi terms "where the wind comes out" and "where the wind goes in" are an apt description of the midpoint horizon cave where the forces of destruction emerge and return.

A corner can be described by either of its defining directions or by a combination of both. For example, the southeast corner of a solstice-based model is described by modern informants in the following ways (Sosa 1989:132): *ti lak'in* "toward east"; *lak'in nohol* "east south"; *lak'in yeetel nohol* "east within south"; and *nohol yeetel lak'in* "south within east."

If the corner can be described by either of its defining directions then an argument can be made that the statement "in the east" can refer to the southeast or northeast corners.[4] The Dresden New Year phrases regarding the erection of the world trees use the directional terms to specify a particular point in both time and space. The layout of the Yucatec village and the Postclassic New Year ceremonies make it clear that this occurs at the midpoints on the sides of the world. The Mayan directional terms could, therefore, be used to indicate the corners, sides, and midpoints of the world square. When I use the terms *cardinal point* or *direction* in this book I am not implying that the Maya structured their world according to the modern system of coordinates, but the two systems are parallel because the midpoints and cardinal points are based on the same natural observation, the rise and set points of the equinox sun.

In a ritual the important points on the perimeter of the world are the midpoints and corners. If a text states a specific location such as "he did it in the north," it is likely that it refers to either the midpoint or corner. In the Cross Group the north references found in the midpoint-oriented Temple of the Cross probably occurred at the north midpoint, while the north references in Temple 14, which is situated in the northwest corner of the Cross Group, probably occurred in the northwest. The context dictates which meaning is intended.

In addition to this question about the cardinal points, there is a second question in the directional debate: do the directional glyphs for north and south also refer to zenith and nadir, respectively? The Tikal twin pyramid complexes form quadrilateral world models (see fig. 4). Clemency Coggins

(1980) interpreted these complexes as cosmograms that represent the passage of the sun. In this model the east and west pyramids represent the rise and set points of the sun, while the north and south buildings represent the zenith and nadir positions. To orient this cosmogram to the natural world requires turning the twin pyramid complexes on their sides. In Coggins's interpretation the ruler illustrated on the north stela would be conceptually performing rituals at the zenith in the sky, "heaven." Although there is absolutely no question that the north and south directional glyphs were used to refer to the midpoints on the sides of the world, there is little hard evidence that they also refer to zenith and nadir or up and down.

Some of the cited evidence is based on the notion that deities and ancestors live in the sky. It is a European Christian belief that heaven is directly up and hell directly down. The Maya ancestors lived in the caves surrounding the community, as did many of the deities. Furthermore, in some of the early Maya maps east is positioned at the top of the page, not north. The modern Tzotzil consider east "up" and west "down" (Robert Laughlin, personal communication, 1993).

In the text of Copan Temple 11 the place names of north-oriented rituals have been interpreted to mean at "the crossroads of the sky" and at "holy heaven" (Schele, Stuart, and Grube 1989). Barbara Tedlock (1993) concluded that these are names for zenith, but they are equally descriptive of the midpoints. The modern Tzotzil refer to sacred mountains where one can talk to the ancestors as "holy heaven" (Fabrega and Silver 1973:257).

The inscriptions of Rio Azul Tomb 12 have been used as evidence in the zenith and nadir debate (Bricker 1988; Tedlock 1993). The walls of the tomb are oriented toward the four directions. One black glyph is painted in each corner. The corner glyphs have yet to be completely deciphered, but they name the corners or some aspect of the corners (see chapter 2). Each side is labeled with two glyphs. The wall glyphs all begin with the same animal head main sign prefixed with a variable and T584 sign. The animal head that is read first has not been deciphered. The east variable is *kin* "day or sun"; west is *akbal* "night"; north is a moon cartouche; south is a star sign most frequently associated with Venus. The T584 sign is likely a shortened version of the *ahau* compound. The second glyph is the appropriate direction for that side of the tomb. In the case of the eastern glyphs, the phrase probably reads "animal head *k'inich ahau* east."[5] Six glyphs that form a sentence run along the top band of the eastern wall: they can be paraphrased as "On 8 Ben 16 Kayab, Ruler X of Rio Azul was buried at 6 Cloud Sky" (Stuart and Houston in press).

This Calendar Round date has three potential Long Count positions (A.D. 398, A.D. 450, A.D. 502). On the night of one of the three possible Long Count dates for the burial of the ruler, the moon was near its zenith while Venus was conceptually near the nadir in the underworld. Victoria Bricker (1988) suggested that the moon compound and Venus compound are literal references to these celestial bodies and that the directional glyphs are references to the position of these bodies at zenith and nadir. To orient these events to the natural world requires turning the tomb on its side with the north wall up and the south wall down.

The most serious flaw in this argument is that there is no evidence that the Rio Azul Calendar Round even occurred on this date. If it did and if the celestial signs in these compounds are literal references, why is the *kin* "sun" in the east when it is supposed to be under the earth with Venus?[6] In the world model the location that is aligned with the noonday position of the zenith sun is the center of the world. The top of a center-oriented pyramid or temple/pyramid is the replication of that location, not the north midpoint.

As discussed in chapter 1, the Maya often performed both clockwise and counterclockwise ritual circuits around their quadrilateral spaces. When a counterclockwise ritual circuit is applied to the quadrilateral world model, walking in a northerly direction along the east side of the square represents the annual path of the sun as it moves from the southeast corner (sun rise on winter solstice) to the northeast corner (sun rise on the summer solstice). Walking along the north side of the square represents the day of the summer solstice as the sun moves from the northeast corner (summer solstice sunrise) to the northwest corner (summer solstice sunset). The west side of the square represents the southern return journey of the sun from the northwest corner (summer solstice sunset) to the southwest corner (winter solstice sunset). The south side represents the night of the winter solstice when the sun passes from the west under the earth to the east. In a clockwise ritual circuit, the reverse is true. An argument can be made, therefore, that the north and south midpoints are aligned with both the zenith and nadir positions of the sun on the solstices. Such an interpretation adds another layer of meaning to the north and south midpoints. Also, the night sky pivots around the north celestial pole, which hovers over the north midpoint.

These celestial attributes do not negate the fact that the south and north midpoints are terrestrial locations. There are some examples where south-oriented locations have death-related imagery. The summer solstice is strongly associated with the onslaught of the rainy season, while the winter solstice is associated with the dry season. Life and death imagery associated with north and south are likely related to these seasonal changes. This does not mean that south was related to the underworld. Where, then, is the nadir of the underworld illustrated or replicated in Maya space? I have no answer, but perhaps it is more important to ask whether the Maya had a need to replicate this supernatural space. Until we have a better understanding of Maya deities and supernatural locations these questions will remain unanswered.

NOTES

INTRODUCTION

1. The combination of limestone and water seepage within the cave creates numerous varieties of spectacular rock formations. The technical term for mineral deposits and formations found in caves is *speleothems*. Stalactites (dripwater formations hanging from the ceiling) and stalagmites (dripwater formations embedded in the floor) frequently join and form a column that appears to hold up the roof of the cave. Flowstones occur when mineral deposits form as a result of water flowing over the walls or floor. These often look like waterfalls frozen in time.

2. The precolumbian history of the Maya region is divided by modern scholars into the Preclassic (pre-300 A.D.), Early Classic (A.D. 300–600), Late Classic (A.D. 600–900), and Postclassic (A.D. 900–1500) periods. There is abundant and growing archaeological evidence for the ritual use of caves extending well back into the Preclassic period. Although many ritual caves are in a natural state, numerous others have been modified with architectural features such as altars, stairs, niches, walls, and even small houses.

3. There is a long tradition of inconsistency in the spelling of Mayan words. Recently the Guatemalan government has officially adopted a system created by native speakers, which some authors are now using. I continue to use the spellings found in my previous publication for reasons of consistency and because not all Maya groups have embraced this new method.

4. The Mathews and Schele list of Palenque rulers includes two lords nicknamed Chac Zotz (Tablet of the Slaves) and Xoc (Palace Tablet). David Stuart (1986) has demonstrated that Chac Zotz did not rule but held a secondary office. It is now apparent from Stuart's work that the so-called *xoc* glyph first identified as the name of a ruler is not part of the nominal phrase. It is likely that the subject of this passage was not a human (see chapter 7, note 7, for a review of the Palace Tablet).

5. Dancing was an important part of Maya ritual. Many examples of actors dancing are known. They usually stand in an animated pose with one foot raised. The verb for

dancing has recently been identified (Grube 1992). Dances appear to be named after the object the actor carries or a costume element. In some examples the object is an idol. There were many kinds of dances, quite likely for different purposes. In the Postclassic Peten Itza area part of the dance involved communicating with the idol. The motivation for modern Aguateca dancing was temporarily to release the ancestors from the otherworld, "to untie them" (McArthur 1977). Dances were an important part of the Postclassic New Year ceremonies and Period Ending ceremonies.

6. There has been some resistance to the application of the framing convention to all parts of the Palenque Cross Group Tablets (Schele and Freidel 1990:470; Schele 1992). These three tablets illustrate the same two figures, a short and tall actor (figs. 48, 49, 50). The pre-accession event of Chan Bahlum II (at age six years) consistently frames the short actor, while his accession text consistently frames the tall actor. Most researchers agree that the text framing the tall actor explains who he is, what he is doing, and when he is doing it. This caption text identifies him as Chan Bahlum on the occasion of his accession. George Kubler (1969) identified the small actor as "he of the pyramid" based on the appearance of this title in the text adjacent to him, ignoring the calendar round date in the text. Schele (1976) identified the short actor as Pacal II based on the Pacal nominal glyph in this text. She interpreted the scene to represent the transfer of power from the dead Pacal II to Chan Bahlum II on the occasion of his accession, also ignoring the calendar round date in the text.

When parentage statements were identified in the text, it became apparent that the subject of the text was "the child of Pacal," that is, Chan Bahlum. Following Kubler's notion that the text in proximity to the actor should name the actor, Floyd Lounsbury proposed that the short actor was Chan Bahlum at the age of six. He suggested that the scene illustrates both a pre-accession and accession event in which "time is displayed in a horizontal spatial dimension" (Lounsbury, personal communication, 1986): the scene represents two rituals performed at the same location but on different dates. Lounsbury presented this interpretation during his 1975 Yale seminar (Lounsbury, personal communication, 1986). In reviewing the history of the interpretation of these figures, Merle Greene Robertson (1991) noted that he presented his interpretation at a 1974 Dumbarton Oaks workshop. This date seems to be in error. In any case, Lounsbury's insightful interpretation was not published and other researchers who heard the presentation did not cite or disseminate it.

Based on formal analysis of the tablets, Flora Clancy (1986) succinctly demonstrated that the figures were not interacting but directing their attention to the central icon. This means that the theme of the Cross Group is not power transfer between the actors. While working on a paper about the relationship between text and image in 1986, I independently came to the same conclusions as Lounsbury and Clancy (Bassie-Sweet 1987, 1991:201–9). If we move beyond the Cross Group and look at other examples of the object held by the short actor we find that all the actors receiving these objects are framed with pre-accession texts (Bassie-Sweet 1991:209–19).

Schele and Freidel (1990:470; Schele 1992) apparently remain unconvinced. Their conviction seems to rest on their belief that the scene is a transfer of power symbols between the two actors, yet they present no argument that this is the case. Their statement that it is unlikely that a six-year-old child would hold symbols of power is not supported by Classic Maya practices. On Yaxchilan Lintel 2 and Lintel 52 the young Shield Jaguar (age six and fourteen, respectively) is pictured holding power symbols. Schele and Freidel's statement that the proportions of the short actor do not conform to the child displayed in the Bonampak murals is countered by the fact that these proportions do conform to those used on Yaxchilan Lintel 2. In this scene the ruler Bird Jaguar stands beside his six-year-old son on the occasion of a pre-accession event. The child-to-adult ratio is the same as that between the Cross Group actors. Furthermore, Schele and Freidel's assumption that a six-year-old Chan Bahlum should have the same proportions as an average modern six-year-old is questionable.

Their final argument seems to imply that they believe that the pre-accession caption does refer to the short actor:

> In the heir-designation event, the six-year-old child was not the main actor, either at Palenque or at Bonampak. The child was displayed as the heir, but the father, who was the acting king, oversaw that display. At Bonampak, Chaan-Muan went to war, not the child, and at Palenque Pacal memorialized the thirteenth-haab anniversary of this heir-designation in the Tableritos from the Subterranean building of the Palace without mentioning Chan-Bahlum at all. Chan-Bahlum, the six-year-old child, was the recipient of the action in the heir-designation rites, but the source of those actions was his father Pacal. (Schele and Freidel 1990:470)

The notion that Chan Bahlum would not be illustrated as a central actor during his own pre-accession event is counter to the scene found on the Dumbarton Oaks Tablet, where the twelve-year-old Kan Xul is illustrated performing a pre-accession event. He is flanked by his parents, who play secondary roles.

To me the important point in this debate is not the interpretation of one single monument but the way the Maya indicated to the viewer what was happening in the image. Researchers must apply the framing convention across the board, not just when it suits their interpretation.

One final comment concerns the unusual knotted clothing worn by the small actor. This costume was originally identified as death-related imagery based on the interpretation that the small actor was a dead Pacal. In some pottery scenes similar but not identical garments are worn by skeletal supernaturals who have traditionally been identified as creatures of the underworld. Because the underworld was a place of death, some researchers have concluded that when humans wear such a costume it is an indication that they are dead. Such a conclusion is not warranted, given that living humans often dressed in the costume of supernaturals. Furthermore, Stephen Houston and David Stuart (1989) have demonstrated that many of these skeletal supernaturals are named in accompanying texts as animal counterparts not underworld deities (see the explanation of animal counterparts below in this chapter).

7. I employ the Thompson correlation constant of 584,285.

8. I use the terms *years* and *months* for the tun and uinal periods only as a method of comparing units. The uinal is not equal to the Gregorian month, which is derived from the cycles of the moon, but rather is 20 days long. Likewise, the tun is not 365 days but 360.

9. Bishop Diego de Landa (1525–79) was the third bishop of Yucatan. He produced a descriptive document primarily concerned with the customs of the Maya of northern Yucatan (Tozzer 1941).

10. For example, if we begin the count with Imix in the east, Ik (the next day) is assigned to north; Akbal (the following day) to west; and so forth. Because twenty (the number of day names) is divisible by four (the number of directions), the end of the twenty-day cycle brings us back to Imix in the east. These directional associations for day names are illustrated in a cosmogram found in the Madrid codex. The day names labeling the border of this cosmogram are oriented in the same manner as the 819 Day Count (there is one error: the day signs Eb and Caban have been transposed). A second calendar asso-

ciation is found in the path of black dots that loops around the corners and encloses the square. The corners of the square are marked with footprints indicating this is a road. Each successive day in the 260-day Tzolkin cycle is represented by a dot and/or its day number and name in this border circuit.

11. Vertical entrances are created when the roof of the cave weakens and collapses. The debris from the collapse often forms a mound on which vegetation grows (the presence of moisture and soil accumulation makes the cave opening very fertile). Large trees growing from the mouth of a cave are common. In northern Yucatan the hollows formed by sinkholes were important locations for cacao groves.

12. The human soul differed from that of other creatures and things. The Tzeltal say that humans are different from animals because only they have the soul called *ch'ulel* "holy one" (Hunn 1977:59). In Pinola it is said that "it is thanks to the *ch'ulel* that we are able to talk" (Hermitte 1964:140).

13. Despite the fact that it is not descriptive of these exceptions, I retain the term *animal counterpart* as the generic term for this concept. Scholars have coined many other terms, such as birth-spirit, birth-guardian, guardian spirit, spirit counterpart, soul-bearer, companion spirit, destiny animal, and co-essence.

14. The political and religious hierarchy of the modern supernaturals usually reflects that of the community or the family (Villa Rojas 1945:112; Hermitte 1964:46). In precolumbian Maya art deities are shown in hierarchical compositions where they appear to be submissive or subordinate in relation to another deity.

15. Four screen-fold manuscripts survive: the Dresden, Madrid, Paris, and Grolier. The first three were discovered in various European libraries and are named for the cities that now house them. The Grolier was allegedly discovered in a dry cave and subsequently exhibited at the Grolier Club (Coe 1973).

16. On Tikal Stela 31 there is an illustration of a supernatural hovering over the protagonist Stormy Sky. The supernatural has a square eye, which is a common trait of deities and is clearly not human. The other iconographic details in the image are related to the deity GIII (see chapter 7), suggesting that this supernatural is GIII. The supernatural's position over the ruler is comparable to the other illustrations of deities hovering over rulers on Ixlu Stela 2, Jimbal Stela 1, and Tikal Stela 5, Stela 11, Stela 22, and Stela 25. The supernatural wears a curl-snouted animal in his headdress. An illustration of a deity wearing an animal head is found on Copan Stela P, where both Paddler deities wear animal headdresses. There is nothing in this image that is inconsistent with other illustrations of deities.

The curl-snouted animal is also used in the name phrase of Curl Snout, Stormy Sky's father. Based on this, the supernatural has been identified as Curl Snout. I believe this identification to be wrong. At Palenque and Copan some of the ancestors wear elements of their nominal glyphs in their headdresses. It has been assumed that these elements are a means of identifying the actors, yet these actors are explicitly named in the accompanying caption texts. What then is the purpose of these headdress elements? Given that Classic elite names are most often those of deities and animals, I think it is likely that the headdress elements represent not the name of the wearer but the attributes of the deity or animal for which the actor was named. I interpret the curl-snouted animal to be a reference to an animal associated with this supernatural. The supernatural is probably a deity, quite likely GIII, and Curl Snout may have been named after the curl-snouted animal associated with GIII.

On the Temple of the Inscriptions sarcophagus the soul of Pacal II is illustrated with the torch of God K in his forehead. This has been interpreted to mean that Pacal experienced an apotheosis as God K. The Tzeltal animal counterparts of powerful individuals do not die but join the supernatural government of the ancestors. With this in mind, it is equally likely that Pacal's soul is being illustrated as the lightning of God K (see chapters 2 and 7). There is therefore little evidence that rulers became deities after their deaths.

17. Although the cross of the famous black Christ of Esquipulas was acquired in the usual manner, the Chorti believe it was found in a cave south of the town (Brady and Veni 1992:155). The Virgin of Cancuc was a precolumbian stone idol that was originally worshiped in a nearby cave (Calnek 1988:55).

18. The objects in which offerings were made to a deity were often decorated with the deity's likeness or attributes. This gives us some insight into the nature of the deities who were worshiped by the Maya. For example, Early Classic incensarios and offering bowls often feature the deity GI (Hellmuth 1987). Some stone incensarios from Palenque feature human faces, suggesting that they are representations of ancestors. The inscriptions on several of these objects point to such an interpretation.

19. On Seibal Stela 10 the location of the north-oriented Period Ending is stated using the Seibal emblem glyph. On Dos Pilas Stela 15 an elite lord is also said to perform a Period Ending event there; the location is referred to as a seat, a designation used to indicate an association with the sides of the world (see chapter 2). At Tikal Period Ending events are also performed at locations with north directional associations. The locations are identified both in the text and in the image using the Tikal emblem glyph. Emblem glyphs are used as place name indicators in several other images. At Yaxchilan and Yaxha the emblem glyph is used as a location indicator. On these monuments these ruler performs various rituals while standing on emblem glyphs.

20. There are, however, some puzzling gaps in the time frame between the death of one ruler and the accession of the next.

21. Some accession narratives state that the ruler was seated as *ahau*. Yet this title was used not only by the ruler but by other members of the ruling lineage including women. As an example, the father and grandfather of the ruler Pacal carried the *ahau* title, but neither was recorded as having ruled. The descent line at Palenque passed from Chan Bahlum I to his daughter Lady Kanal Ikal then to her young grandson Ac Kan. At the premature death of Ac Kan, the rule passed briefly to Ac Kan's mother, Lady Zac Kuk (the daughter of Lady Kanal Ikal), and then to his younger brother Pacal (Bassie-Sweet 1991:241–47) (see table). Both Lady Kanal Ikal and Lady Zac Kuk carry the *ahau* title.

22. Classic period lords are often illustrated participating in hostile acts against foreigners. Certain Classic phrases have been interpreted as references to war against other polities. There is considerable debate over the nature of the hostilities and the end results. Warfare to obtain captives for ritual sacrifice, to seek revenge, to advance a political position, or to gain an economic edge is documented in contact period literature. These motives were not mutually exclusive and were probably all employed from the beginning of Maya culture.

23. Stuart has argued that the phonetic rendering of this office is *sahal* (cited in Houston 1993:130). In early publications it was called *cahal*. References to the *sahal* have a limited distribution, with the majority occurring in the monuments of the Piedras Negras and Yaxchilan areas.

24. This is not to say that these lords were the only ritual specialists in the community. It seems likely that ceremonies for individuals and kin groups would have been carried out by lower-status ritual specialists.

CHAPTER 1. THE PARTS OF THE UNIVERSE

1. The *Chilam Balam* books are postconquest manuscripts written in European script. They deal with many subjects, including the creation and destruction of the world.

2. These incantations are a collection of Yucatec chants used during healing ceremonies (Roys 1965). In his translation, Roys often used "sky" for *can* "serpent" because he felt it was more appropriate. I have modified his translation to conform to the original Maya text and enclosed the revisions in square brackets.

3. Parts of the world model are embedded in many aspects of Maya life. Sosa (1985:247) noted the structural parallel between wasp's nests and the guardian deity's cave. A similar parallel can be found in the construction of beehives. In Yucatan the beekeeper constructs a hive by stopping up the ends of a hollow log with wooden plugs. "A small entrance hole is made in the center of a small square or circular depression cut in the center of the side of the hive; over the entrance hole a small cross is cut" (Redfield and Villa Rojas 1934:48). The guardian deity known as Hobnil Bacab was the patron deity of bees. These beehives with their cross-marked entrances are symbolic representations of his horizon cave (see chapter 2 for further discussion of beehives and the horizon).

4. This replication is also found in the objects used in ritual settings. For example: for the Chorti, "The milpa and altar represent the universe in miniature. . . . The candles set up at the four corners of the altar are said to be its corner posts (as if it were a house) and its boundary markers (as if it were a milpa)" (Wisdom 1940:430).

5. Some authors have characterized modern rituals that reflect the quadrilateral structure as vestiges of a long forgotten idea and have suggested that the modern Maya are ignorant of the "real" meaning of their cosmology. I strongly disagree. The modern world view reflects the present Maya world as precisely as the ancient models reflected Postclassic and Classic societies. Modern cave rituals are not remnants of precolumbian cave cults, but expressions of modern Maya world view and beliefs.

6. The ancestral grandparents called Xpiyacoc and Xmucane were both diviners and daykeepers. Xpiyacoc was a marriage broker and Xmucane a midwife (Tedlock 1985). It is hard to say whether all the sea deity names refer to separate deities or whether some or all of them are titles of the ancestral grandparents. I lean toward the latter view.

7. Every day the sun emerges out of the earth in the east, arcs across the sky, and descends back into the earth in the west. During the annual cycle, the sun's rise and set points on the horizon change on a daily basis. Beginning with the vernal equinox (approximately March 21), the sun rises and sets due east and due west of the observer. On subsequent days the sun rises and sets at points north of these coordinates until it reaches its most northerly rise/set points on the summer solstice (approximately June 21). The sun moves south, returning to the due east/west coordinates on the autumnal equinox (approximately September 21), and continues south until the winter solstice (approximately December 21). The sun then moves north until it again reaches the due east/west coordinates on the vernal equinox and begins the annual cycle once more.

The cardinal points of east and west are established by the rise and set coordinates of the equinox sun. The north and south cardinal points are easily established as the midpoints on the horizon between the rising and setting coordinates of the sun on any given day of the year. On the most basic level, it is the location of the sun that establishes the cardinal points.

In the Maya area the daily path of the sun is not perpendicular to the earth but rather arcs across the sky toward the south. The time of zenith passage (when the sun passes directly overhead at noon) is established by the latitude of the observer's location. For the Maya area, which encompasses approximately latitudes 14.5 to 21.5, zenith passage occurs between May 1 and 21 and again between July 24 and August 12. It is likely that the solstices, equinoxes, and zenith passages of the sun have been observed by the Maya at least since the beginning of the Classic period (Aveni 1980).

8. In a Zinacantan house the center is marked by a hole in which offerings were buried when the house was first built (Vogt 1969:461). The center of a Chimaltenango house and cornfield is the site of rituals when the maize is about to be planted (Wagley 1941:34–35). The center of a Yucatan milpa is often marked by an altar on which offerings are made to the four Chacs and Balams before sowing (Redfield and Villa Rojas 1934:134). The Kekchi mark their cornfields with a cross. During the milpa ceremony, the farmer scatters chicken blood at the foot of the cross and toward the four sides. Copal incense is then directed to the four corners (Carter 1969:41).

9. Another example of this is found in the Tzeltal town of Amatenango: the village is a rectangle, yet the villagers draw it as a square (Nash 1970:xviii).

10. They also demonstrate that temples could represent caves (see chapter 3).

11. What became of Middle of the Plain is unknown.

12. These shrines had directional associations: Auilix was a temple/pyramid on the east side of the main plaza, while the west side had the temple/pyramid of Tohil. Hacauitz's shrine bordered the south side, although its doorway faced outward to a smaller plaza.

13. Some of the traits of the tobacco-smoking God L are agedness, black body markings, jaguar features, an owl headdress, a long string of beads, and a merchant bundle. The owl headdress frequently has a sky sign with a numerical coefficient attached to it. The Postclassic portrait glyph for God L is prefixed with a *naab* "sea" sign with water falling from it and he wears a waterlily blossom in his headdress on Lords of the Underworld Vase 1 (Coe 1978). He is often pictured sitting on a jaguar bench, suggesting that he is a member of the supernatural government. Although it has been proposed that God L is a major deity of the underworld based on his association with caves (Coe 1973:14), I believe he belongs in the category of creator deity.

14. A column of day signs without numbers runs down the left side of each page. Each column consists of a day sign repeated thirteen times followed by a second day sign repeated thirteen times. These day signs represent the day before New Year's day (the last day of Uayeb/the seating of Pop) and the first day of the New Year (1 Pop).

The first scene is framed by the calendar sign for the last day of Uayeb and illustrates an event that occurred on that day. The second and third scenes are framed by the calendar sign for the next day (the first day of the New Year) and illustrate sequential events on that day. The four pages together represent the passage of four consecutive years. The two day signs are each repeated thirteen times to indicate that the four-year passage of time recurred thirteen times in a row. Four multiplied by thirteen gives a fifty-two year cycle. Hence, these pages represent a complete cycle of the fifty-two year calendar round.

In order to make these series of years conform to the standard counterclockwise ritual circuit of a New Year ceremony (east, north, west, and south), page 26c and page 28c would have to be reversed. Although Thompson argued for this "correction," there are still so many unsolved problems with these pages that I remain neutral on this point.

15. Kelley (1976:177) argued that the opossums in the scene were the Mams, but the syntax of the sentence implies that "the black something [Uayeb idol according to Love] is his Mam, God A is his burden." The possessor of God A in the scene is the opossum actor. This implies these two phrases are a couplet that means "his idol and burden is the Mam called God A."

16. The first deity shares the attributes of the God G illustrated in the second scene of the second page, but he is missing God G's *kin* infix. God A and God A1 are both death deities related to the underworld.

17. In a previous publication I incorrectly suggested that the Chac and tree were equivalent (Bassie-Sweet 1991:121).

18. Whenever the Maya created a space, a ritual circuit was performed, which often included the placing of offerings at the midpoint of the space. The offerings by the Dresden deities are the antecedents for this action.

19. Each of these names was prefixed with an appropriate directional color. Each brother also had a unique name: south—yellow (*kan*): Hobnil, Kanal Bacab, Kan Pauah Tun, Kan Xib Chac, Kan u Uayeyab; east—red (*chac*): Can Sicnal, Chacal Bacab, Chac Pauah Tun, Chac Xib Chac, Chac u Uayeyab; north—white (*sac*): Sac Cimi, Sacal Bacab, Sac Pauah Tun, Sac Xib Chac, Sac u Uayeyab; west—black (*ek*): Hosan Ek, Ekel Bacab, Ek Pauah Tun, Ek Xib Chac, Ek u Uayeyab.

Several Classic pottery scenes illustrate sets of four Bacabs, Chacs, and Pauahtuns. The title *pauahtun* found in nominal phrases appears with a four prefixed to it. The *bacab* and *chac* titles are often preceded by a directional glyph. This information suggests that these deities were also associated with the four directions during the Classic period.

20. The Bacabs were above the Pauahtuns in the hierarchy. Although the Pauahtuns are mentioned in the *Ritual of the Bacabs*, it is the Bacabs who have the power to remove the illness carried by wind. In modern hierarchical structures, the wind deities are assistants not principal deities. The Postclassic hierarchical relationship between the Bacabs and the Chacs is unclear.

On a Classic period Ponoma panel a *sahal* lord (secondary lord) carries Pauahtun's name as a title. The principal lord on this monument is named with the *bacab* title. On Lords of the Underworld Vase 11 four Pauahtuns appear in a subordinate position to a Chac (Coe 1978). These examples suggest that the hierarchical structure found in the Postclassic also occurred in the Classic with the Pauahtuns at the lower end.

21. As noted, the *Popol Vuh* describes the creation of the world as though it was the creation of a milpa. The Kekchi method of making a milpa recorded at the turn of the century by Carl Sapper (1897:285) demonstrates the parallel between these creations, but also adds the concept of the world trees. The Kekchi farmer goes to a wild area and measures out as much land as he can travel in one day and then "places at each of the cardinal points a small tree; after a year he returns to the place, burns copal to the Tzultacca [mountain valley deity] and prepares his maize fields in the direction in which the smoke of the copal travels." The sides of his milpa are oriented to the four directions, so it is clear that the trees stand at the midpoints on the sides of the quadrilateral cornfield.

22. The trees wear clothing marked with footprints, which are used to indicate a road in other contexts in the codices. It has been suggested that the Dresden footprint represented the goal of a pilgrimage (Forstemann 1901). The midpoint of the quadrilateral world was the goal of a ritual procession during the New Year ceremonies. The idol and his tree/standard might also be marked in this way because they were taken on pilgrimages from a midpoint to the center and then back out to another midpoint.

23. The notion that the cave can be opened and closed is observed in Tzotzil Chenalho, where the frog who is the servant of the rain god is asked to open the door of the cave so that the petitioner can communicate with the rain deity (Guiteras 1961:288). The caves of Tzeltal Pinola are also thought to have doors that are opened and closed. At Tzeltal Amatenango a person may go to petition the cave owner on Thursday, "when the earth is open" (Nash 1970:24). In many areas the cave is only open on certain days. This may

reflect the precolumbian practice, in which rituals could only be performed on certain days of the tzolkin.

24. The only problem with this interpretation is that the upper band should represent either the ecliptic or the celestial equator. The Three Hearth Stones constellation is not between the turtle and these paths as illustrated in the Madrid codex, but below the turtle.

25. Although it has been suggested that the turtle here is also a reference to the Turtle constellation in Orion, this constellation is not on or near the ecliptic and cannot, therefore, function as part of the zodiac.

26. It has been noted that the Milky Way was personified as "a double trunk tree, a double-headed serpent, an umbilical cord connecting heaven, earth, and the underworld, a white road on which the stars and sun traveled, and other related sacred metaphors" (Hunt 1977:151). These all seem to be valid metaphors for this starry road.

27. The southern midpoint is also celestially marked in a number of ways. At summer solstice sunset and winter solstice sunrise, the Milky Way borders the edge of the horizon and the constellation known as the Southern Cross marks the south midpoint. At spring equinox sunrise and autumn equinox sunset, the rift road and Scorpio crossroads point toward the south midpoint.

28. The bicephalic monster is also known by the nicknames celestial monster, cosmic monster, and Venus/sun monster.

29. Cauac monsters are discussed in chapter 2.

30. This bicephalic monster has been interpreted to be the Milky Way on winter solstice at 7 P.M. (Schele 1992:136). The Milky Way does not arch from east to west at this time. It arches from the northeast corner across the sky to the southwest corner of the world forming a diagonal across the sky and is thus inappropriate for a doorway that is aligned with the southeast and southwest corners of the world.

31. Because many of the watery supernatural scenes in Maya art have incorrectly been associated with the underworld rather than with the mythological sea, several researchers have concluded that the underworld was wet. The Yucatec Maya relate wet caves to the sea and dry caves to the underworld (Redfield and Villa Rojas 1934).

32. Landa stated that there was "the prince of all the devils, whom all obeyed, and they call him in their language Hunahu" (Tozder 1941:132). This seems to parallel the *Popol Vuh*, where Hun Hunahpu is left at the entrance to the underworld. Landa's inclination to label all Maya deities as devils and his Christian world view of heaven in the sky may have prevented him from appreciating the different categories of Maya deities associated with the nether regions of the earth.

33. The children of the ancestral couple were called Hun Hunahpu and Vucub Hunahpu. These brothers lived on the surface of the earth somewhere near the eastern edge of the world. Hun Hunahpu and his brother played ball every day. Angered by the ballgame noises above their heads, the underworld gods sent a challenge to the brothers. Hun Hunahpu and Vucub Hunahpu journeyed to the underworld and after a series of defeats were sacrificed at the western ballcourt. Hun Hunahpu's decapitated head was placed in a gourd tree by the ballcourt road. When Blood Woman, a daughter of an underworld lord, ventured near, the head of Hunahpu spit in her hand, magically impregnating her. Fleeing the underworld, she found refuge in the home of Hun Hunahpu.

Blood Woman gave birth to the hero twins Hunahpu and Xbalenque, who grew up to be accomplished ballplayers and hunters. In several episodes the hero twins encountered a number of supernaturals living on the surface of the earth. We are not told the origins of these entities, but the hero twins were able to overcome them. Eventually the loud ballplaying of the twins resulted in an invitation from the underworld lords. The hero twins defeated the lords through transformations, superior wit, and the help of the sky deity called Heart of Sky, Hurricane. The lords of the underworld were not destroyed; the boys merely took away some of their power. Unable to resurrect their father and uncle (Hun Hunahpu and Vucub Hunahpu), the twins left them at the ballcourt entrance to the underworld with the promise that humans would worship them. The twins went on to become sun and full moon or at least to be associated with those celestial bodies.

34. This competitive nature of the deities is also evident after the final creation of humans. These first four lineage heads were so perfect that they could see and understand all that the deities could (Tedlock 1985:166) Recognizing the danger in creating beings with equal power, the creator deities decided to take away part of their vision so they would only see things that were nearby. This firmly placed humans in the lower ranks of the hierarchy. For some Maya groups, the attribute that sets the ritual specialist apart from the common person is an ability to see and understand.

35. God A is a skeletal deity with black spots on his body. Eyes, often with the nerve hanging from them, decorate his hair and collar. These have been nicknamed death eyes. His name glyph is a portrait of a skeletal head with a T24 suffix. A title is also associated with him: a portrait glyph with a closed eye and a death eye attached as a suffix. Both glyph portraits are used in calendar contexts, where they stand for the day name Cimi "death," a known name for a death deity. A third nominal glyph for God A is phonetically spelled *cisin*, another known name for a death god (Fox and Justeson 1984:39).

The second death deity found in these New Year pages is designated God A1. This deity has death eyes, bones, and *akbal* signs in his headdress; a bone-decorated cloak; a dark eye band; and a *cimi* death sign on his cheek. In some cases, his nominal glyph is a portrait with his facial markings, but in the New Year scene it is a jawless head with a four prefix. This may indicate that there were four death deities, each related to one of the directions. In Classic pottery scenes his name has the same jawless quality. God A1 also carries the *cimi* closed eye title used by God A. On Madrid page 64c his name glyph is conflated with this title. Although they appear to have similar traits, God A and God A1 are clearly separate gods, as they are illustrated together on Madrid 19b and Pearlman 60 (Coe 1982:109). In the Postclassic Uayeb ceremonies the deity who is parallel to God A1 is *Uax Mitun Ahau* "six underworld lord."

The Postclassic God A1 appears in several Classic pottery scenes. A skeletal deity similar to God A appears in a mythological scene on a Tonina stucco frieze associated with the north. Another skeletal deity hovers inside the *cauac* cave on Piedras Negras Stela 5. At the present time, these Classic skeletal deities can only be related to the underworld through analogy with Postclassic beliefs.

36. There are four Itzamna and Ix Chel couples named in these incantations, one for each direction and its associated color. Itzamna and Ix Chel are the creator couple in Pokoman myth. In other sources Ix Chel is said to be the grandmother of the Bacabs or the mother of Itzamna's wife (Tozzer 1941:10).

37. Many female deities found in Maya art have attributes associated with the moon. It is likely that some of these females are related to different aspects of the moon: young with waxing and old with waning.

38. I identified God K's full figure glyph as a reclining baby (Bassie-Sweet 1991:27), but Stephen Houston (1987) has shown good reason to identify this form with a dwarf.

39. In some pottery scenes Chac is also illustrated with a serpent's foot.

40. *Na* has a variety of meanings. It is unclear what meaning is intended here.

41. On Copan Temple 11 there is an 819 Day Count passage containing three parts that can be paraphrased as "the yellow God K was set up; his foot, his animal counterpart,

God K; at the south sky seat." Houston and Stuart (1989:8) have offered an explanation of the second phrase:

Data from Copan raises another point about the serpent. We suspect that in some instances what concerned the Maya was not the snake, but God K's leg, which often ends in a reptilian head. On the East Door, south Jamb of Copan Temple 11, an inscription implies that y-ok, "his foot," is the way of God K. This reference explains scenes on Classic Maya pottery that display large, coiled serpents attached to God K's foot. In these images, the God K image is diminutive or absent altogether, perhaps indicating that some isolated serpent images in Maya art are to be understood as God K's foot.

I disagree with this interpretation. If the foot decipherment is correct, this phrase could be a couplet that reads "his foot; his animal counterpart; God K." Translated into an English couplet this would read "God K's foot, God K's animal counterpart." The foot of God K is the lightning/serpent; his animal counterpart is also the lightning/serpent. I interpret this phrase as a couplet referring to lightning. What concerned the Maya was not the foot of God K, but the spirit of lightning that resided in his serpent leg and foot. When rulers were illustrated grasping the leg of the God K mannikin scepter they were conceptually taking hold of lightning and the power that it contained.

42. The God E maize deity in the third Dresden scene may be related to a later Quiche patron deity who seems to have replaced Middle of the Plain. His name was Corn Tassel.

43. Lords of the Underworld Vase 11 illustrates four Pauahtuns in the process of being dressed. The woman behind the upper right deity holds the Pauahtun's headband.

44. In the Classic inscriptions the main sign is either the T548 *tun* "drum" sign or T528 *tun* "stone" sign, giving the pronunciation of his name *pauahtun* (Coe 1973:14). Karl Taube (1989:36) has suggested that the element in the center of the net bag is *wah* "tortilla, tamale or general sustenance." He argues that this element represents the *wah* sound in Pauahtun. Although I agree with the identification of this sign with corn, I question whether its function is purely phonetic with no semantic value.

45. The turtle shell is also a symbol for the earth, with its feet representing the corners of the world. When the Pauahtun is seen wearing a turtle shell, his appendages are symbolically emerging at the corners of the world. He is frequently illustrated at the corners of quadrilateral spaces.

46. The opposite corner of the bench illustrates a similar actor wearing the net bag headdress of Pauahtun. He faces a young actor dressed in the waterlily headdress of the Bacab. This Bacab imitator holds a rope, perhaps the rope that encircles the quadrilateral world. The two center supports of the bench illustrate two human actors with waterlily headdresses facing each other. I speculate that the human actors on this bench are likely to be the ancestors of the owner of the bench.

CHAPTER 2. ILLUSTRATIONS OF HORIZON CAVES

1. The sign for the month name Ch'en "cave" is composed of a pictograph of a *cauac* cave with a black prefix. In some examples the black prefix is replaced by crosshatching in the cave, making this a black cave.

2. The 819 Day Count passages place God K at each of the midpoints.

3. A section in the *Book of Chilam Balam of Chumayel* makes reference to corn contained inside "the one stone, the mighty pointed stone, the stone column, the mighty pointed clashing stone" (Roys 1933:66), suggesting that this stone was the stalagmite of the cave.

4. Other T528 signs include a flint sign along with the *cauac* cluster. As noted, the rain god's lightning was manifested as his flint axe.

5. Early forms of the T528 cauac sign have a layered element in place of the corn curl element (see fig. 17c). In the Supplementary Series Glyph G9 this early variant substitutes for a mirror sign. J. Katheryn Josserand (personal communication, 1990) has suggested that this early variant might represent a pool of water, with the lines representing ripples. Pools of water within caves were also a focus for rituals. Reflective surfaces such as pools, bowls of liquid, and mirrors were used in divinations. Ritual specialists gazed at the surface and interpreted the movements they saw there. I am inclined to view the layered element as a reference to the shimmering speleothem, which in cross-section is layered, but acknowledge that Josserand's suggestion is equally plausible.

An interpretation that combines both views is that the element represents small stalagmites that are just beginning. These formations look like small craters and often have a pool of water in the indentation on top. In the Tlappanec region of Guerrero these formations are thought to contain the spirit of corn (Heyden 1981:26).

6. There are examples where the teeth of the cauac monster are illustrated as T528 signs. The Chol refer metaphorically to stalactites as the teeth of the cave (Nicholas Hopkins, personal communication, 1989).

7. In some myths it is said that the beating of the rain god's drum creates thunder and lightning. Following personal observations and those made by Barbara MacLeod and Dennis Puleston (1978) that dripwater formations are natural drums, I speculated that the dripwater formation was the rain god's drum and the source of thunder and lightning (Bassie-Sweet 1991:118). I suggested that the replacement of the T548 *tun* "drum" sign with the T528 *tun* "stone" sign was based on the fact that they are both the same thing: the stone and drum of the rain god.

8. Several pottery scenes show supernaturals immersed in water with fish swimming between their legs. Nicholas Hellmuth (1987) categorized many of the motifs associated with this location.

9. Another example of the high-mountain and low-water nature of ritual locations is found at Santa Eulalia. The ceremonies performed for the New Year include a pilgrimage to the sacred hill of the ancestral couple (high-mountain place) and another to a pool of water in the sacred cave of Yalan Na' (low-water place) (La Farge 1947:122). The Quiche lineage patrons were placed in a canyon (low) and on mountains (high).

10. At Zinacantan the ritual specialists make a pilgrimage to a distant mountain called Junior Large Mountain in order to petition for rain. It is thought that inside this mountain is a large lake.

11. In the *Ritual of the Bacabs* incantations a passage identifies the birth cave as the place of "lady sprout of the waterlily": "He would fall behind the east [serpent], at the place of Ix Kuknab" (Roys 1965:8).

12. The caption text refers to this location as being in the north. Directions can be used to describe the corners as well as the midpoints and sides of the world (see appendix).

13. The Temple 14 Tablet location has been interpreted by other authors to be a plaza based on the fact that at Machaquila the plaza has a partial quatrefoil shape embedded in its surface and the monuments illustrate a ruler performing rituals at a *naab* quatrefoil. Thus, Schele and Grube (1990:4) state: "We believe that the Maya called their plazas nab and that they thought of them as the surface of water, perhaps the ocean in which the earth rest." While a plaza may have been viewed as the surface of the earth or a plain, there is no ethnohistorical or linguistic evidence that Maya plazas were thought to be the sea.

14. The northwest panel illustrates a serpent with the quatrefoil shape in its forehead. A *cauac* element hangs from its lower jaw. The northeast jamb is a monster head also with the quatrefoil shape and *cauac* elements.

15. The Dresden world trees have a serpent draped in their branches. Landa noted that the New Year tree/standard was decorated with an insigne representing water.

16. The Shell Wing Dragons are serpentlike animals with a shell "wing." These little shell monsters seem to be appropriate symbols for the spirit of wind that lives in shells and water, but their identification remains elusive.

17. Kan Xul is performing a ceremonial dance, but his raised foot and the position of the axe indicate that he is in midswing.

18. In some Classic illustrations the serpent has a deer ear or antler. Some of the illustrations of horned serpents use the antlers of a white-tailed deer, which have the same branched shape as lightning. These branched horns are in contrast to the small pointed horns of the brocket deer. The idea of conflating a serpent with a deer, one of the few New World animals with a horn, may rest in the concept of the whirlwind/horn.

19. One Tzeltal tale describes a horned rock that had a spring emerging from it (Karasik 1988:208–9). The spring was created by a horned serpent who lived under the rock and plowed up the earth with its horns. The serpent destructively dug up the land including the cornfields, so the people went to the rock on the Day of the Cross and prayed. The rock and the earth lord were pleased by this action so the rock "hid" the serpent. To this day the people continue the Day of the Cross celebration to placate the deity. The Day of the Cross is a time when the modern Maya renew their tree/crosses and make petitions for rain. The association of a destructive force (the horned serpent) with the Day of the Cross ceremonies is reminiscent of the role of the world tree in the New Year ceremonies.

20. The illumination of lightning on water has the same quick movement as a snake moving on water.

21. Several *Ritual of the Bacabs* incantations refer to the birth caves as *tan yol can* "the heart of the sky" and *tan yol caan* "heart of the serpent." Roys (1965) translates *yol* as "heart," but it also carries the meaning spirit, soul, and innermost recess. The wind comes from the innermost recesses of the cave passage.

22. The number *can* "four" also substitutes for sky and serpent. This is not based on the mere similarity in sound of these terms but on shared value: there are four cave passages at the midpoints and at the corners of the square. The head variant of the number four is the sun, which incorporates the four corner points in its kin sign.

23. The *Ritual of the Bacabs* incantations demonstrate that the cave passageway was thought to be layered like the celestial sky. The five in *Na Ho Chan* may be related to the fifth layer of the cave.

24. Even today there is a strong belief that the cenotes of the site have passageways that lead to various sacred locations. Across the Maya area similar beliefs are held. The residents of Tila believe the cave at the edge of the town continues all the way to Palenque, while a cave near Copan is thought to extend to Quirigua. Many researchers dismiss these claims as fabrications, but their importance lies in the fact that they reflect Maya world view and a basic belief concerning caves.

25. In this particular example, there are two jaws that form a mirror image. As the south side of the lid represents the south side of the world, each jaw may represent one of the corner caves. Pacal falls midway between these two caves, that is, at the midpoint cave. Some examples of full frontal cauac monsters are also mirror images.

26. The Principal Bird Deity is the nickname for a supernatural bird who appears in a variety of contexts (Bardawil 1976). In several pottery scenes more than one bird is

illustrated, suggesting that there may have been at least one bird for each direction. Despite any strong evidence that this supernatural bird was a deity, I retain the name as a nickname.

27. The location of precolumbian altars is consistent with modern locations. There is archaeological evidence for precolumbian altars inside caves, on the slopes of mountains, and at spring locations. In a family compound altars are most often found on the back wall of the main structure opposite the doorway or in a separate shrine or oratory.

28. The *Ritual of the Bacabs* incantations refer to the directions as the four resting places, and one of the deities is *Yum Ho-can-lub* "father four-resting place" (Roys 1965:7, 149, 161). *Lub* is the flat stone at the crossroads where travelers often rest their packs.

29. In a comparison with the quadrilateral model, the house represents the square, the doorway represents one of the midpoint locations, and the altar represents the opposite midpoint. The post at this location represents the midpoint world tree. In the Tzeltal area the spirit of the house is said to reside at this center post of the rear wall (Nash 1970:11).

30. Some pottery vessels are cosmograms. Circular, shallow bowls are often decorated with water symbols to represent the sea on which the world floats. The quatrefoil cave opening is carved on the bottom of a Tikal burial bowl (Coe 1976:17). This suggests that the bowl itself is a symbolic cave.

31. The seat sign occasionally has the form of the day sign Muluc, which is a pictograph of a cave with a circle element in the center. Muluc has the meaning "hidden water," an appropriate description of the horizon cave.

32. Like the cauac monsters that are labeled with glyphs and symbols to emphasize certain aspects or to specify the name of the mountain cave, benches are also so marked. Benches occur in the text of Quirigua Stela C in reference to the setting up of stone idols at the beginning of the current era; there are references to a jaguar bench, a serpent bench, and a *naab* bench (see chapter 4).

33. The Tree of the Sea place name is composed of the *naab* sign with the pictograph of a tree prefixed to it. This tree sign also appears in "the tree of the stone" phrases (see chapter 5). In some Piedras Negras name phrases the pictograph of the tree carries a phonetic *ma* suffix. In one example it carries a phonetic *la* prefix. Stuart suggests that these phonetic complements indicate a reading of *lakam*, which has many meanings, including big and standard. On Copan Stela A the phonetic spelling *lakam(a)* precedes the *tun* sign. Some researchers have ignored the pictographic value of the tree and chosen the meaning "big." Given that tree/standards played such a paramount role, such a choice seems unjustified.

I believe the Tree of the Sea compound represents a tree/standard located at a water shrine. Such an occurrence is common in the Maya area. The Temple of the Inscriptions narrative records an axe event at the Tree of the Sea location (Looper and Schele 1991). The verb has been interpreted to mean that the location was damaged by foreigners. This brings to mind the extensive efforts at Dos Pilas to protect its sacred cave from attack during the last wars of that site (Brady 1991; Demarest 1993).

The Zinacantan hamlet of Sek'emtik has a sacred mountain called K'uk Ch'en "quetzal cave" named after a tree called K'uk Te "quetzal tree" that grows there (Vogt 1969:169). K'uk Witz "quetzal mountain" is a common mountain name in the Chiapas highlands. The Palenque place name K'uk Lakam Witz seems to fall into this kind of naming practice (Korelstein n.d.).

34. The triple form of these "fish-in-hand" locations suggests the possibility that they may refer to three locations rather than three names for the same location. Evidence for this interpretation is found in the Cross Group narratives, where there may be a reference

to three "fish-in-hand" events rather than one. An event on 2 Cib 10 Mol is stated in parallel passages in each of the Cross Group Tablets. On the Cross Tablet a fish-in-hand event by Chan Bahlum follows this event. This passage begins with what has been interpreted to be a distance number of three days, suggesting the fish-in-hand occurred three days after the 2 Cib event. The 2 Cib event on the Sun and Foliated Cross narratives is not followed by this event but by an event at dawn the next day. Chan Bahlum is said to perform a ritual to purify the *k'inich kuk balam na* "the sun-eyed Quetzal Balam house." The next passage states that Chan Bahlum performed a "fish-in-hand" event. It too begins with the same alleged three day distance number. Because of the intervening day in the Sun and Foliated Cross narratives, this alleged distance number would have to be counted from the 2 Cib date. Josserand (1991) has demonstrated that when a story backs up in time it signals a new episode. Such an episode break here does not seem appropriate. Another interpretation is possible. Instead of representing a time period of three days this glyph may indicate that three fish-in-hand events were performed (David Stuart, personal communication, 1986).

35. This does not invalidate its association with gourds or with backbones, for the world tree was metaphorically represented in many ways.

36. In the Palenque Temple of the Inscriptions text the T559 sign appears in association with the glyphs for east and west. Interestingly, the *kin* sign is on the right in the context of west (fig. 42a), but is to the left with the east glyph (fig. 42b). The date of the associated event is July 1, when the sun is north of the quadrilateral midpoint (the sun is to the left of the midpoint tree when the observer is looking east, and to the right of the midpoint tree when looking west).

37. The appearance of the mirror sign in the context of the world tree and midpoint cave is probably related to the use of mirrors as divination tools. Ritual specialists studied the reflections of light in mirrors and other reflective surfaces. It is likely that the surface of such material represented the surface of the calm sea upon which the world floated. The images within the mirror represented the supernatural world. At the midpoint one could look into the cave at the supernatural world. There is therefore an equivalency between cave openings and the surface of a mirror.

38. The *tzuk* head and *tzuk* sign substitute in a female name phrase that appears at Naranjo and a panel in the Saenz Collection in Mexico City. The name phrase is "Lady 6 Sky Lord of the Side" and she carries the *bacab* title.

39. This bound figure may be the crocodile that represents the earth. If so, it may be bound to represent the tied up (safe) earth.

40. On Tonina Monument 26 the phrase *lakam-tun* "the tree of the stone" is replaced with *tzuk lakam* "side tree." On the Palace Tablet a T528 *tun* glyph is suffixed with the *tzuk* sign, making it "the stone of the side."

CHAPTER 3. COSMOGRAMS

1. GII has the same diagnostic traits as God K. How the four directional God K deities mentioned in the Classic 819 Day Count related to GII is unclear.

2. A number of place names in the hieroglyphic text are used to designate mythological locations as well as local ritual sites (Tedlock 1985; Schele and Freidel 1990; Bassie-Sweet 1991; Schele 1992; Stuart and Houston in press). When a text or scene illustrates such a place and the actor is clearly a historical person, it is relatively certain that the location was a local version of the mythological site. Some place names appear to name the horizon area in either general or specific terms.

The Cross Group inscriptions state that the Palenque Triad of deities were born at or from a location called *Matawil* (Stuart and Houston in press). On the Tablet of the Foliated Cross, which illustrates Chan Bahlum at the birth cave of GII, the shell on which the young Chan Bahlum stands is labeled with the *Matawil* sign, indicating this place sign's association with the cave (fig. 49). Further evidence that *Matawil* was associated with a cave location is found on a looted panel from the Yaxchilan region illustrating two individuals performing a fire-drilling rite associated with the act of divination (Stuart and Houston in press). The location symbol is composed of the skeletal jaws of the cave. The text within these jaws ends with the *Matawil* sign. The iconography of the Cross Group indicates that each member of the Palenque Triad was born at a different cave location. I suggest that *Matawil* was a general name for the supernatural space at the horizon, probably the sea. The Triad emerged from this supernatural place by different cave openings, each oriented to a different direction.

On the Tablet of the Cross Lady Beastie (the mother of two of these deities) is said to perform a Period Ending event at this *Matawil* place. This sign also occurs as the main sign for the emblem glyph associated with this woman (that is, she was a *Matawil* lord).

3. The modern Chol living in the region of Palenque go to the mountain southwest of Palenque to petition Don Juan, the supernatural owner of the mountain (Cruz, Josserand, and Hopkins 1980). Pilgrims also come from the farthest regions of Chol territory such as Tumbala. Don Juan has been directly related to the rain deities of other areas (Cruz, Josserand, and Hopkins 1980:116). The cave is located at the north slope of Don Juan Mountain and Ausencio Cruz (personal communication, 1993) reports precolumbian material at this location. At nearly 1,200 meters Don Juan mountain makes an impressive home for deities and ancestors. The mountain ridges to the south and east of Palenque also contain precolumbian ritual caves (Rands, Bishop, and Harbottle 1978).

4. It has been argued that the cave rituals illustrated on the Cross Group tablets actually occurred inside the Cross Group temples (Schele and Freidel 1990). The excavation of the Cross Group demonstrates that it was constructed on bedrock. The Cross Group narrative includes a past tense event in A.D. 692 followed by a future tense event just three months later. This indicates that the Cross Group was built circa A.D. 692, so it is clear that the location of these rituals could not have been the Cross Group buildings.

5. On each of the Cross Group staircases there is a text referring to the birth of its respective deity. The birth verb incorporates a hand over the T526 *cab* cave sign (the representation of a horizon cave). The Palenque birth verb was initially thought to be related to the concept of touching or experiencing the earth for the first time (Lounsbury 1976). This is in accord with my evidence that it represents a horizon cave, from which the deities emerged into the world. Several authors have recently suggested that the T526 sign carries no semantic value and records only a phonetic *cab*. There may be contexts where this is true, but these examples may simply be cases where we do not yet understand the cultural connotations.

6. The Tablet of the Cross also records the birth of GI Senior and Lady Beastie (the mother of GI and GIII). An episode states that GI Senior ritually prepared (the God N verb) the house of the north called "Raised-up Sky" and then GI was born at *Matawil* (MacLeod, cited in Schele 1992:129). The Temple of the Inscriptions Tablets state that Raised-up Sky was the seat of GI. My interpretation of the Cross Tablet passage is that GI Senior ritually prepared the north cave for the birth of GI.

7. A Late Classic example of the association of buildings and caves is found at Yaxchilan. The highest hill at the site (eighty-eight meters) rises in a series of natural terraces with coulees on either side. Three of the lower terraces were modified by the

Maya and buildings were erected on them. Three of these buildings had stalactite columns in front of them (Maler 1901–3:168). The stalactite in front of Structure 33 is delicately carved with a scene of hand-scattering similar to those carved on Yaxchilan stelae. The top of the hill includes three buildings: Structures 39, 40, and 41. An enormous stalactite (280 cm long) was positioned there (Maler 1901–3:183). Formal access to the top of the hill is gained by walking up the coulee from the plaza to a staircase leading up the steep northeast escarpment of the hill. On the southwest side of the coulee near the staircase is a ritual cave (Tate 1992:150).

Further association between caves and these buildings is found in the solar alignment of the doorways of Structure 33 and Structure 41, which are oriented to the rising sun of the summer solstice (Tate 1992:112–15). The tops of the doorways in Structure 41 are shaped like half quatrefoils, and on the summer solstice the rising sun forms a quatrefoil cave shadow on the interior of the rooms, as though the light of the sun validates this doorway as a representation of the quatrefoil cave of the horizon. In the Nahuatl village of Amatlan a permanent altar is maintained on the hill where the rising sun first touches the earth (Sandstrom 1991:248).

8. A number of temple/pyramids were decorated with *cauac* symbols that further associate them with the rain god's mountain/cave. The doorway is often decorated to imitate the mouth of the cave.

9. Some sources seem to imply that the Maya "heaven" was located in one of the celestial layers. This can be reconciled with the notion that ancestors lived at the horizon because these layers were thought to occur not only above, in the sky, but at the horizon and inside the directional mountains as well (the cave passageways).

10. The text that runs around the outside edge of the lid is a narrative divided into three episodes. It relates the deaths of Palenque rulers beginning with Chaacal I (A.D. 524) and ending with the death of Pacal II (A.D. 683). Two of these Palenque rulers were women, Lady Kanal Ikal and Lady Zac Kuk (the grandmother and mother of Pacal, respectively). This narrative also includes the deaths of their consorts Pacal I and Kan Bahlum Mo (Bassie-Sweet 1991:246). The ancestors on the box are displayed, not in the order of their deaths but in conjunction with the text that appears above their heads.

The first episode of the sarcophagus narrative begins on the east side with an undeciphered phrase and relates the deaths of Chaacal I, Kan Xul I, Chaacal II, Chan Bahlum I, Lady Kanal Ikal, and Ac Kan. The death of Ac Kan occupies the entire north rim of the sarcophagus. This chronology leaves out the death of Pacal's namesake, Pacal I. His death occurred after Lady Kanal Ikal's death but before Ac Kan's. The second episode begins on the west rim by backing up in time to the death of Pacal I and then relates the deaths of Lady Zac Kuk and Kan Bahlum Mo. The third episode backs up in time again and tells of the birth and death of Pacal. It occupies three glyph blocks on the west rim and the entire south rim. This episode includes the statement that Pacal was the child of Lady Zac Kuk and Kan Bahlum Mo and that he had participated in four katun ending ceremonies before his death.

In a previous publication I proposed a revised genealogical chart for the Palenque rulers (Bassie-Sweet 1991:206) (see table). Two factors were involved in creating the chart: the reading of hieroglyphic texts as narratives and a change in the death date of Lady Kanal Ikal. In regard to the death date, I questioned whether the head used in the numerical position for the month Ceh was actually "the end of Ceh" as proposed by Lounsbury (1974). It has since been demonstrated that in the contexts of Glyph F of the Supplementary Series this sign is a substitution for the T128 sign used in "end of" constructions (Schele 1990). The possibility that the death date was incorrect led me to question the widely accepted model of the Palenque descent line. My revision of the descent line does not, however, hinge on Lady Kanal Ikal's death date. In fact, using Lounsbury's date strengthens my position that both Ac Kan and Pacal were sons of Kan Bahlum Mo and Lady Zac Kuk, who was the daughter of Lady Kanal Ikal and Pacal I.

The strongest evidence that Ac Kan was the child of Lady Zac Kuk and Kan Bahlum Mo is found in the placement of the text and image on the sarcophagus lid. The passage on the south rim deals solely with Pacal. Under this episode are portraits of Pacal's parents, Lady Zac Kuk and Kan Bahlum Mo. The text states that they were Pacal's parents and the image illustrates them as ancestors living in the sacred caves surrounding the community. In Lounsbury's dating the first episode ends with the death of Ac Kan. The passage referring to Ac Kan is the sole inscription on the north rim that places considerable emphasis on him. Below his death statement are again the portraits of Lady Zac Kuk and her husband, Kan Bahlum Mo. Ac Kan has been deliberately placed in a parallel context with Pacal.

A second parallel with Pacal is found in the placement of quatrefoils on the lid. The north and south edges of the sarcophagus lid each have three quatrefoil openings with the same three individuals pictured inside. Their name glyphs include titles indicating subordinate rank (the *sahal* and God C titles). Whoever these figures may be, it is clear from their titles that they held offices. Their position on the edges of the quadrilateral world indicates that they were also members of the ancestral government.

I have suggested that these individuals were the patrilineal descendants of Pacal II (Bassie-Sweet 1991:246). Below these lords on the sides of the box are portraits of Pacal's father, Kan Bahlum Mo. I believe their position at the borders of the Palenque world and above Kan Bahlum Mo strengthens the argument that they were paternal ancestors of Pacal. Their position on the north side above the death statement of Ac Kan suggests they were also his ancestors.

When the descent line passed from Chan Bahlum I to Lady Kanal Ikal, rulership remained in Chan Bahlum's lineage because children always belong to their father's lineage. In order for Ac Kan and Pacal to be legitimate rulers, their father had to be a member of the founding lineage. Kan Bahlum Mo carries the Palenque emblem glyph, which indicates that this was the case. These two lords became rulers because they were the grandsons of Lady Kanal Ikal, but they were eligible for this position because of their father's descent line. Kan Bahlum Mo's descent line from some earlier ruler was of paramount importance. The three quatrefoil lords were surely his paternal ancestors.

The legs of the sarcophagus also illustrate these three secondary lords. Their position at the corners of the Palenque world suggests roles similar to those of the secondary Pauahtun deities, who are also frequently depicted at these locations.

Based on an interpretation of the God C title as mason or architect, it has been suggested that these lords "were the master artists who designed the sarcophagus and the temple about it" (Schele 1992:45). This follows Stuart's notion that the *lu* "bat" phrase found on some monuments represents the signature of the artist. Such an interpretation seems unlikely, given the position and repetition of these three lords on the sarcophagus.

11. The employment of a skyband to indicate the east and west sides of the world demonstrates that skybands could also represent the annual path of the sun along the horizon.

12. Pacal has a bone element on the end of his nose that is reminiscent of the Zinacantan soul, which can sit on the tip of its owner's nose (see chapter 6).

13. A second subject mentioned on this monument has been interpreted to be a relative or subordinate of Yax Pac. It would appear that on the occasion of Yax Pac's accession anniversary this relative took an office of some kind.

14. Specifically which ancestors are represented in this illustration is unknown. The north side has two anthropomorphic figures with *cab* "bee, beehive" signs for heads. They hold the calendar round for Yax Pac's accession in their hands and sit on the first katun anniversary phrase. These *cab* supernaturals are reminiscent of the Yucatec Maya bee deities who live at the horizon.

15. The Seibal emblem glyph is preceded by T606:23 *tan(a)* "in front, in the middle." Visits by foreign lords are documented in several Classic narratives. One of the verbs used in these narrative has been deciphered to mean "to arrive" (Grube and MacLeod, cited in MacLeod 1990). Another verb is a pictograph of an eye and has been phonetically translated as "to see" (Stuart 1987; Houston 1987). The implication is that these lords witnessed a particular event. The attendance of foreign lords at a community event is in accord with a Postclassic tradition noted by Bartolomé de las Casas. He stated that after the selection of a lord the elite from other towns were invited to the accession ceremonies. The invitation was extended to friend and foe alike. If these lords could not attend they sent a brother or other representative. In addition, foreign visitors also attended the five or six annual religious ceremonies of the town "because although they all hold the same celebrations, they are accustomed to honor another by attending" (Miles 1955). One reason that a foe might attend such a ceremony or conduct a pilgrimage through hostile territory is that the journey provided an opportunity for the entourage to survey the conditions in other regions. Traders and pilgrims made very good spies. Several researchers have suggested that these visits by foreign Classic lords document alliances between polities. If the Postclassic was any indication, this may not have been the case.

Naj Tunich cave is located in the southeast of the Peten. Its tunnels, which extend over three kilometers, include altars oriented to dripwater formations, stalagmite idols, and ceremonial pottery. Areas for private and public ceremonies have been identified (Brady, Veni, Stone, and Cobb 1992). The largest number of Classic hieroglyphs and drawings yet discovered in a cave environment are found on various stone formations as well as the walls of the cave. These inscriptions contain a number of "arrival" and "witness" verbs indicating that lords documented their participation in cave rituals there (Stuart and Houston in press). The wide variety of emblem glyphs used in the name phrases of these individuals suggests that Naj Tunich was a pilgrimage goal for Maya from many regions (Brady and Brady n.d.). How Naj Tunich developed a reputation as a particularly sacred location and who controlled and maintained the site is presently unknown.

16. Two stelae were also placed in the center of Copan. Stela 3 was set up near the center of the main plaza. Both sides of Stela 3 illustrate an actor. At the base on either side of Stela 3 are place names. One appears to be a T528 *cauac* cave variant; the other is a cave cartouche with either a *kin* sign or "mat" sign in the center. One side of the cave is cross-hatched to indicate the dark zone of the cave. The north/south orientation of the monument suggests that it illustrates two rituals performed at either the north or south midpoints. Stela 2 was erected at the north end of the ballcourt, suggesting it may represent a north event.

17. The text relates a number of events, including a mythological one. There is an eroded section, which makes the identification of both actors as 18 Jog uncertain.

18. Birds were a common ritual offering in caves (Norman Hammond, personal communication, 1989). In the *Ritual of the Bacabs* incantations a macaw is said to warm the first corn kernels behind the acantun (Roys 1965:111). The cave of Pecmo, where the Kekchi worship the mountain deity, is located on Macaw Rock (Sapper 1897:281; Thompson 1975:xxix). At Copan there are several references to a Macaw Mountain.

19. The glyph phrase on the back of Copan Stela B that refers to Macaw Mountain also includes a compound composed of a sky sign prefixed with the number four and a long-nosed serpent. I have interpreted this to mean that Macaw Mountain is one of the four midpoint sky seats. The last event on Copan Stela A contains a series of undeciphered actions that also suggests this. The Stela A passage includes a reference to four sky locations; four lords; a place at the side of the sky and at the side of the world; and the directions east, west, south, and north. Like the Stela B Macaw Mountain example, each sky compound is prefixed with the number four. Although the meaning of the passage remains somewhat obscure, it seems to indicate that each lord performed a ritual at one of four directional sky locations situated at the side of the sky as well as the side of the world, the midpoints of the quadrilateral world.

Each sky location is distinguished by a different prefix. The second example, which is paired with the direction west, has the same long-nosed serpent found on Stela B, which is also associated with the west. Three of the four sky locations employ the standard T561 sky sign, but the main sign of the second location is a conflation of the sky sign and the head variant of the seat sign. This west sky location is being emphasized as a seat.

CHAPTER 4. THE RENEWAL OF THE WORLD

1. The Quiche day name Wind is said to be "symbolic of the destructive forces of the universe embodied in the stone idols" (Bunzel 1952:280).

2. The notion that the four directions are a source of destructive powers is also found at Chenalho:

Man unfailingly intervenes in order to prevent the annihilation of both sun and moon, which would entail the destruction of human existence. The evil beings that come to devour the sun and moon are thought to attack from the cardinal sides of the heavens, which are also related to colors: the north is white, the west is black, the south is yellow, and the east is red. (Guiteras 1961:287)

3. The many parallels between the human New Year ceremonies described by Landa and the Dresden New Year ceremonies have been recognized since the beginning of Maya studies (Thomas 1882). The Dresden New Year pages illustrate a model for humans to emulate each time one of these important calendar cycles was repeated. It must be kept in mind that Landa's account of these events is brief and at times contradictory.

4. Taube (1988a:276–79) argued that the idol was related to the current year, and I agree. It is likely that the two heaps of stones do not represent two separate mountains but rather one mountain with a cleft or split at the top similar to the cauac monster illustrated on the Tablet of the Foliated Cross.

5. This stone appears to be a permanent fixture at the house of the lord.

6. This placing or seating of the idol at the midpoint occurred at the end of Uayeb and at the seating of the month Pop. The sign for Pop reflects this location: it is composed of the *kan* sign and "mat" seat sign inside a cave opening (see chapter 7 for discussion of the "mat" sign). On a Chinikiha stela the Pop sign is composed of a skeletal head with the "mat" and *kan* sign infixed on the ear and eye, respectively. A similar skeletal head represents the cave opening on the altar of Copan Stela D.

In modern New Year ceremonies the Year-bearer deity is greeted at the appropriate mountain location. He is thought to be seated at this location, just as the Postclassic ceremony involved physically seating the idol at the midpoint.

7. The moving of the guardian idol from the symbolic midpoint cave to the center of the community and back to a midpoint is similar to a Quiche Postclassic ritual, where the idol was taken from the cave, brought to the temple for worship, and then returned to the cave (Carmack 1981:186).

8. A tun ending happened every 360 days, while the all-important katun ending occurred at the end of every 20 tun periods.

9. I interpreted the phrase as intransitive (Bassie-Sweet 1991:181), but the verb is transitive (Schele 1992:123).

10. This pair of Classic deities is often associated with Period Ending events. On several bones from Tikal Burial 116 they are illustrated paddling a long canoe full of supernaturals: hence their name, the Paddlers. Although their names are most often portraits, *akbal* and *kin* signs within modified paddle cartouches are also used. One of the Paddlers is an old supernatural with a stingray spine through his nose. The other Paddler appears in many other contexts. He is patron of the month Uo, head variant of the number seven, and a variant of Glyph C of the lunar series. In most examples this deity is portrayed as a roman-nosed god with a twisted cord over the nose and/or jaguar features. Occasionally, he has *kin* "sun, day" sign markings. In Glyph C the portrait can be replaced with just the deity's eye and twisted cord, suggesting that the deity can be identified on the strength of this diagnostic trait alone. It has been argued that this supernatural represents the night sun on its journey through the underworld, and he has been given the nickname Jaguar God of the Underworld. I prefer the descriptive but neutral name Twisted Cord Deity for this figure.

The appearance of the Twisted Cord Deity in Glyph C of the lunar series strongly suggests he has moon associations; I have argued that he is associated with the full moon and Xbalenque (jaguar sun) of the *Popol Vuh* (Bassie-Sweet 1991:192). The Twisted Cord Deity is discussed further in chapter 7.

11. This compound has been translated as "lying down sky" and interpreted as a reference to the world at creation: "this is the perfect description of space at the beginning of creation before the sky has been lifted away from the earth when it was lying-down on the earth" (Schele 1992:125). I do not find this a convincing interpretation because the Maya stories referring to the creation, destruction, and re-creation of the world do not make reference to the sky being separated from the earth. There always seems to be a sky and sea. The earth rises from the sea and is subsequently flooded.

12. This is the case with the Aztec. In the *Popol Vuh* obtaining fire was of paramount importance to the first four heads of the Quiche lineage.

13. The activities of women were greatly focused on the hearth area. It is therefore expected that the concepts associated with the three hearth stones would involve goddesses. For the central Mexican Cuicatecs, the goddesses of sustenance were manifested as three skulls, the three hearth stones, and the three stars of Orion's belt (Hunt 1977). In some Maya areas the three female supernaturals associated with corn are the three daughters of the rain deity. These women personify the spirit of corn.

14. It is interesting that the T501 *naab* sign for the sea is used in some contexts for the phonetic sign *ba*. In some contexts *ba* has the meaning "first."

15. In the *Ritual of the Bacabs* an incantation associates Itzam Cab (a deity closely related to or equal to Itzamna) with the three stones of the hearth (Roys 1965:50).

16. Various monuments record Period Ending ceremonies at five-tun, ten-tun, thirteen-tun, and fifteen-tun intervals as well. It is unclear whether the world was in danger at every tun ending or just at the all important katun ending. Certainly the katun endings received the most attention.

17. The seating verb used in these phrases is the same as that for the "seating" of the ruler during the accession rituals. It is also the same verb used in the expression for the seating of the month, such as the seating of Pop at the beginning of the New Year.

18. The Temple of the Inscriptions passages that refer to the 9.12.0.0.0 Period Ending of Pacal contain an episode naming a series of headdress elements for each of the Palenque Triad (Macri 1988). Their order implies that these passages refer to Pacal dressing in the costumes of each member of the triad: a white headband, a necklace, earrings, and a headdress specific to the deity. The headdress of GI is distinguished by the Quadripartite Badge, while that of GIII is the so-called Jester God, nicknamed for its resemblance to the hat of a European court jester.

19. It is not my intention to imply that the deities of the Palenque Triad were equal to the ordering deities of the Dresden codex.

20. A number of locations are specifically named as places where mythological rituals or events occurred at the end of the previous era. The black Vase of the Seven Gods illustrates such a scene (Coe 1973:106). Stacked *cauac* heads form the frame of a house decorated with crossed bones, death eyes, and a reptilian monster. God L sits inside this cave house on a jaguar bench. The ends of his mat loincloth are raised above his thigh, which suggests that the display of this symbol of authority was important. He gestures toward two tiers of deities who sit before him. All seven deities are dressed in similar clothes but wear a distinctive headdress. These supernaturals seem to be a council with God L in charge. This scene may illustrate the west midpoint. The place name of God L's house is prefixed with black and the background of the vase indicates that this is a black place. If this was related to color/directionalism then this cave was associated with the west. At GIII's west cave God L appears holding up the bench, which also has a jaguar head attached to it.

In Mesoamerica bundles were often used to contain idols and implements for rituals. There is a bundle set before each tier of deities as well as one behind God L on his bench. It is possible that these bundles contained the stone idols mentioned in the Quirigua text. If this is the case, a number of scenarios are possible. This scene could illustrate the setting of the stone at the western cave or could illustrate these deities picking up the stones in preparation for their journey to the three locations named in the Quirigua narrative. The texts are so brief and so poorly understood that we can only speculate.

21. This is a common motif of Period Ending scenes. How and when these individuals were killed is not completely certain in all cases. On Dos Pilas Stela 2 the captive Jaguar Paw is illustrated crouching at the feet of Ruler 3 on 9.15.4.6.11. He also appears at Ruler 3's feet on Aguateca Stela 2, but the occasion is the 9.15.5.0.0 Period Ending nearly a year later (Bassie-Sweet 1991:52).

22. The concept of human sacrifice during the creation of quadrilateral space also occurs in Zinacantan (Hunt 1977:276).

23. The notion that the creation of ritual space involved penis perforation is found on Madrid page 19, where five deities surround a house: the cord joining them runs through the penis of each deity.

24. The God L on the jambs of the Temple of the Cross is illustrated with the ends of his loincloth untied. God L's loincloth is marked with footprints, suggesting that the loincloth represents the cord or path around the world. When the ruler untied his loincloth to perform his bloodletting, he may have been symbolically untying the cord that secured the world.

A bound crocodile is illustrated in several Period Ending scenes such as the Piedras Negras niche scenes and the Paris codex Period Ending scenes. The crocodile is most often used as a metaphor for the surface of the world. In these Period Ending ceremonies the bound crocodile might be a metaphor for the bound, and therefore safe, earth.

25. Another title related to the Period Ending function of the lord is found on Yaxchilan Stela 16. In this narrative Shield Jaguar is called a five *katun ahau* in reference to his age. He also carries the title "he of three tree/standards" in reference to the three Period Endings during his life when he set up the tree/standard of the stone idol.

26. The names of many of the elite members refer to the most powerful of the animal counterparts or to deities. The use of God K (a lightning deity) and Chac in personal names is widespread.

27. The Postclassic ruler title *batab* is derived from *bat* "stone axe." As noted, Chac's axe was considered to be lightning, the most powerful of the animal counterparts and the ultimate precolumbian weapon. *Batab* was a highly appropriate title for a ruler who had the spiritual power to command this supernatural force.

CHAPTER 5. GUARDIAN IDOLS

1. *Acante* has such meanings as thunder tree, set-up tree, and wooden shaft. There has been a tendency to view the Acantun and acante as one (Taube 1988a:241), but I believe that they are two related but separate concepts: a stone belonging to the guardian deity and his tree/standard.

2. I interpret the *Ritual of the Bacabs* incantation that indicates that the Acantun was cast down and broken to mean that the disease was able to come into being because the Acantun was not functioning.

3. Incensarios, which often display the face of the supernatural to which the offering was directed, are occasionally carved with the face of the personified *tun* sign.

4. It is interesting to note that many of the so-called alabaster offering bowls are actually made from speleothems (Jamie Awe, personal communication, 1994).

5. For example, seven stalactites were broken off and erected on a stone altar situated in front of a large flowstone at Naj Tunich cave (Brady, Veni, Stone, and Cobb 1992:78). At Yaxchilan numerous dripwater formations were erected in front of various temples (the largest stalagmite was over 280 cm long). At Copan speleothems have been found in house and stela caches alongside the more common offerings of flint and obsidian (Strömsvik 1941). The Dos Pilas Cave survey, the first systematic appraisal of cave features in relationship to a site, has documented the wide use of speleothems in many ritual contexts (Brady 1991). Stalagmites are also found on modern Tzeltal house altars (Deal 1988:74). Modern ritual specialists from all over Tabasco and Chiapas make pilgrimages to the sacred cross and cave on the mountain high above the town of Tila (Alfonso Morales, personal communication, 1986; personal observation, 1993). The focus of the cave rituals is a dripwater column idol known as Señor Tila.

6. As noted, the association of corn and dripwater formations is found in the Tlappanec region of Guerrero. The cave of their rain deity contains dripwater formations that are worshiped as gods (Heyden 1981:26). Corn is said to have come first from the small speleothems caused by dripping water.

7. To erect a stela, a cache offering was placed near or under the site where the stela would be. The commonest offering was flint and obsidian. At Copan stela caches for Stela 1, Stela C, and Stela I contained speleothems as well.

8. Many of the carved stelae were painted, but in most cases the paint only survives in the protected recesses of the carving. This means that many of the uncarved stelae found at various sites may have originally been painted with commemorative information as well.

9. Tikal Altar 4 is a round sculpture. The top is badly eroded, but appears to show an actor emerging from a serpent mouth. The sides illustrate four Pauahtuns emerging from quatrefoil openings decorated with cauac monster mouths. Each Pauahtun holds up a dish with a different offering. The surface of the altar is the round disk of the world with its quadrilateral nature established by the symbols carved on its sides. Offerings placed above the Pauahtuns would be symbolically offered to those locations.

10. Stelae and altars share another characteristic with idols and offering dishes: they are all often ritually killed. The Maya deliberately smashed these objects, defaced them, or drilled a hole in them. For example, Tikal Stela 31 (circa A.D. 450) was removed from its unknown original location and re-erected inside of Structure 33-2nd sometime during the eighth century (Coe 1976). Prior to the building of a new temple on top of this structure, the stela was burnt and shattered and the numerous incense burners surrounding the stela were smashed. The room was then filled in. As long as an idol existed, the Maya may have believed that the supernatural expected to receive offerings there. The destruction of the idol was, therefore, not necessarily an act of rejection or disregard but may have simply been a means of ending the idol's life. Many of the stelae have only the nose defaced. In Zinacantan the soul is thought to be able to sit on the tip of the nose. If this was true during the Classic period, the destruction of the nose after the death of the ruler might prevent his soul from returning to the image.

CHAPTER 6. THE RULING ELITE

1. The descriptions of these caves vary. In San Miguel Acatan the animal counterparts are said to live in "tiny houses situated in large rocks high up on mountain sides" (Siegel 1941:70). In Zinacantan the animal counterparts are in corrals next to the ancestors' house in the senior cave (Vogt 1969).

2. For example, the Tzotzil of Chenalho have a benevolent deity called Manohel-Tohel who led humans out of the caves and provided them with their soul and body (Guiteras 1961). The Chorti wind deities are said to "blow the first breath into newborn children, without which the latter would die, and they reclaim the breath at death" (Wisdom 1940:397).

3. The concept of the animal counterpart appears in classifications of animals. The Tzeltal word for animal is *canbalam* "serpent jaguar" (Hunn 1977). This term employs the two strongest animal counterparts: the lightning/serpent and the jaguar.

4. In an interesting story from Amatenango the ancestors were said to live in a cave on a nearby mountain (Nash 1970). When a young boy entered the cave and did not find them, their house, or their possessions, the consensus of the village was not that they did not exist but that they had moved to a new cave.

5. The exception is All Souls' Day, when they return to communicate with their living relatives.

6. In Pinola the sacred cave is said to be the seat of the spiritual government (Hermitte 1964:46–47). A secretary, policemen, and a judge live in this cave and assist the ancestors and important ritual specialists in deciding the destiny of their subjects.

7. In the seventeenth century Núñez de la Vega noted that the identity of a person's animal counterpart was assigned by a ritual specialist, who determined this according to the day on which the individual was born (Blom and La Farge 1927:369). The ancient almanacs that contained this information were produced, maintained, and interpreted by the ritual specialists, who thus controlled a powerful tool for social management and authority.

8. The function of the *ik* "wind" sign is in dispute (Stuart, cited in Schele 1992:154).

9. Grube and Nahm (cited in Schele 1992:44) have argued that the *ahau* sign is used outside of the day name contexts as a sign for flower. The association of the day sign Ahau with flower is well attested (Thompson 1950; Kelley 1976).

Evidence for their interpretation is found in the head variants used for the number three, the number thirteen, and the patron of Mac. These variants all represent a youthful head wearing the headdress of the so-called Waterlily Serpent. This headdress is composed of a waterlily pad and blossom. Often a fish nibbles at the blossom, just as fish nibble on real waterlily blossoms that bloom underwater. Although this flower is stylized into a simple circular element in most examples, it is clearly a flower on Bonampak Panel A (this same stylized flower sign appears in other contexts such as the Palenque House E facade). On Dresden page 9b the sign used for the number three is composed of T345 and the *ahau* sign in a fringed cartouche. This mutual substitution of the flower of the Waterlily Serpent and the *ahau* sign is convincing evidence that the *ahau* sign represents a flower.

10. This interpretation also gives us insight into why the Maya offered flower blossoms to their deities; they were symbolic souls. It is not surprising that many Mesoamerican descriptions of "heaven" refer to it as a place filled with flowers.

11. In the Ixil area both a jaguar and a serpent are said to guarded the cave (Colby and Colby 1981:175).

12. Seibal uses the Three Stones of the ancestral couple's cave as the main sign of its emblem glyph. The jaguar *way* has a waterlily on its forehead, perhaps a reference to his relationship with these ancestral sea deities.

13. In the Yaxchilan inscriptions the *way* of Lady Great Skull is said to be *kaanal chak bay kan* (Houston and Stuart 1989:7). We have seen that lightning can be represented by a serpent.

In some cases, it is difficult to ascertain the role of the serpent or even to identify the actor in a scene. Yaxchilan Lintel 25 is a prime example. This scene illustrates a woman kneeling before a serpent. A male actor dressed in war regalia emerges from its mouth. Following a suggestion by Peter Furst, several authors have characterized this serpent and many others like it as visions resulting from bloodletting. *Vision serpent* has become the standard term used to describe these supernaturals, but it is an inaccurate and misleading label that should be discarded.

The text begins in the upper right corner with a date that we know from other texts to be the accession of Shield Jaguar. This sentence, which relates a fish-in-hand event by Shield Jaguar, moves across the top of the lintel and down the left side. By reading the text, the viewer is brought to the serpent and the male actor. Based on this framing device, I concluded that this actor was Shield Jaguar (Bassie-Sweet 1991:147).

The remainder of the text is divided into two blocks that I interpreted as a continuous phrase. By reading this caption text the eye is drawn to the kneeling woman. Her personal name (Lady Xoc) appears at I1. The phrase ends with a place name "the center of the water shrine, Yaxchilan emblem glyph place (split sky)," which rests on the body of the serpent (I3). I interpret this place name to be the Yaxchilan senior ancestral cave (see below).

Schele and Freidel (1990) see these blocks as separate sentences that identify each of the actors. Because the second glyph in the upper text includes a glyph that in other contexts appears to relate to the house of the founding ancestor, they identify the male actor as the first ruler in the Yaxchilan dynasty. Until the finer decipherments of the text are made, we are left with two possibilities for the male actor: Shield Jaguar and the founding ancestor.

Given these two possible identifications, we can speculate on what the serpent represents: a human emerging from a cave passageway; a soul in the form of a human body emerging from a cave passageway; a soul in the form of a human body being enclosed by its serpent animal counterpart; or a human and his serpent animal counterpart. At this point we can only speculate.

14. Modern descriptions of the soul's passage to the supernatural world often involve a journey down a road and across a river or body of water. In some cases the soul arrives at a crossroads and must make a choice that will lead to a good location or one of hardship. The road to this final destination is the cave passage. Cave passages often branch into two roads and many contain a river or body of water.

15. One of the more interesting examples of the multivocal nature of symbols is found on the Tablet of the Cross world tree. As a representation of the crossroads at the north midpoint, the horizontal branches of this tree represent the north side of the world. A double-headed serpent is draped in the branches, suggesting it represents the path of the sun on summer solstice. The ends of the branches terminate in stylized flowers that have the form of a serpent's head. In the context of the world model, these flower serpents mark the summer solstice rise and set points, which can also be illustrated as serpent/cave passageways. In a comparison with the Xiu tree, these serpent flowers also represent the souls of the ruling elite.

16. At Seibal there are three prominent elevations of land joined by causeways: Group A (north), Group D (east), and the plaza of the round structure (south). Norman Hammond (personal communication, 1990) has suggested that the three stones sign may refer to the three hills of Seibal. This may be why this particular ancestral name was chosen. The concept of naming three elevations of land as the three hearth stones occurs at Zinacantan, where the ancestral mountain and the two nearby peaks are called the Three Hearth Stones (Vogt 1969:378; Hunt 1977:159).

17. Yaxha is situated beside a lake of blue-green water. Although the name describes the lake, the lake itself is a representation of the great sea. In the Lacandon area the name of the sacred cave is the same as that of the adjacent lake.

18. For example, on Yaxchilan Stela 4 the location symbol is composed of the head variant of the seat sign with the Yaxchilan split-sky sign infixed in its head. On Yaxha Stela 3 the location symbol is composed of the Yaxha sign followed by the sky seat sign (see fig. 39b).

19. There is a place name at Tikal that is composed of a *yax* "first" sign and the main sign of the Tikal emblem glyph. This compound is followed by or conflated with a variant of the seat sign. On Stela 1 (circa 9.1.0.0.0) the *Yax* Tikal Seat Place forms part of the zoomorph on which the ruler stands. Like the cauac monster zoomorphs, this indicates the location of the event. It also appears in the text as the place name of the event. The *Yax* Tikal Seat Place is also the location of the illustrated action on Stela 39. There it is attached to the lower register on which the ruler stands. In this example a sky sign also appears in the compound. The text of Stela 39 states that the event happened at the *Yax* Tikal Sky Seat Place.

Emblem glyphs are also used in place names in conjunction with a sign that represents a ballcourt. The two mythological ballcourts of the *Popol Vuh* were located at the horizon at the cave entrances to the supernatural world. In regard to the world model, these ballcourts were at the east and west midpoints. The *Popol Vuh* and the imagery associated with ballcourts suggest that the ballcourts found at Maya sites also replicate one of the mythological mountain locations. The emblem glyph appears in the name of certain ballcourts, specifying that they represented the ballcourt of the mythological mountain that was also the location of the ancestral cave.

20. This woman does not appear in other inscriptions, so her identity is uncertain.

21. The Tikal emblem glyph is used as a location indicator on a censer idol found in a private collection (Berlo 1980:347). The censer shows an actor sitting on a pillow labeled with the Tikal emblem glyph. I would interpret such an actor as an ancestor sitting on his bench at the Tikal ancestral cave.

22. The *yax* prefix in this sign may indicate an association with the ancestral sea deities. Another possibility given the diffusion of its members to other settlements in the Peten is that the *yax* refers to the first Tikal ancestral cave.

23. The choice for burial sites was not necessarily dictated by the direction of the ancestral cave; other factors seem to enter into the equation. For example, they chose to bury Ruler A on the east side of the main plaza in a replication of the eastern mountain.

24. There are some references to lords at Dos Pilas who seem to predate Ruler 1. It is possible that the kinship ties were between one of these individuals and some member of the ruling Tikal lineage.

25. This text is on Miscel. Bone 28, Burial 116. The death dates of six individuals are recorded on this bone. Their relationship to one another is unknown. There is Classic and Postclassic evidence that the family and foreign elite often sent personal articles to be placed in the ruler's tomb. Articles were sent by both ally and foe. In the brief number of texts that refer to both the death and burial of a ruler, the time lapse is about three days, so there would be a time element involved for rulers who died suddenly.

26. Stuart and Houston (in press) read this cross-hatched sign as *ha* "water" rather than *naab* "sea."

27. On Dos Pilas Stela 15 Ruler 2 (Shield God K) stands on a band of *cab* and *cauac* elements, indicating his location is a symbolic horizon location. Below is a location symbol composed of a full figure *k'inich* prefixed to a zoomorphic head with a waterlily infix. A captive sprawls below. The ruler is decorated with waterlily pads and blossoms, and a heron stands to his left. The main text begins with a series of three events on the 9.14.10.0.0 Period Ending. The first event is Ruler 2's hand-scattering at an *ik* water shrine. The next event introduces a new subject, an individual called Smoking GI. He performed a *nawah* event at the center of the Seibal ancestral cave (the Three Stones Place), which is also said to be a seat. This action is followed by the erection of a world tree again by Smoking GI but at a third location, the *K'inich* Mountain of Aguateca. Four months later Ruler 2 set up a *k'inich* stone idol and danced at the Dragon Water Place. By reading this last action, the viewer is brought to the image that illustrates Ruler 2 on this occasion. The dwarf that often accompanies dancers is to his right. In the band of *cab* and *cauac* signs on which the ruler stands is a small inscription that backs up the timeframe 227 days to a star/shell event.

The meaning of the Stela 15 narrative is uncertain. The 9.14.10.0.0 Period Ending required actions by Smoking GI at other locations. He may have carried out part of the Period Ending ritual circuit for Dos Pilas, or more likely he carried out or participated in the Period Ending event for another community for which Ruler 2 was responsible. We do know that Ruler 2's role was not limited to Dos Pilas; he was the overlord of the Arroyo de Piedras ahau and performed some event at Tamarindito. Ruler 2's mother was from Itzan and he was married to an Arroyo de Piedras woman.

28. Naj Tunich has become a ceremonial location for Kekchi Indians who recently moved into the area (Brady and Brady n.d.).

CHAPTER 7. SYMBOLS OF POWER

1. Another location for accession rituals is mentioned on the Palenque Tablet of the 96 Glyphs, which begins with the 9.11.0.0.0 Period Ending by Pacal and refers to the preparation of a ritual space. The compound used to describe this space has been read in a number of ways, the most convincing being "white great house" (Hopkins 1989). The narrative continues with the accessions of Kan Xul, Chaacal, and Kuk at this location.

A common interpretation is that the White Great House refers to House E of the Palace. This is based on the fact that the background color of House E is white and a bench with accession information on it was found there. This is also the location of the Oval Palace Tablet, which some researchers believe is an accession tablet. I have interpreted the White Great House compound as a reference to a cave location (Bassie-Sweet 1991:116). Although I prefer the natural cave interpretation, I acknowledge the possibility that it may refer to the seating of the lord at the center of the community, with House E being a likely candidate.

House E is one of the earliest in the Palace complex and predates the ritual dedication mentioned on the Tablet of the 96 Glyphs. If the White Great House is House E, the preparation must refer to a renovation of it that required the Maya to purify it ritually again.

2. During precolumbian rituals, bloodletting was performed, and Furst (1976) has suggested that the physical jolts of such acts induced visions. Although I think this is possible, it should be kept in mind that the act of bloodletting had many purposes. The use of hallucinogenic drugs and alcohol to attain altered states has also been noted.

3. In this scene his parents sit on either side preparing to give him the objects in their hands. The text that refers to this event is still poorly understood. Although some of the proposed decipherments such as "he entered the sleeping place of the 9 Chacs" and "he stepped onto the mountain" have been interpreted to represent a temple ritual, they can just as easily be related to a natural cave.

4. It is interesting that this is the only Yaxchilan lintel where neither actor stands in the dominant full frontal pose.

5. The spiritual power of lightning is also related to divination practices, where the tool used to prognosticate is called "the lightning in the blood" (Tedlock 1982).

6. Several of the piers of Palenque House A illustrate a lord dressed in the headdress. Each lord holds a God K lightning staff. The lord is flanked by a male and female, similar to the composition of the Tablet of the Slaves and Palace Tablet. Some authors have interpreted these scenes as accession rituals, but their parallel form with other Palenque pre-accession rituals leads me to believe they too are pre-accession ceremonies.

7. The Palace Tablet has always been a difficult narrative to understand for a number of reasons. The story begins with the caption text and refers to the birth of a subject on 1 Ahau 3 Uayeb (fig. 65). The nominal glyph is composed of the Jester God head with a number three and yo prefix (this subject was nicknamed Xoc). The timeframe then moves forward by a distance number to a new date of 8 Ahau 18 Xul (some fifty-seven years later), relates a "placing" event, and again names the 3 Yo Jester God. Neither Calendar Round date is directly tied to a Long Count position.

The main text continues the story with the Long Count birthdate of Kan Xul (circa A.D. 644) and states that he is the child of Pacal and Lady Ahpo Hel. It proceeds through a series of events climaxing with Kan Xul's accession in A.D. 702. These include a pre-accession event involving the Palenque Triad when Kan Xul was seven years old. The main text ends with still undeciphered events in A.D. 720 that make reference to both

Kan Xul and the 3 Yo Jester God. Because it was assumed that the 3 Yo Jester God nominal glyph named a contemporary historical person, the birthdate of the caption text was placed at the closest Long Count position (A.D. 650) to the birth of Kan Xul. This placed the subsequent 3 Yo Jester God event in A.D. 706, some four years after the accession of Kan Xul and fourteen years before the final event of the main text.

These assigned Long Count positions for the caption text can now be questioned because it is quite likely that the subject of the caption text birth and "placing" event was not a historical person (Josserand, Hopkins, and Bassie-Sweet n.d.). The "placing" event is a positional verb that in other contexts refers to the placing of an object. This is often followed by the name of the object, and in the Palace Tablet example it is followed by the phrase "its name is 3 Yo Jester God." This event frames the central actor and explains the action of the central actor receiving GIII's Jester God headdress. It is likely that 3 Yo Jester God is the name of the headdress.

The image shows us who gave the headdress and who received it, but the caption text does not tell who these men are or who the flanking female is. The main text does not tell us what is happening in the image, but we can infer from it that the central actor is the protagonist of the story, Kan Xul, and the flanking actors are his parents.

When a story introduces a new Calendar Round date that is not directly tied to a Long Count position by a Distance Number or other such device, we assume that the timeframe of the story is either moving forward or backward to the next occurrence of that date. Applying this simple, well-established assumption to the Palace Tablet means that the last Calendar Round date of the caption text must be the first occurrence of 8 Ahau 18 Xul before or after Kan Xul's birth. As Kan Xul is illustrated in the scene, it is quite certain that it is the later at 9.11.1.13.0, when Kan Xul is nine years old. This date is 220 days after the pre-accession event of his older brother, which is pictured on the Temple 14 Tablet.

The caption text is divided into two blocks of text that frame the central actor. The sentence referring to the placing of the 3 Yo Jester God begins at the bottom of the first block (S5), continues at T1, and concludes at the bottom of the second row (U6). In order to read this sentence, the reader is drawn across the body of the central actor. It has been argued that this kind of framing device indicates to the reader which event of the story is being illustrated (Bassie-Sweet 1991:38–76).

The interpretation that the 3 Yo Jester God headdress referred to a human subject led many researchers to believe that Palenque experienced some kind of upheaval and that Xoc was an interim ruler of some kind. Much of this speculation can now be set aside because there was no Xoc.

8. In place of the personified flint, there is a supernatural without the *cauac* elements or eccentric flint shape. It has been assumed that this supernatural is equivalent to the personified flint.

9. On Lintel 3 of Tikal Temple I the text states that an undeciphered action was conducted on the *tok pacal* of Jaguar Paw of Site Q. In the inscriptions of Tortugero the flint shield plays an important role in "star over *cab*" events associated with war. It is likely that the capture of a lord involved confiscating these symbols (John Carlson, personal communication, 1992).

10. It is interesting that the shield has the form of the quadrilateral world with the corners marked with circles.

11. Although the standing youth does not appear in any of the other Piedras Negras monuments, it has been proposed that he was a relative of the Piedras Negras ruler (Schele and Miller 1986:149). It has been suggested that the scene is "an initiation ritual in which

royal youths for the first time donned battle dress or engaged in bloodletting" (Schele and Miller 1986:149). Another interpretation is that the scene is the initiation of the standing youth with the kneeling youths acting as representatives of their lords (Schele and Mathews 1991:231). Given that it is unlikely that the Piedras Negras ruler would initiate young Lancanha, Bonampak, and Yaxchilan lords, the latter interpretation seems more probable. I would qualify it by saying that the kneeling youths might be attending a ceremony in which the standing youth is joining their ranks. There are also many other interpretations that are just as likely.

12. I follow Houston's (1993) designations of these monuments.

APPENDIX. DIRECTIONAL TERMS

1. Stuart (cited in Schele 1992) has demonstrated a phonetic value of *och k'in* for the west glyph.

2. In Classic Period texts two different glyphs were used to express the concept of north: *na* or *nal* and *xaman*. The *na* sign has a wide variety of meanings, such as house, first, mother, contemplate, understand, or divine. The main sign of the *xaman* sign is composed of a serpent segment, which I interpret as a reference to the serpent/sky cave passage associated with the north midpoint (Bassie-Sweet 1991:173). Yucatec *nohol* "south" has been suggested as a reading for the south glyph. Although there are no substitution patterns or phonetic evidence to substantiate this, it is a likely reading given the survival of the other directional terms and their direct relationship to directional glyphs.

As noted, the Paddler deities location called *Na Ho Chan* (Na Five Sky) is described as a mountain of the *xaman* "north" (see chapter 4). The *na* "north, first, house" in this expression may refer to the north, to the fact that it is the house of the Paddlers, or to the fact that the first T528 stone was placed there. When epigraphers phonetically decipher a glyph, it is often difficult to choose from the many meanings of a word. I suggest that many of the seemingly divergent meanings are actually intrinsically related.

3. This arrangement is found in the Madrid cosmogram. Although most native maps place east at the top of the page, the Madrid has east at the bottom and west at the top. The viewer holding the page is situated in the position of the rising sun with north on his or her right hand and south on the left.

4. A page illustrating a katun wheel in the *Book of Chilam Balam of Chumayel* has its corners marked with similar terms: *ti likin uaye* "to east here" (southeast) and *ti nohol uaye* "to south here" (southwest) (Gordon 1913:72).

5. The *ahau* sign is usually composed of T584 and T687a signs with phonetic complements to indicate a reading of ahau. There are examples of the *k'inich ahau* title that use just the kin sign with T584 and T687a prefixes. It is therefore likely that the east compound is read *k'inich ahau*.

6. Copan Stela 13 and its altar may shed some light on the Rio Azul compounds. These monuments are located in the hills to the east of the site. It is interesting that the text on the Stela 13 altar runs around its perimeter. In order to read the text, the viewer is led on a circuit around the altar just as the preparation of ritual space requires a circuit. The text of the altar begins with an action that has been characterized as a dedication event. I believe this refers to the establishment of an ordered space or object (i.e., the ritual circuit around the house that makes it a safe place to live or the establishment of a ritual space around an object such as an idol). It is followed by the name of the object or space that has been put in order: "7 skeletal head, animal head, *k'inich ahau*, east sky seat." As discussed in chapter 2, the east sky seat refers to the

east midpoint on the side of the quadrilateral world where the eastern guardian deities lived and to those locations in the local landscape that represent that sacred space. The "7 skeletal head, animal head, *k'inich ahau*" phrase appears on Stela A, where it refers to a *lacam tun* "the tree/standard of the stone." I interpret this object to be the world tree set up at the midpoint during the Period Ending ceremonies, which in turn was the replication of the world tree set up by the deities following the last round of world destruction and re-creation. The Copan and Rio Azul animal heads are similar. It may be that the Rio Azul phrases are the proper names for the idols, seats, or tree/standards on the sides of the world.

REFERENCES

Adams, Richard
  1986 Río Azul. *National Geographic* 169(4):420–61.
Andrews, E. Wyllis, IV
  1943 *The archaeology of southwestern Campeche.* Contribution to American Anthropology and History, no. 40. Washington, D.C.: Carnegie Institution.
  1970 *Balankanche, throne of the jaguar priest.* Middle American Research Series, Pub. 32. New Orleans: Tulane University.
Ashmore, Wendy
  1989 Construction and cosmology: Politics and ideology in lowland Maya settlement patterns. In *Word and image in Maya culture,* ed. William Hanks and Don Rice, 272–86. Salt Lake City: University of Utah Press.
  1991 Site-planning principles and concepts of directionality among the ancient Maya. *Latin American Antiquity* 2(3):199–226.
Aveni, Anthony
  1980 *Skywatchers of ancient Mexico.* Austin: University of Texas Press.
  1986 The real Venus-Kukulcan in the Maya inscriptions and alignments. In *Sixth Palenque round table, 1986,* ed. Merle Greene Robertson and Virginia Fields, 309–21. Norman: University of Oklahoma Press.
Bardawil, Lawrence
  1976 The Principal Bird Deity in Maya art: an iconographic study of form and meaning. In *The art, iconography, and dynastic history of Palenque: Part III,* ed. Merle Greene Robertson, 181–94. Pebble Beach, Calif.: Pre-Columbian Art Research, Robertson Louis Stevenson School.
Bassie-Sweet, Karen
  1987 Illustrated stories: The relationship between text and image. Paper presented at the 86th annual meeting of the American Anthropological Association, Chicago.

1991   *From the mouth of the dark cave: Commemorative sculpture of the Late Classic Maya.* Norman: University of Oklahoma Press.

Baudez, Claude
1985   The sun kings of Copan and Quirigua. In *Fifth Palenque round table, 1983,* vol. 7, ed. Merle Greene Robertson and Virginia Field, 29–27. San Francisco: Precolumbian Art Research Institute.

Berlin, Brent, Dennis Breedlove, and Peter Raven
1974   *Principles of Tzeltal plant classification.* New York: Academic Press.

Berlin, Heinrich
1958   El glifo emblema en las inscripciones mayas. *Journal de la Société des Américanistes* 47:11–19.
1959   Glifos nominales en el sacrfago de Palenque. *Humanidades* 2(10):1–8.

Berlin, Heinrich, and David Kelley
1961   *The 819 day count and color-direction symbolism among the Classic Maya.* Middle American Research Series, Pub. 26, 9–20. New Orleans: Tulane University.

Berlo, Janet
1980   Teotihuacan art abroad. Ph.D. diss. Yale University.

Blom, Frans, and Oliver La Farge
1927   *Tribes and temples.* Middle American Research Series, Pubs. 1–2. New Orleans: Tulane University.

Brady, James
1991   The Petexbatun regional cave survey: Ritual and sacred geography. Paper presented at the 47th International Congress of the Americanists, New Orleans.
n.d.   The Gruta de Jobonche: An analysis of speleothem rock art. Unpublished paper in possession of author.

Brady, James, and Sandra Brady
n.d.   The rebirth of an ancient Maya pilgrimage center. Unpublished paper in possession of author.

Brady, James, and George Veni
1992   Man-made and pseudo-karst caves: The implications of subsurface features within Maya centers. *Geoarchaeology: An International Journal* 7(2):149–67.

Brady, James, George Veni, Andrea Stone, and Allan Cobb
1992   Explorations in the new branch of Naj Tunich: Implications for interpretation. *Mexicon* 14(4):74–81.

Bricker, Victoria
1988   A phonetic glyph for zenith: Reply to Closs. *American Antiquity* 53:352.

Bruce, Robert
1975   *Lacandon dream symbolism.* Mexico City: Ediciones Euroamericanas Klaus Thiele.

Butlar, Mary
1934   A note on Maya cave burials. *American Anthropologist* 36:223–25.

Bunzel, Ruth
1952   *Chichicastenango: A Guatemalan village.* Seattle: University of Washington Press.

Calnek, Edward
1988   *Highland Chiapas before the Spanish conquest.* New World Archaeological Foundation, vol. 55. Provo: Brigham Young University.

Carlsen, Ruth, and Francis Eachus
　　1977　The Kekchi spirit world. In *Cognitive studies of southern Mesoamerica*, ed.
　　　　　Helen Neuenswander and Dean Arnold, 36–63. Dallas: Summer Institute of
　　　　　Linguistics Museum of Anthropology.
Carlson, John
　　1981　A geomantic model for the interpretation of Mesoamerican sites: An essay
　　　　　in cross-cultural comparison. In *Mesoamerican sites and world views*, ed.
　　　　　Elizabeth Benson, 143–211. Washington, D.C.: Dumbarton Oaks.
Carmack, Robert
　　1981　*The Quiché Maya of Utatlán*. Norman: University of Oklahoma Press.
Carter, William
　　1969　*New lands and old traditions: Kekchi cultivators in the Guatemalan lowlands*.
　　　　　Jacksonville: University of Florida Press.
Ciaramella, Mary
　　in press　The weavers in the codices. In *Research Reports on Ancient Maya Writing*.
　　　　　Washington, D.C.: Center for Maya Research.
Clancy, Flora
　　1986　Text and image in the tablets of the Cross Group at Palenque. *RES* 11:17–32.
Coe, Michael
　　1973　*The Maya scribe and his world*. New York: Grolier Club.
　　1978　*Lords of the underworld*. Princeton: Princeton University Press.
　　1982　*Old gods and young heroes*. Jerusalem: Israel Museum.
Coe, William
　　1976　*Tikal: A handbook of the ancient Maya ruins*. Philadelphia: University
　　　　　Museum.
Coggins, Clemency
　　1980　The shape of time: Some political implications of a four-part figure. *American
　　　　　Antiquity* 45:727–39.
Colby, Benjamin, and Lore Colby
　　1981　*The Daykeeper: The life and discourse of an Ixil diviner*. Cambridge, Mass.:
　　　　　Harvard University Press.
Cruz, Ausencio, Kathryn Josserand, and Nicholas Hopkins
　　1980　The cave of Don Juan. In *The third Palenque round table, 1978: Part II*, vol.
　　　　　5, ed. Merle Greene Robertson, 116–23. Austin: University of Texas Press.
Deal, Michael
　　1988　Recognition of ritual pottery in residential units: An ethnoarchaeological model
　　　　　of the Maya family altar. In *Papers of the New World Archaeological Founda-
　　　　　tion, no. 56*, ed. Thomas A. Lee, Jr., and Brian Hayden, 61–90. Provo: Brigham
　　　　　Young University.
Demarest, Arthur
　　1993　Violent saga of a Maya kingdom. *National Geographic* 183(2):95–111.
Douglas, Bill Gray
　　1969　Illness and curing in Santiago Atitlan, a Tzutujil-Maya community. Ph.D. diss.
　　　　　Stanford University.
Edmonson, Munro
　　1971　*The book of counsel: The Popol Vuh of the Quiche Maya of Guatemala*. Middle
　　　　　American Research Institute, no. 35. New Orleans: Tulane University.
Eliade, Mircea
　　1958　*Patterns in comparative religion*. London: Sheed and Ward.

Fabrega, Horacio, and Daniel Silver
1973   *Illness and shamanistic curing in Zinacantan.* Stanford: Stanford University Press.

Fash, Barbara, William Fash, Sheree Lane, Rudy Larios, Linda Schele, Jeffrey Stomper, and David Stuart
1992   Investigations of a Classic Maya council house at Copan, Honduras. *Journal of Field Archaeology* 19(4):419–42.

Forstemann, Ernst
1901   Commentary on the Maya manuscript in the Royal Public Library of Dresden. *Papers of the Peabody Museum of American Archaeology and Ethnology, Harvard University* 4(2):42–266. Cambridge, Mass.: Peabody Museum.

Fought, John
1972   *Chorti (Mayan) texts.* Philadelphia: University of Pennsylvania Press.

Fox, James, and John Justeson
1984   Polyvalence in Mayan hieroglyphic writing. In *Phoneticism in Mayan hieroglyphic writing*, ed. John Justeson and Lyle Campbell, 17–76. Institute for Mesoamerican Studies, Pub. 9. Albany: State University of New York at Albany.

Furst, Peter
1976   Fertility, vision quest and auto-sacrifice: Some thoughts on ritual bloodletting among the Maya. In *The art, iconography, and dynastic history of Palenque: Part III*, ed. Merle Greene Robertson, 181–94. Pebble Beach, Calif.: Pre-Columbian Art Research, Robertson Louis Stevenson School.

Girard, Rafael
1962   *Los Mayas eternos.* Mexico City: Antigua Librería Robredo.

Gordon, George
1898   Caverns of Copan, Honduras. *Memoirs of the Peabody Museum of American Archaeology and Ethnology* 1:137–48. Cambridge, Mass.: Peabody Museum.
1913   *The book of Chilam Balam of Chumayel.* Anthropological Publications, vol. 5. Philadelphia: University of Pennsylvania, University Museum.

Gossen, Gary
1974   *Chamulas in the world of the sun.* Cambridge: Harvard University Press.

Grube, Nikolai
1989   A glyph for *way*: Sorcery, nagual, transformation. Unpublished paper in possession of author.
1992   Classic Maya dance. *Ancient Mesoamerica* 3:201–18.

Grube, Nikolai, and Linda Schele
1991   *Tzuk in the Classic Maya inscriptions.* Texas Notes on Precolumbian Art, Writing and Culture 14. Austin: University of Texas at Austin.

Grube, Nikolai, and David Stuart
1987   *Observations on T110 as the syllable* ko. Research Reports on Ancient Maya Writing, no. 8. Washington, D.C.: Center for Maya Research.

Guiteras, Calixta
1961   *Perils of the soul.* Glencoe, N.Y.: Free Press.

Hanks, William
1984   Sanctification, structure, and experience in a Yucatec ritual event. *Journal of American Folklore* 97(384):131–66.

Hellmuth, Nicholas
1987   The surface of the underwaterworld. Ph.D. diss. Karl-Franzens-Universitt. Culver City: Foundations for Latin American Anthropological Research.

Hermitte, Esther
   1964   Supernatural power and social control in a modern Maya village. Ph.D. diss.,
          University of Chicago.
Heyden, Doris
   1981   Caves, gods, and myths: World-view and planning in Teotihuacan. In *Meso-
          american sites and world-views*, ed. Elizabeth Benson, 1–35. Washington, D.C.:
          Dumbarton Oaks.
Hopkins, Nicholas
   1989   A Classic Cholan reading of the 96 glyphs. Paper presented at the Seventh
          Mesa Redonda de Palenque.
Houston, Stephen
   1983   A reading of the flint-shield glyph. In *Contributions to Maya hieroglyphic
          decipherment I*, ed. Stephen Houston. New Haven: HRAFlex Books.
   1987   The inscriptions and monumental art of Dos Pilas, Guatemala: A study of
          Classic Maya history and politics. Ph.D. diss. Yale University.
   1993   *Hieroglyphs and history at Dos Pilas: Dynastic politics of the Classic Maya.*
          Austin: University of Austin.
Houston, Stephen, and David Stuart
   1989   *The* way *glyph: Evidence for co-essences among the Classic Maya.* Research
          Reports on Ancient Maya Writing, no. 30. Washington, D.C.: Center for Maya
          Research.
Hunn, Eugene
   1977   *Tzeltal folk zoology.* New York: Academic Press.
Hunt, Eva
   1977   *The transformation of the hummingbird.* Ithaca and London: Cornell University
          Press.
Josserand, J. Kathryn
   1991   The narrative structure of hieroglyphic texts at Palenque. In *Sixth Palenque
          round table, 1986*, vol. 8, ed. Merle Greene Robertson and Virginia Fields,
          12–31. Norman: University of Oklahoma Press.
Josserand, J. Kathryn, and Nicholas Hopkins
   1991   *A handbook of Classic Maya inscriptions, Part I: The western lowlands.* Final
          performance report for the National Endowment for the Humanities. Grant
          RT-21090-89.
Josserand, J. Kathryn, Nicholas Hopkins, and Karen Bassie-Sweet
   n.d.   The Palenque Palace Tablet. Paper in possession of the author.
Justeson, John, and Peter Mathews
   1983   The seating of the *tun*: Further evidence concerning a late Pre-Classic lowland
          Maya stela cult. *American Antiquity* 48:586–93.
Karasik, Carol
   1988   *Mayan tales and dreams from Zinacantan.* Collected and translated by Robert
          Laughlin; edited by Carol Karasik. Washington, D.C.: Smithsonian Institute Press.
Kelley, David
   1976   *Deciphering the Maya script.* Austin: University of Texas Press.
Kerr, Justin
   1989   *The Maya vase book.* Vol. 1. New York: Kerr Associates.
Korelstein, Audrey
   n.d.   The ethnoarchaeologist as detective: The case of the Quetzal mountain.
          Unpublished manuscript.

Kubler, George
  1969   *Studies in Classic Maya iconography.* Memoirs of the Connecticut Academy
         of Arts and Sciences, vol. 18. New Haven: Connecticut Academy of Arts and
         Sciences.
  1972   The paired attendants of the temple tablets at Palenque. In *Religión en Meso-
         américa 42*, 317–28. Mexico City: XII Mesa Redonda, Sociedad Mexicana de
         Antropología.
La Farge, Oliver
  1947   *Santa Eulalia.* Chicago: University of Chicago Press.
La Farge, Oliver, and Douglas Byers
  1931   *The Yearbearer's people.* Middle American Research Series, Pub. 3. New
         Orleans: Tulane University.
Laughlin, Robert
  1975   *The great Tzotzil dictionary of San Lorenzo Zinacantan.* Smithsonian
         Contributions to Anthropology, vol. 19. Washington, D.C.: Smithsonian
         Institute Press.
  1977   *Of cabbages and kings.* Smithsonian Contributions to Anthropology, vol. 23.
         Washington, D.C.: Smithsonian Institute Press.
Looper, Matthew, and Linda Schele
  1991   *A war at Palenque during the reign of Ah-K'an.* Texas Notes on Precolumbian
         Art, Writing and Culture, no. 25. Austin: University of Texas.
Lounsbury, Floyd
  1974   The inscription of the sarcophagus lid at Palenque. In *Primera mesa redonda
         de Palenque, Part II*, ed. Merle Greene Robertson, 5–19. Pebble Beach, Calif.:
         Pre-Columbian Art Research Institute.
  1976   A rationale for the initial date of the Temple of the Cross at Palenque. In *The
         art, iconography, and dynastic history of Palenque: Part III*, ed. Merle Greene
         Robertson, 211–24. Pebble Beach, Calif.: Pre-Columbian Art Research, Robert
         Louis Stevenson School.
  1982   Astronomical knowledge and its uses at Bonampak, Mexico. In *Archaeoastronomy
         in the New World*, ed. A. F. Aveni, 143–68. New York: Cambridge University
         Press.
Love, Bruce
  1991   A text from the Dresden New Year pages. In *Sixth Palenque round table, 1986*,
         vol. 8, ed. Merle Greene Robertson and Virginia Fields, 293–302. Norman:
         University of Oklahoma Press.
MacLeod, Barbara
  1990   The God N/step set in the primary standard sequence. In *The Maya vase book*,
         ed. Justin Kerr, vol. 2, 331–47. New York: Kerr Associates.
MacLeod, Barbara, and Dennis Puleston
  1978   Pathways into darkness: The search for the road to Xibalba. In *Tercera mesa
         redonda de Palenque*, vol. 4, ed. Merle Greene Robertson and Donnan Call
         Jeffers, 71–77. Palenque: Pre-Columbian Research Center.
Macri, Martha
  1988   A descriptive grammar of Palenque Mayan. Ph.D. diss. University of California,
         Berkeley.
Maler, Teobert
  1901-3 *Researches in the Usumatsintla Valley.* Peabody Museum Memoirs, no. 2.
         Cambridge, Mass.: Peabody Museum.

Mathews, Peter, and Linda Schele
1974   Lords of Palenque—the glyphic evidence. In *Primera mesa redonda de Palenque, Part I,* vol. 1 ed. Merle Greene Robertson, 63–75. Pebble Beach, Calif.: Pre-Columbian Art Research, Robert Louis Stevenson School.

McArthur, Harry
1977   Releasing the dead: Ritual and motivation in Aguacatec dances. In *Cognitive studies of southern mesoamerica,* ed. Helen Neuenswander and Dean Arnold, 3–33. Dallas: Summer Institute of Linguistics Museum of Anthropology.

Mendelson, Michael
1959   Maximon: An iconographical introduction. *Man* 59:57–60.

Miles, Suzanna
1955   Sixteenth century Pokom-Maya. Ph.D. diss. Radcliffe College, Harvard University.

Nash, June
1970   *In the eyes of the ancestors.* New Haven: Yale University Press.

Navarrete, Carlos, and Eduardo Martnez
1977   *Exploraciones arqueológicas en la Cueva del los Andasolos, Chiapas.* Mexico City: Universidad Autónoma de Chiapas.

Oakes, Maude
1951   *Two crosses of Todos Santos.* New York: Pantheon.

Pendergast, David
1970   A. H. Anderson's excavations at Rio Frio Cave E, British Honduras (Belize). Royal Ontario Museum Art and Archaeology Occasional Paper 20. Toronto: Royal Ontario Museum.

Pohl, John, and Bruce Byland
1990   Mixtec landscape perception and archaeological settlement patterns. *Ancient Mesoamerica* 1(1990):113–31.

Proskouriakoff, Tatiana
1963   Historical data in the inscriptions of Yaxchilan, Part 2. *Estudios de Cultura Maya* 3:149–67.

Rands, Robert, Ronald Bishop, and Garman Harbottle
1978   Thematic and compositional variation in Palenque region incensarios. In *Tercera mesa redonda de Palenque,* vol. 4, ed. Merle Greene Robertson and Donnan Call Jeffers, 19–30. Palenque: Pre-Columbian Research Center.

Redfield, Robert, and Alfonso Villa Rojas
1934   *Chan Kom.* Washington, D.C.: Carnegie Institute.

Reents, Doris
1985   The Late Classic Maya Holmul style polychrome pottery. Ph.D. diss. University of Austin, Texas.

Ricketson, O. G.
1928   Astronomical observatories in the Maya area. *Geographical Review* 18:215–25.

Ringle, William
1988   *Of mice and monkeys: The value and meaning of T1016, the God C hieroglyph.* Research Reports on Ancient Maya Writing 18. Washington, D.C.: Center for Maya Research.

Rivard, Jean-Jacques
1971   *A hierophany at Chichen Itza.* Miscellaneous Series, no. 26. Museum of Anthropology. Greeley: University of Northern Colorado.

Robertson, Merle Greene
1991   *The sculpture of Palenque.* Vol. 4. Princeton: Princeton University Press.

Robicsek, Frances
1975   *A study in Maya art and history: The mat symbol.* New York: Museum of
        the American Indian, Heye Foundation.
Robicsek, Frances, and Donald Hales
1982   *Maya ceramics vases from the Classic Period: The November Collection.*
        Charlottesville: University Museum of Virginia Bayly Memorial Building.
Roys, Ralph
1931   *The ethno-botany of the Maya.* Middle American Research Series, Pub. 2. New
        Orleans: Tulane University.
1933   *The book of Chilam Balam of Chumayel.* Carnegie Institution of Washington,
        Pub. 523, Contribution 31. Washington, D.C.: Carnegie Institution.
1943   *The Indian background of colonial Yucatan.* Washington, D.C.: Carnegie
        Institution.
1965   *Ritual of the Bacabs.* Norman: University of Oklahoma Press.
Ruppert, Karl
1940   A special assemblage of Maya structures. In *The Maya and their neighbors:*
        Essays on Middle American anthropology, ed. C. L. Hay, R. Linton, S. Lothrop,
        H. Shapiro, and G. Vaillant, 221–30. New York: D. Appleton-Century Co.
Sandstrom, Alan
1991   *Corn is our blood.* Norman: University of Oklahoma Press.
Sapper, Carl
1897   *A trip to the highlands of Anahuac: Travels and studies of the year 1888–1895.*
        Brunswick: Friedrich Viewig and Son.
Schele, Linda
1976   Accession iconography of Chan Bahlum in the Group of the Cross at Palenque.
        In *The art, iconography and dynastic history of Palenque: Part III,* ed. Merle
        Greene Robertson, 9–34. Pebble Beach, Calif.: Pre-Columbian Research
        Institute.
1990   *End of expression at Copan and Palenque.* Copan Notes, no. 69. Austin:
        University of Texas.
1992   *Notebook for the Maya hieroglyphic writing workshop at Texas.* Austin:
        Institute of Latin American Studies, University of Texas.
Schele, Linda, and David Freidel
1990   *A forest of kings: The untold story of the ancient Maya.* New York: William
        Morrow.
Schele, Linda, and Nikolai Grube
1990   *The glyph for plaza or court.* Copan Notes, no. 86. Austin: University of Texas.
Schele, Linda, and Peter Mathews
1991   Royal visits and other intersite relationships. In *Classic Maya political history:*
        Hieroglyphic and archaeological evidence, ed. T. Patrick Culbert, 226–52. New
        York: Cambridge University Press.
Schele, Linda, Peter Mathews, and Floyd Lounsbury
1990   *Untying the headband.* Texas Notes on Precolumbian Art, Writing and Culture,
        no. 4. Austin: University of Texas.
Schele, Linda, and Mary Ellen Miller
1986   *Blood of kings.* Fort Worth: Kimbell Art Museum.
Schele, Linda, David Stuart, and Nikolai Grube
1989   *A commentary on the restoration and reading of the glyphic panels from*
        Temple 11. Copan Notes, no. 64. Austin: University of Texas.

Schellhas, Paul
  1904 *Representation of deities of the Maya manuscripts.* Papers of the Peabody
        Museum of American Archaeology and Ethnology, Harvard University, vol.
        4, no. 1. Cambridge, Mass.: Peabody Museum.
Siegel, Morris
  1941 Religion in western Guatemala: A product of acculturation. *American Anthro-
        pologist* 43(1):62–76.
Sosa, John
  1985 The Maya sky, the Maya world: A symbolic analysis of Yucatec Maya
        cosmology. Ph.D. diss. State University of New York at Albany.
  1989 Maya concepts of astonomical order. In *Symbol and meaning beyond the closed
        community,* ed. Gary Gossen, 185–96. Albany: State University of New York
        at Albany.
Strömsvik, Gustav
  1941 *Substela cache and stela foundation at Copan and Quirigua.* Contributions
        to American Antropology and History, vol. 7, no. 37. Washington, D.C.:
        Carnegie Institution.
Stuart, David
  1986 Paper presented at Blood of Kings symposium. Fort Worth, Texas.
  1987 *Ten phonetic syllables.* Research Reports on Ancient Maya Writing 14.
        Washington, D.C.: Center for Maya Research.
Stuart, David, and Stephen Houston
  in press *Classic Maya place names.* Washington, D.C.: Dumbarton Oaks.
Tate, Carolyn
  1986 The language of symbols in the ritual environment of Yaxchilan, Chiapas. Ph.D.
        diss., University of Texas at Austin.
  1992 *Yaxchilan: The Design of a Maya Ceremonial City.* Austin: University of Texas
        Press.
Taube, Karl
  1988a The ancient Yucatec New Year festival: The liminal period in Maya ritual
         and cosmology. Ph.D. diss. Yale University.
  1988b A prehispanic Maya katun wheel. *Journal of Anthropological Research*
         44(2):183–203.
  1989 The maize tamale in Classic Maya diet, epigraphy, and art. *American Antiquity*
        54(1):31–51.
  1992 *The major gods of ancient Yucatan.* Washington, D.C.: Dumbarton Oaks.
Tedlock, Barbara
  1982 *Time and the highland Maya.* Albuquerque: University of New Mexico Press.
  1993 The road of light: Theory and practice of Mayan skywatching. In *The sky
        in Mayan literature,* ed. Anthony Aveni, 18–42. Oxford: Oxford University
        Press.
Tedlock, Dennis
  1985 *Popol Vuh.* New York: Simon and Schuster.
Thomas, Cyrus
  1882 A study of the manuscript Troano. *Contributions to North American Ethnology*
        5:1–237. Washington, D.C.: U.S. Department of the Interior.
  1888 Aids to the study of the Maya codices. In *Sixth Annual Report of the Bureau
        of Ethnology (1884–1885),* 251–357. Washington, D.C.: U.S. Government
        Printing Office.

Thompson, J. Eric S.

1930   *Ethnology of the Mayas of southern and central British Honduras.* Anthropological Series, 17(1). Chicago: Field Museum of Natural History.

1934   *Sky bearers, colors and directions in Maya and Mexican religion.* Carnegie Institution of Washington, Pub. 436, Contribution 10. Washington, D.C.: Carnegie Institution.

1939   *The moon goddess in Middle America with notes on related deities.* Carnegie Institution of Washington, Pub. 436, Contribution 10. Washington, D.C.: Carnegie Institution.

1950   *Maya hieroglyphic writing: An introduction.* Carnegie Institution of Washington, Pub. 589. Washington, D.C.: Carnegie Institution.

1962   *A catalog of Maya hieroglyphs.* Norman: University of Oklahoma Press.

1970   *Maya history and religion.* Norman: University of Oklahoma Press.

1972   *A commentary on the Dresden Codex.* Memoirs of the American Philosophical Society 93. Philadelphia: American Philosophical Society.

1975   Introduction. In *The hill-caves of Yucatan,* by Henry C. Mercer, vii–xliv. Norman: University of Oklahoma Press.

Tozzer, Alfred

1907   *Comparative study of the Mayas and Lacandones.* Archaeological Institute of America. London: Macmillan and Co.

1941   *Landa's Relacin de las cosas de Yucatan: A translation.* Papers of the Peabody Museum of American Archaeology and Ethnology, Harvard University, vol. 18. Cambridge, Mass.: Peabody Museum.

Villa Rojas, Alfonso

1945   *The Maya of east central Quintana Roo.* Carnegie Institution of Washington, Pub. 599. Washington, D.C.: Carnegie Institution.

1947   Kinship and nagualism in a Tzeltal community, southeastern Mexico. *American Anthropologist* 49:578–87.

1988   Appendix. In *Time and reality in the thought of the Maya,* 113–59. Norman: University of Oklahoma Press.

Vogt, Evon

1969   *Zinacantan.* Cambridge, Mass.: Harvard University Press.

1976   *Tortillas for the gods: A symbolic analysis of Zinacanteco rituals.* Cambridge, Mass.: Harvard University Press.

Wagley, Charles

1941   *Economics of a Guatemalan village.* Memoir 58. Menasha: American Anthropological Association.

1949   *The social and religious life of a Guatemalan village.* Memoir 71. Menasha: American Anthropological Association.

Webster, David

1989   *The House of the Bacabs, Copan, Honduras.* Studies in Pre-columbian Art and Archaeology 29. Washington, D.C.: Dumbarton Oaks.

Wisdom, Charles

1940   *Chorti Indians of Guatemala.* Chicago: University of Chicago Press.

INDEX